THE EXPERIENCE OF A LIFETIME

Living Fully, Dying Consciously

THE EXPERIENCE OF A LIFETIME

Living Fully, Dying Consciously

Carolyn North

Amber Lotus
San Francisco
1998

For information, write to Amber Lotus
P.O. Box 31538, San Francisco, CA 94131

Cover photograph: Leslie Cooper
Cover design: Sara Glaser
Text design: Sara Glaser and Carolyn North

ISBN: 1-56937-218-7

ACKNOWLEDGMENTS

Thank you, my friends Lynn Hendrix, Jim Hickman, "Alice" and Duncan Campbell, for sharing with me the ultimate gift of friendship: your dying process.

Their partners and families have graciously given me permission to tell their stories, as well as reading and correcting what I have written. My thanks go to:

Ruth and Verne, Susan and Roger, Barton and Evie Hendrix; Skip, Pam and Scott Smith.

Paul and Beth, Brian Hickman, Steve Hickman, Joe Mayfield.

Conrad Martel; Virginia, Bruce and Linda, Carol and Doug Campbell.

For reading from the manuscript with care, and being honest with me no matter what, I am deeply grateful to Sharon Armstrong, Steve Ajay, Anne Hudes, Richard Cook, Kelly Lohman-Basen, Liz Jones, Susan D'Alcamo, Alicia Ostriker, Viven Feyer, Karin McPhail, Effie Brown, Joan Levinson, Mike Litchfield, Kathie Weston, Elise White, Adrienne Robinson and Mark Sommer. Just a few years ago Lynn and Jim and Duncan were also amongst my best critics, giving their acute intelligence to whatever I wrote. Duncan was still around to read the first chapter shortly before he died, and to listen while I read to him parts of the second. His advice to me was to not use such big words.

My thanks to Snooey Heslen, who made me welcome at her home at the edge of the meadow in Putney, Vermont; to Regine Schwenter who kept the kids quiet while I worked in the loft at Shenoa; to Sara McCamant, whose sanctuary of a garden needed weeding exactly when I needed to take breaks, and to the blessed Navarro River in Northern California, on whose forested banks I always do my best work.

Thank you, Sara Glaser, for the pleasure of making every book we do together beautiful.

To Jerry Horovitz, who took a chance on this book as the first on his list at Amber Lotus, my deepest gratitude. His sharp reading of the stories, his honest feedback and honorable way of doing business and art, has been heartening in a world where balance and right-livelihood are rare.

To Joanna Smith, Kathy Cave, Richard Hack, my brother Leon Cooper and my daughter Rebecca Strauss for their loving care of my sister while she lay dying.

And finally, to my husband, Herb, who is my first critic, computer expert and best friend, I can only bow with gratitude for hanging in there with me through these years of caregiving, loss and grief, and for being right there in the room or at the other end of a telephone, day or night, even when he doesn't appear on the page.

This book is for him, who took care of me while I took care of them.

CONTENTS

Introduction

*Birth is not a beginning,
death is not an end.*
There is existence without
limit. There is continuity
without starting point.
CHUANG TZU

uring the past four years I have lost over thirty significant people in my life. Many were in their primes—between the ages of forty and sixty—and most died of either cancer or AIDS. Two were young adults who committed suicide. Each was what one friend called "the irreplaceables."

I was bereft, leveled by loss. I took it personally. I felt under siege, abandoned, outraged. Many of the witnesses of my life were gone and I felt myself, as do many members in the gay community whose circle of friends gradually disappears, a lone survivor.

During the first year there were often four or five people in jeopardy simultaneously—as there are at this writing, including my younger sister. One week I went to three memorials, and in between sat in a hospital lobby while a friend had a mastectomy. I had to grieve hard and fast to be ready for the next assault. Exhausted by despair, I sought the help of a therapist who informed me that I was suffering from multiple-bereavement syndrome, and I would do well to get out into nature as much as possible and to take up some hand work to calm me under stress. And to cry a lot, and to yell.

This I took quite seriously. I went for long walks, often on cliffs by the sea, and in that first year made thirty-three patchwork quilts, one after the other. Sewing scraps of color into multi-colored patchwork designs over and over seemed to save my sanity. The therapist also suggested I speak to people about my situation as often as I could get someone to listen. This I was a bit more reluctant to do, assuming that nobody likes a whiner, until one day I received phone calls from two close colleagues within an hour of each other.

"Listen," said Duncan, who was HIV positive, "I'm calling to let you know that I've finally gotten my AIDS diagnosis. It's PCP. I can't handle telling Jessica right now—would you be willing to tell her?"

I assented, but my stomach churned with grief. At the time, Jessica,

Duncan and I were working together with improvisational theater as a healing mode. I knew that Jessica would take Duncan's news at least as hard as I did. Then the phone rang again. Incredibly, it was Jessica.

"Hi," she said. "I'm afraid I've got some bad news. You know that routine mammogram last week? Well, they want to do an immediate biopsy. It doesn't look too good. I don't know how I'm going to tell Duncan. Could I ask you to let him know?"

It took me days, but I finally relayed the news to each of them, never mentioning the macabre synchronicity that had put me in the middle. I knew then I would have to take a step.

I would not only talk to people about my experience, I decided, I would immerse myself in the subject of Death. Since bereavement was clearly on my plate for the duration anyhow, instead of protecting myself and flinching I would embrace it, dive into it, take the damned bull by the horns! And perhaps, if I learned something useful from this Death project, I would write about it and let others know what I learned.

I began with reading the *Tibetan Book of the Dead,* and from there searched out every book on death and dying I could find—the biology and psychology of death to the anthropology and theology of death. I went to meetings of the local near-death survivors group, and interviewed people who had "died"—been clinically pronounced dead and lived to tell the tale. Mostly, though, I observed my dying friends—and myself—with a new kind of eye and mind, and a heart held as open as I could hold it.

What I was interested in understanding was how facing death might define how we lived; how the way we lived might define how we died. In short, I wanted to know whether it was possible to live well while preparing for death, and then to die well when it was time to die.

The answer I gradually have gotten was that it is.

Gloriously so. Revelationally so. I have learned that when the process of dying is accepted, the growing awareness that emerges when soul and body actively prepare for this great transition, seems to corroborate all the wisdom traditions of the world.

The good news is that Death happens, and it is OK. The loss, for those left behind, is excruciating, but what we can learn in the process is a gift beyond compare if we can allow ourselves to see it that way.

This book, quite deliberately, is not about assisted suicide, abortion, right-to-life, or any of the issues currently being hotly debated in our culture. I am interested, here, in the more ordinary experience of death that is the fate of most of us: the death that happens, willy-nilly, when our time has come.

This book, therefore, is about myself, what I have learned from my research, and what I have observed in the intimacy of walking the path with friends as they prepared for their passage. It is about their experience as they communicated it to me, and about my experience watching them decline physically and emerge spiritually. It is about the caregivers' role, and the reactions of family and friends; it is about resistance and acceptance and coping.

The stories are true stories, although I have taken the liberty of changing names and fictionalizing at will to protect privacy where appropriate. Between each story, I have taken a brief look at some personal issues inspired by the story; growing older, facing my own mortality, how my own life and death fit into the larger universe. In both story and musing commentary I have been asking the question,

"Can we prepare for death in a way that is Whole—physically, emotionally, mentally, psychologically and spiritually? And more deeply, how can we use this experience to learn how to love?"

ONE

Lynn's Story

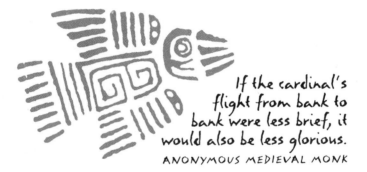

If the cardinal's
flight from bank to
bank were less brief, it
would also be less glorious.
ANONYMOUS MEDIEVAL MONK

ynn and I first met in the middle of the Pacific Ocean. I was in the Galápagos Islands on an adventure, following in Charles Darwin's footsteps in preparation for writing a book, and she was there studying plant succession on a recent ash fall near the rim of the Fernandina volcano. I had been told at the Darwin Research Station that an American botanist would soon be arriving on the islands, but as I had been out in the field, I had not yet crossed paths with her.

The little fishing boat she was on broke down, and the little fishing boat I was on picked up their distress signal and sped through open water to their rescue. My first impression was of a lithe, open-faced young woman walking the plank between our two vessels, a straw hat perched low over her eyes and the churning sea just inches beneath her boots. Giving us a shy grin, she handed over her backpack before quickly tip-toeing the length of the plank, arms out for balance. I grabbed it and reached out a hand to her as she jumped down from the gunwale.

Even then, at the age of thirty-two, the cancer that would kill her before her forty-fourth birthday was likely already lurking within her bones.

Hitching a ride with the fishermen, our boat towing the crippled one behind it, we anchored in a cove near Santiago Island for the night. Leaning companionably against the coiled rope with the fishermen, we feasted on freshly caught *bonito* fried over coals on board, and traded jokes in two languages with the fishermen. They threw bits of fish skin into the water to attract sea lions who arrived in numbers, cavorting in the swells around our boat along with the night-feeding gulls.

The dark sea was lit with phosphorescence where the sea lions swam, streams of sparklers following in their quick wakes as they flapped their tail flippers, turned and dove. The starry sea matched the star-filled sky, a moving embroidery of light stitched by sea lions at play.

"They perform for you!" the fishermen laughed, scattering more fish into the water for them to catch, while Lynn and I leaned out over the side of the boat as far as we dared. Briny and fishy, the sea lions skimmed inches beneath our faces, at one with the water, and they churned up light and effervescence with every flip and swish of their streamlined bodies.

Later, after the fishermen had discreetly peed over the side and walked the plank to sleep on the other boat—pointing first at a bucket for us— we lay side by side on the deck in our sleeping bags, gazing up at the Southern Hemisphere sky and having our first exchange of stories in what would become a close, committed friendship.

We talked, that first night, about family. The family she described to me sounded idyllic—the kind I had always longed to belong to. She came from people grounded and educated for generations in the same land. Since childhood she had hiked in the mountains with parents and siblings, who celebrated their extended group of relatives and friends with harvests from their gardens and family-special ice cream concoctions they were famous for. They were the "base of her being," she said fondly.

I, at thirty-five, still shaken by my father's recent early death, and coming from a chaotic bunch of angry Russian Jews, could hardly picture the world she described. A bit nervously, I told her about madness and danger growing up in Brooklyn, and how the notion of a family ice cream dish was like something from another planet. I confessed that my family of origin was a group I chose to avoid, but that my husband and three children were of another order entirely, wherein I was attempting to create the kind of loving family I never had.

We listened to each other with fascination, as if we had come from opposite sides of the world, and by the time we fell asleep next to each other on the rolling deck, we were mutually enchanted. So we decided to disembark on Santiago together and traverse the lava flow that bisected the south side of James Bay from the north, where there was purported to be a long white-sand beach and an extensive lagoon where, in some seasons, they said, flamingos came.

Our plan was to hide everything but the clothes we were wearing and our notebooks and cameras, and carry on our backs all the water and food we would need for a week. We could, we decided, do the trek in a single day if we started out well before dawn. So after a day of planning and preparation, we took off. I drew the short stick and got to carry the full gerry can of water on my back. Everything else was packed in by Lynn.

The sun at the equator, reflecting off black lava, creates a blinding, shimmering heat that sucks the moisture out of your body as you breathe. Waking in the dead of night, we made ready by drinking as much water as we could swallow, packing up our camp, and hoisting the too-heavy packs onto our backs. Trudging single file in the dark across tuff plain to the hard edge of basalt we went, in a single heave, from soil to rock. Crust crackled beneath our boots. The lava field seemed empty of all signs of life except for ourselves.

"Not all," Lynn observed as we made our way, by flashlight, around pressure ridges and piles of exploded rock shards. "You'll see, when we peek into fissures where ash has collected, we'll find the most amazing treasures."

And she was right. Once there was light to see by, she showed me, with the unerring instinct of a born field biologist, miniature plants gaining rootholds in places I would never have thought to look. We found prickly cacti tucked in the depressions of spatter cones; patches of lichen on sea-facing slabs; even a Galápagos tomato plant with tiny yellow flowers near the entrance of a lava tube.

Lynn was gleeful at this find and photographed it from every angle, snipping off a specimen and pressing it between the pages of her notebook. I followed her like a novice, kneeling cautiously beside her, the water's dead weight on my back. I asked questions about everything—the plants, the geology, the rainfall—which she answered at length, often searching for examples in the lava to illustrate a point.

As the sun reached the zenith, we walked together in silence, reserving our strength for putting one foot ahead of the other on the field of barren, black lava which seemed to go on forever. The relatively recent flow had spilled from a tuff cone in the highlands and bisected what had once been a broad tuff plain, creating an endless dark desert separating grassy oases on either side. Stopping for lunch after hours of walking, we still could not see any green indicating the plain on the other side of the flow.

Later, as the sun was lowering, the sight of grass and some trees became just visible in the distance ahead. We picked up the pace a bit and talked again, about our work.

Lynn, as a scientist, was impassioned by the natural world in all its diversity. She wanted to see everything there was to see and to understand how it all went together. She was a woman in love with the world. I caught her enthusiasm the way I had caught her backpack on the fishing boat—with a flash of fun and recognition. Here was somebody I could wonder with; a woman not embarrassed to talk to birds, to babble gleefully at the sight of an unexpected flower. And where had I found her? Off the coast of an uninhabited island, in an archipelago known to sailors as *Las Encantadas,* 600 miles away from the Ecuadorian mainland. In the middle of the sea.

Wherever else?

With the tenderest of fingers, she bent over and cradled a bit of green hidden inside a shallow fissure, showing me its structure and telling me about its prototype on the mainland.

"This may have gotten here on a living raft," she mused. "In big storms on the mainland, sometimes whole clumps of a riverbank break off and make it out to sea. If it eventually gets washed up onto some island—and the Galápagos are the only islands anywhere in these waters—why then, it's likely to find a foothold. And then," she added, "the seeds or insects or whatever had caught a ride on the raft has to adapt to these new conditions in order to get established."

"Sounds like what people have to do, too," I mused.

"I find the natural world totally amazing," Lynn remarked that night, settled in our hastily assembled camp a few yards from the edge of the lava field where we had finally arrived shortly after sundown, exhausted and with burning feet. On the equator night falls quickly, with little transition from the light of day. The sky, jam-packed with stars, seemed to come right down to the land all around us. From a distance, the sea hit the tideline rocks with a muffled thunder. "Nature has dreamed up absolutely everything you could possibly imagine; every shape, every color, every activity."

"I think what fascinates me most, though," I said, "is what you can't see, what you can only intuit. The subtle stuff, like the patterns behind all the details. It's not something you can actually pick up and look at, but it's what everything comes out of. Sort of like the cookie dough before the cookie cutter makes all the cookie shapes."

"Why bother going beyond what you can see for miracles?" she asked, yawning. "To me, what I can see is more than enough to keep me busy for the rest of my life."

"Sure," I agreed, "but to me it's not that you're going *beyond* the natural world, you're just extending your definition of the natural world to include what isn't physically visible." I was getting too tired to express myself clearly. She said nothing, and for awhile I thought she had fallen asleep. Then I heard her murmur,

"I'm not sure I understand what you're talking about."

At the first light of dawn, eager to watch the sun rise over the ocean on our first morning, we hurriedly laced up our boots, packed some crackers and sardines, binoculars and sunscreen into the day pack—and moleskin for my blistered feet—and picked our way across the grassy tuff toward the beach.

Even before we got to the sea-worn lava boulders at the edge of the sand, we could hear it above the sound of the surf—a great whirring and honking, as of a thousand flying creatures in the sky. We ran the rest of the way, scrambling over the rocks and dropping down onto the smooth white sand and stood gaping. Above us the sky was filled with the great flapping wings of the flamingos, their underfeathers a hot fuchsia, like fire. Packed in close formation, long necks extended and legs trailing they raced out toward sea in jubilation of the waves.

We were stunned into breath-held stillness.

Their flight took them out, out, a distant cloud moving against the blue of the sky until we could hear them no longer. And then, as a flock, the cloud turned and headed back toward land. Their honks grew louder and louder, and then we could feel the wind of their wings as, flapping hard, they sailed above us once more and dropped, flamingo by flamingo, into the lagoon behind a ring of mangroves at the back of the beach.

For a moment Lynn and I grasped hands, a sister-bond forged. The flight of the flamingos had connected us forever.

And we both understood, without words, that we each knew it.

We continued on in silence, taking off our boots and exploring the fine-sand beach until we found a place where the mangroves parted and a path of mud and roots led to the lagoon. On a smooth stretch of clear, shallow water, the sky and tree-studded escarpment on the other side reflected in its surface, the flamingos calmly browsed. We squatted at the edge of the lagoon, the only humans in Paradise. Lynn took out her camera and quietly stalked the birds, squinting for a long time before she clicked the shutter. At the sound, which reverberated in that still, pristine place, they drifted together into a far corner of the lagoon away from us. Even whispers made them shy.

Calmly feeding, they probed with dark beaks into the muddy bottoms, stirring up food with their feet. Lynn lay belly down at the edge of the water, her camera poised. Eventually, the flamingos fanned out again, each pink body reflected in the slick mirror of the lagoon, long curved necks meeting at the surface, bills busy in the mud.

I wondered if, in my most creative imagination, I could have ever invented an enormous pink bird with brilliant fuchsia undersides? A big pink-winged creature that was shy, and scooped up algae and flocked in remote lagoons. How did Darwin's natural selection work, that something like a flamingo could emerge from the evolutionary process?

Questions tumbled pell-mell into my mind, but none were ready to be asked, and commentary seemed trite. All I wished for was solitude to observe and to think, and since Lynn was also in a pensive mood we agreed to go our separate ways for awhile—she to the beach, and me to remain at the lagoon.

She left shortly after, and I meandered slowly around the lagoon, gazing down into the water to see an illusion of clouds, hillside and flamingos extending deep into the earth, and deeper, ever-so-slightly distorted by faint ripples from the birds' quiet steps.

I felt I was finally in the Galápagos I had come to experience. And with a friend as a bonus! Now I would try and see whatever it was that Darwin saw and perhaps begin to perceive what, for me, was real.

After about an hour I made my way through the mangrove cover to the open beach and looked for Lynn. Her day pack was stashed in the shade of a mangrove tree, but she had wandered almost out of sight along the tideline. Strolling toward her at the edge of the lapping waves, I stopped and watched her gaze out to sea with her ankles in foam, rapt, totally nude. Unaware of being witnessed, she raised her arms to the sides as if opening to the whole ocean and sky, and then with a great whoop she ran forward, jumping over the low surf and diving straight into an oncoming swell.

For a few moments she had disappeared, but then her head bobbed into sight. Noticing me on the beach, she slicked the hair out of her eyes, waved exuberantly, and shouted for me to join her.

Two years later, awaiting the news of her biopsy with her mother in the waiting room at the Stanford Medical Center, that was the image that kept playing in my mind. Her strong, young body free and ecstatic beneath a summer sky on a beach at the edge of the beyond, diving into the embrace of an unsullied sea.

The diagnosis was of metastasized breast cancer and included two spots on her spine. She would need a mastectomy, chemotherapy and radiation. She was thirty-four years old.

She began to keep a journal at this time, which I would neither know about nor see until after her death, ten years later. From the first entry:

I want to keep a notebook of all the thoughts and feelings and random analogies that go thru my head. It's for me, but it's also, someday, for others. It's a kind of grasping at immortality, I suppose, an attempt to cheat Death: "You may take my body, but a part of me will have escaped your grasp. I'll scatter words and drawings and smiles with friends like a trail of crumbs marking my passage.

Shortly before her mastectomy, she wrote:

With both doctors, softer words couldn't hide the starkness of the message: "You'll die of this. We just don't know when." I came out from both conversations utterly exhausted, numbed. The weight of that burden is too great to carry steadily; it's too heavy an awareness; it mashes me flat...So I'm girded for battle and must live a double reality. On the one hand a fight for life with all my will and strength and stubbornness; a hope for the miracle cure or the inexplicable remission; the expectation of years ahead for all my plans and hopes. On the other hand the inexorable deadliness of metastasized cancer, the grim statistics, the urgency of doing now what I may not get a chance to do tomorrow. It's not a bad way to live....The gift in it is the intensification of each day, each moment—a Zen state? The trick is to keep the balance.

Right now the balance is there. It's like riding the buses in Peru. As they whipped around hairpin turns on mountainsides and squeezed past trucks on narrow roads crumbling down cliffs, my first response was to scrunch down in my seat and squeeze my eyes closed tight. Then I realized I was missing the view that way, it was out of my hands anyway and I might as well sit up and enjoy the ride. So for me, now, the first and most important order of business is to enjoy the view, no matter where the bus eventually ends up.

There are so many books and seminars and classes now on death....I suppose it's good that it's no longer taboo, but right now I want nothing to do with any of that. It's not simply that I'm "in the stage of denial" or something, but rather a fear of being influenced. If it's to be my death, I want to do it my way—to go thru my own evolution, think my own thoughts, make my own discoveries, face my own fears and grow my own way. I don't want that process affected by majority vote of how I "ought" to feel. Sometime I may well want to do that reading—I may want the help that sharing of experience might give—the data-gathering scientist in me may simply get curious. But not just yet.

After the mastectomy, she writes:

And so—medical ages later—I return to my notebook. There's not much time in the midst of medical activity to be contemplative. You focus on one detail at a time, taking them as they come. And that's how the whole mas-

tectomy seems to me from here—a collage of details, some fading, some vivid, all somewhat unreal. The bustle of a teaching hospital. The entourage that came with the doctor on his visits and stood in a silent, observing row behind him.... "Here's an interesting specimen, class!" The feeling of ritual, of being a sacrificial victim as I took a pre-surgery shower in the 6 am hospital quiet, and a line of song kept running through my head.

"Little lamb, little lamb, little innocent lamb; I'm gonna love God til I die...."

The bright lights in the OR; my fuzziness in ICU, finally waking up after 5 days feeling like Me again. Realized again how severe is sensory deprivation in a hospital, how walled-in your world. Still remember the wonder I felt after the biopsy, coming out into warm sunshine, green and rustling leaves, fragrant breeze. It seemed miraculous to me that there could be so much color and diversity in the world.

"But I *like* my bras sloppy!" Lynn insisted to the saleswoman in the lingerie fitting room at a local Department Store. The three of us were squeezed into a tiny cubicle, our reflections in the mirror giving the impression of a crowd. Fitting prostheses for women with breast cancer was evidently a new specialty amongst the personnel, and the saleswoman's eyes betrayed her fear.

I pretended to be at ease with the whole procedure, casually keeping busy by stuffing rejects back into their boxes and helping Lynn tighten brastraps. All the while, beads of sweat gathered into rivulets and dripped unseen down my sides.

"I'm afraid you won't be able to wear sloppy bras anymore," scolded the woman, gingerly avoiding a touch on Lynn's scar as she held the false breast up for the fitting. Lynn's face turned stiff.

The smell in the cubicle sickened me—a stench of stale perfume mixed with the faint antiseptic sourness of medicated flesh. My gorge rose. Despite myself, I envisioned Lynn striding free over dark lava, the fresh winds of the Pacific Ocean blowing her hair back from her face.

She fumbled inexpertly at the contraption harnessing her chest, and gazed at herself in the mirror. The woman was growing more and more nervous, and I could practically hear her thinking, *So young...thank God it's not me.*

Thank God it's not me, too, my mind echoed inadvertently, choking me immediately with a rush of guilt.

Lynn regarded me in the mirror for confirmation. "Well, what do you think?"

"What do I think?" I wanted to scream. "I think I want to vomit, to bash that mirror into smithereens, to pull you out of here and run with you up to the mountains and make this whole horrible thing go away! *That's* what I think!"

What I said was, "If it feels OK, I'd get it."

The saleswoman looked infinitely relieved.

Despite everyone's great anxiety, after the mastectomy and then the ongoing trial of chemotherapy and radiation, Lynn's cancer went into remission. Signs of the hot spots on her spine had disappeared, and given a clean bill of health by her doctors, she returned to central Washington and her normal existence. She resumed teaching at a small college in Yakima and planned field trips to exotic parts of the world. And invited me to come and visit her in Washington.

Not long after her final chemotherapy treatment, I left the children with my husband and flew to Washington to spend a week with her. In the evenings we sat and talked late, and during the day I mostly followed her through her routine, sitting in on some of her classes, meeting her friends and colleagues, watching sunsets over the canyon. And on the weekend, we took a camping trip to what she referred to as her "favorite place on the planet."

She wanted to surprise me, so she wouldn't tell me where we were going. We took a route through a canyon lined with quaking aspen and drove through green farmland for miles. The land became rocky, and then rather barren, and still we drove. When I regarded her questioningly, she just smiled. Soon we were in a wasteland of jumbled rock and after awhile, in a cleared space on the side of the road, we stopped and parked.

"This it?" I asked, gazing around and trying not to sound disappointed.

"Almost," she replied quixotically, hauling the backpacks out of the trunk. Shouldering our gear—helping each other wriggle into the straps, just as we had in the Galápagos—we started hiking along a bare-ly marked trail indicated in the rocks. Our destination was still not clear, and I wondered what strange compulsion all that medication may have provoked in my friend.

But then, ahead, sticking up out of the landscape like a mirage, was a wooded butte about ten acres square, with nothing around it to indicate how it might have been formed. It was like an island of forest in a sea of rocks. Lynn stopped, breathed in deeply and turned to me with sparkly eyes.

"Ta-da!" she sang. "We're going up there!"

Following her along the rock trail had been an ankle-twisting exer-cise, but climbing the side of the butte—called "Meek's Table"—seemed to me downright hazardous, especially for someone whose body had just been weakened by surgery and chemotherapy. Lynn's footing however, was secure and she took it slowly, actually waiting to help me up some of the steeper places.

At the top, a final hoist put us up and over, and we went from bad-lands to a wondrous, primeval forest with stately trees rising like wise old sentinels above the world.

"See?" she exclaimed with satisfaction.

I could only stand and stare. How did this place get here? Was this all that was left of an ancient woodland after the impact of a meteor?

Behind us the forest dropped off to a wasteland of barren rock as far as the eye could see, but spread out before us was a storybook grove of magical trees, the ground beneath them fragrant with grasses and wild-flowers, the land springy with thousands of years of untroubled mulch.

"Shangri-la," she said softly, and then, "After I die when I am ninety, this is where I want to be."

For a moment, a shadow passed before my sun, but she had said, "when I am ninety...."

Hadn't she?

That evening, sitting by the fire after a supper of rice, canned sar-dines and avocados—for old times' sake—she pulled a hair from her head and showed me how it registered each treatment of the chemo with evenly-spaced thinnings of the strand.

"It's banded, like the trunk of a tree," she observed. "Interesting, huh?"

"It's quite amazing that you never actually lost your hair," I commented admiringly. "What a constitution!"

"No baldy, I," she retorted with a grin.

But later, when we stripped out of our clothes to snuggle into our sleeping bags for the night, I could see by the firelight that her perfect body, once unblemished and firm, was puckered and scarred where the surgeon had cut, and had faded bruises where needles had rudely gained entry.

The day after the eclipse of the sun, which occurred that same year, she wrote in her journal:

We <u>saw</u> it !!!

It was iffy right up to the last minute—"37% chance," "25%," "50%," "skies clear overhead but low clouds to the east." We started off under varied skies, trying to be optimistic/realistic/fortified against disappointment. Climbed the Dolph's hill of gold dried grass with a sweeping view of lower valley, ridges, Mt. Adams—a magnificent way to begin any day. A pilgrimage. Then we used our viewers and pinholes and binos, and saw the <u>chunk</u> out of the sun and moving fast—really as if being eaten. WOW! 45 minutes—more people coming—looking at reflected crescents of sun with clouds across them. Then—the eerie purple pink light of the sun fading—and fading—dimmer and dimmer—and TOTALITY. Lights in town, stars out. Unspeakably awesome. The absolute roundness of that sharp-edged black— big—black sun in black sky. Dark—like twilight, not midnight. White corona. Thru the binocs—3 or 4 glowing red flares around the sun's edge. Taking photos, looking, ahh-ing, looking, trying to absorb <u>everything</u>. And much too soon the timer went off, Ivar called from his stopwatch and we all turned to face the west, children and adults, stunned and joyful, ecstatic, hiding eyes from the returning sun and watching light return to Mt. Adams and our hill.

That summer she made another trip to the Galápagos to continue her plant-succession study of the ashfall on Fernandina, and from there traveled to the jungles of the Amazon, collecting plants. I received several cheery postcards from South America, and a few letters which included odd-shaped seedpods, downy feathers and delicate leaves.

She arrived back well-tanned and brimming with enthusiasm and good health. Life was exciting and she felt strong and fit. As she told me on that visit, "cancer is something that happened in the past...."

Skiing in the Cascades that winter she met Skip, an entomologist with whom she fell madly in love. He was a widower whose first wife had died of cancer when his two children were quite young, and he and Lynn spent a leisurely courtship before establishing themselves as a family. The children, adolescents at the time, were initially cautious about accepting a new mother, but gradually were won over. I tried to imagine my own children in their position, having lost me as their mother. How would they have received a new woman come to take my place by their father's side? In their father's heart? My own heart went out to all of them.

Lynn and Skip and the kids got married, on Meek's Table of course, in the spring.

"He's a brave man, my Skip," Lynn declared to me when they made their first visit as a married couple to San Francisco. "It's not every man who would link up with a lady with only one breast twice in a row."

"He's clearly mad for you, my dear," I countered. She gave me a gleeful hug.

"Why, yes, I'd say he is that," she purred contentedly.

In her journal of this time, she writes:

Well, so now I've come to a new equilibrium. I went thru a time of "fear and trembling"—learned that that old cliché is literally accurate. Actually, I've known it before, that I shake when feeling really vulnerable or threatened—but I've never before had the trembling sneak up on me when I wasn't consciously aware of dealing more or less directly with the fear. (Roethke: "This shaking keeps me steady....")

Then the scan showed no more spread. A shaky relief. Gradually the bands of fear loosened—bit by bit—more relief could creep in. Oh!— whew—yes—a bigger breath—Whew!—Hear, hear it's OK for now! It's

OK! Whew. But we're not done. No, it's a cautious, sober joy. From here it's wait and see, cross your fingers and hope. No one, I realize finally, no one, no matter what happens, no one is ever going to say to me, "Go home. It's over. You're cured."

To live with that uncertainty ever after. There it is. Not surprising. But so absolute—it's that that took some getting used to. After all, everyone has that precise uncertainty in his life, tho the shape may not be so clear. Living with and past the immediacy of it—that's the burden and the gift.

I find in her journal from that same period a quote from one of my letters to her. I had written,

I suppose for every glimpse into the truth, one must pay a price. And we never know, I suppose, what is gift and what is tragedy.

I recall now, that in writing that letter I had been trying to imagine myself in Lynn's position, facing death just as I had found my life partner, just as I was dreaming of the future—and I could not. In my fear, I waxed poetical, philosophical. The wise one. The truth was that I couldn't face what she was facing. Those pretty words were nothing but bluff.

But here, from that same time, are her words:

"Love, look away..." a fragment of song comes to me here, sitting among granite boulders with the steady voice of a waterfall behind me. Last summer in High Sierra I had so recently been told of gloom and death. I felt I had to grasp greedily at each moment as a chance never to be offered again—that never again, for example, might I sit in sunny alpine tundra. Any moment that was less than perfect was cause for distress. This year the knowledge of each moment's uniqueness remains, but the tension of desperate urgency has eased. So "look away" for a bit. Look away for now from looming death pushed to the background. Never forget to savor fully, but relax, let go, be at peace.

It was during this year, when Lynn, Skip and the children were visiting, that I first met Jim. Lynn, Jim and Celia, now his wife, had been friends and fellow hikers since graduate school. Jim had become a botanist and Celia a geologist, and over the years they had teamed up with Lynn and other friends for wilderness trips all over the country.

Taking part in Lynn's extended family, they had a tradition of joining Lynn's parents and brothers every summer on the family camping trip in the mountains. Indeed, they looked almost like family—the same wiry athletic builds, the same open faces and easy smiles.

We all went for a walk in the hills one Sunday, a merry group of some fifteen people that included my husband and adolescent children and a number of large dogs. Such gatherings of good-natured outdoors folk of all ages, which I associated with Lynn's extended circle, were unique in my life and enchanting to me, and I looked forward to each excursion as an adventure.

Celia and Jim had recently moved from the East Coast—she to take up a teaching post and he to edit a natural history journal—and the friends spent much of our walk reminiscing about old times: trips taken together and gossip about mutual friends from school. And, of course, the inevitable teasing and laughter about the family ice cream specials of other years.

"Oh, don't you worry," declared Lynn's father. "We've got all the makings back home, and you'd better come back with us and help us eat it!" And the day did indeed end with a garden feast, followed by one of the famous ice cream extravaganzas that Lynn had described to me that night we slept on the boat anchored off the coast of Santiago Island.

But the day remains unforgettable for me because of a brief few minutes on the trail when I found myself walking alongside Jim and exchanging the new observations of friendly strangers. In the space of about 500 yards, we both recognized that in some mysterious way we were not quite strangers, but rather something more like kin. It was immediately clear to me, and I was to learn years later that it had been equally so for him. On that day, however, we simply smiled, and our eyes held for a short extra moment. But that was all that was needed.

Lynn was in remission for about nine years. We kept in touch regularly by letter and telephone, but our lives took place at a remove from one another.

We established a routine of holiday visits—either here or there or in between—and always spent special time together when she came through on her way to or from study trips to the Galápagos. These days much of our talk revolved around the trials of raising teenagers, balancing work and marriage, recipes using leftovers....We never mentioned cancer.

She and Skip were happy together. At school, they collaborated on a project by adopting an endangered bog in central Washington, studying its wildlife and ecology on a long-term basis. For years, she waxed enthusiastic about their bog, focusing much of her teaching on it and producing a number of scholarly papers. The bog inspired the artist in her too, and she sent me photographs and then drawings of grasses, toads, microscopic organisms. Eventually, the drawings evolved into woodcuts, and the woodcuts evolved into etchings. And all this artistic output, over a period of about five years, went from being the work of a gifted beginner to the work of a consummate artist.

Her compositions, in their intricate detail etched in acid upon metal plates, evoked whole worlds: winter weeds in the bog, cottonwoods in the canyon, spring on Meek's Table. She had a mature and loving eye and worked intensively every spare hour now, spending long evenings and weekends at her etching. Lynn had become, it seemed, as committed an artist as she was a scientist.

And then one day she telephoned from Washington.

"The hot spots are back," she told me simply, without preamble. For a few moments I was immobilized while my brain cranked painfully into gear.

"When did you find out?" I finally whispered. I called up into mind the faith healers of the Philippines, Native American shamans, Tibetan doctors. "Are you...?"

"I'm starting radiation again," she replied matter-of-factly, "which," she rushed to assure me, "is not such a bad thing, because then I can take the quarter off teaching and spend my whole time etching. Skip's building a little studio in the garden for me, so I can do my artwork to my heart's content!"

Oh, Lynn....

In her journal of this time, she writes:
...Scary, but I'm really OK. Have been enjoying one of those joy-

bubbling-up-inside moods, in fact. Only a greedy joyfulness about life makes sense—less seems such a waste.

And

Such beautiful mountains this October. Each weekend I go and think in amazement and longing, "How can I not be always here in this beauty? How can I perhaps not return here again and again and again?"

How can I not be among you, my friends, my family? How can I not be among you? How can I? I so love you all.

The radiation treatment was long, and exhausting. She writes, after it was over:

Five weeks of radiation made me tired. I was angry to lose 2 hrs each day commuting to and from the hospital but the real impact was the exhaustion. For the first time in all of this, a treatment really slowed me down. I'd never before realized what lethargy sheer tiredness can produce. Never before have I been content to spend so much time simply sitting and staring—not reading, not even particularly thinking—just sitting inert in the beanbag, semi-dozing. Movement from this state was an effort. I understand as I never did before what it must be like to suffer a chronic debilitating disease, to be weak from starvation, to lack the strength and zip I've always taken for granted. And in that state of tiredness, it's hard to feel positive, hard not to feel discouraged and frightened. Through my mind went the question, "Is this the beginning of the end?"

Then, of course, the radiation stopped, and slowly, mysteriously—even in the face of medical uncertainty and eventual chemotherapy—a subterranean healing of body and spirit began....

Through that time I focused on rallying my forces. I read Symington's book and tried imagery. I sang songs to myself when I walked. ("We're winning, we're winning my brave little band; We'll munch them and crunch them and get the top hand. We'll find them and mash them and gobble with glee; We'll chase them all out, till of baddies we're free. Away, away....It's the song of the Lymphocyte Army.")

And, as I walked and took deep joy in the flowers and the sun and the spring smells and the dailiness of life, a bounce returned to my step, strength. I stopped worrying, stopped imaging, stopped thinking about cancer cells, confident—because my body tells me so—that all is OK for now.

On the basis of this sense of well-being and strength, Lynn and Skip planned a two-month expedition to South America, starting in Patagonia, where Skip would be collecting insects in Tierra del Fuego, and ending up on Fernandina, where the two of them would climb the volcano to complete Lynn's study of plant succession on the ashfall. *National Geographic* was sponsoring the trip, and would produce the resulting paper. As Lynn put it, "When this trip is finished, I hand all my Fernandina notes over to them—and then it's *theirs!*"

Lynn bought new boots for the trip, declaring that she was making an investment in the future. She showed them off proudly at her parents' house when she and Skip came through on the first stop of their journey. We were all there for a barbecue and the inevitable ice cream special—my family, Jim and Celia, a few friends of Skip's and her parents. Skip unrolled a map of South America and was pointing out their itinerary.

I tried not to stare at her badly-fitting wig, and wondered if she planned to wear it on the climb. I couldn't imagine anything hotter. It also crossed my mind that she might know something about her condition that she was not saying, and had a secret agenda on top of her beloved volcano. I considered discreetly sounding her out, but then didn't know what I'd do if I guessed this was so. Climbing a mountain such as Fernandina in her condition was hardly a commonplace—or commonsense—thing to do.

I wondered about Skip in all of this; had he been cajoled into doing this trip, or was he a man simply willing to take on awesome responsibilities for the hell of it? Did he really believe she could handle the rigors and primitive conditions they were going into? Finally, I asked him outright. His response was hearty laughter.

"I get to carry *everything* on my back," he pointed out merrily. "No doubt *I'll* be the one to collapse first, and Lynn'll have to carry *me* down the mountain!"

Everyone laughed with them, but I wondered if there wasn't forced bravado in the levity, and I wondered if I was the only one who noticed. I wondered myself into a headache, and slipped into the kitchen for an aspirin.

Jim followed. "Howdy," he said quietly, clinking water glasses with me.

"Hi." I had nothing to say. We exchanged skeptical looks, shrugged and he came over and gave me a hug—hard. Then he nodded toward the living room and we took our water back to where Lynn, with a mischievous grin, was unwrapping a large plastic bag tied with criss-crossing rubber bands.

"Come look!" she exclaimed brightly. To my ears it was again a little *too* brightly. "I've got presents for everyone!" My kids jumped up from their chairs and crowded round, while she, savoring the moment, reached in very deliberately and took out a stack of brown T-shirts, which she placed on the coffee table.

Each shirt had been stenciled with one of her drawings of a long-tailed land iguana peering over the rim of a crater. Printed beneath the tail was the word, in bold: **Fernandina, '84.**

"Wear it while I'm up there," she announced, presenting each of us with a T-shirt, "for good luck."

In her journal there is an entry from Fernandina:

The power of names. No—the Belief in the power of names. That primal feeling that to _name_ something is to _control_ it. And yet the tremendous gap between the name and the reality. It's as if I felt that if only I understood enough about my cancer, I could change it. As if, if I show myself smart enough or wonderful enough in dealing with it, some power will grant me reprieve. I _have_ to participate in my health—mind and mystic of me both insist upon it. Yet sometimes I see so clearly the futility of Naming, feel how I lack any real and deep control. On the volcano at Fernandina, in the beauty of this world I want to know forever, I suddenly feel anguish and say to the air and to an iguana, "No. No. No. I don't want to have cancer. I want to be _Well._ I want to be _done_ with all this medical stuff—I'm _tired_ of it. Why can't I look forward to my 90 years?—I've so much to do. Why. Why. Why?

We learned only after they returned that she had in fact broken her pelvis even before she climbed Fernandina! After having come safely through the rigors of travel and camping in Patagonia, and making it in one piece all the way to the shores of the Galápagos, she tripped disembarking from the fishing boat onto the beach at Fernandina. She actually heard something crack, she confessed to me later. She knew Skip would never let her make the climb if she told him about it—so she didn't tell him.

Lynn climbed one of the most rugged volcanoes in the world with a broken pelvis!

"Lynnish…," I heard myself complain when we were together again. Her hair had grown back into a boyish crewcut, and the wig was no longer in evidence. She grinned at me sheepishly.

"It hurt," she admitted. I sighed, my shoulders sagging. "But I made it to the top," she insisted proudly.

"You made it to the top," I repeated.

"Yes, made it to the top," she said yet again, her face gentle, attentive, "and down again, too."

From her journal:

Interesting that all along and still I have a self-image of myself as a healthy *person.* Illness *seems incompatible with* me*, something that attacks from outside, something Other-ly. Until very recently I've also thought of myself as* strong*. That's been modified by fragile bones and episodes of old-lady immobility. But I still feel capable of doing almost everything—just within limits and more slowly.*

But by the following spring those fragile bones did betray her. She and Skip returned to California to have some heroic surgery done on her spine, to shore up some of her crumbling vertebrae with a metal bar. Skip stayed with her in the hospital four days out of every seven, commuting back to Washington to teach three days of classes each week. The rest of us—family and a few local friends—took turns keeping vigil by her bedside, and on the actual day of the operation, while Skip and her parents stayed close by in the hospital, Jim and I took the day off work and went up into the hills to hold our own vigil of prayer.

Along the trail to the ridge we picked wildflowers and new grass, carrying them to a spot where we could look east to the mountains and west to the sea. It was a place each of us had hiked with Lynn, and on this particular day it was clear enough to see, far in the distance, the glint of snow-high peaks in the Sierras.

"Good omen," remarked Jim, spreading the wildflowers in a radiating star. In the center I placed colored stones, one for each vertebra, and at the official starting time of the surgery we sat in quiet meditation. For about an hour we sat without speaking.

"Oo-ooh," Jim murmured at last, shifting his position. When I opened my eyes, there were tears brimming in his.

"I'd like you to know something," he said finally, gazing out across the hills. Interrupting himself, he raised his binoculars to track a large raptor and handed them over to me, excited. "Eagle!" he declared. "It's very rare to sight them!" We watched, taking turns with the binoculars until the eagle had sailed out of sight.

Then carefully, he replaced the binoculars around his neck, sighed, and flashed me an unreadable smile. I was certain he was going to confess to a long-standing love affair with Lynn. My heart immediately went out to what he must be suffering.

"Mmm-m," I murmured encouragingly. Absently fingering a dried bit of root, he sighed again and said,

"Celia and I are going our separate ways."

"No!" I exclaimed, genuinely shocked. The perfect couple with the perfect life. "Really?"

"Yes," he confirmed quietly. Then he looked up sharply and with something of a challenge in his voice, announced, "I'm gay." The root, shredded now, dropped from his fingers.

"You are?" was all I could respond. This was still a rare category in my experience. I had no idea what to say next. "For how long?" I asked. Stupid blunder. "I mean...."

"For always," he replied reasonably. Then he smiled and seeing my confusion, touched my arm. The only thing I could think of at that moment was Celia.

"Celia must be devastated," I offered. He nodded his head.

"Yeah, it's not easy on her," he admitted, "but it hasn't come as a complete surprise. It's sort of been something we don't quite talk about and I think she'd like to keep it that way. But—I can't anymore."

"What will you do?"

"Move to the city, for starters," he replied.

"You know people...?"

"Of course," he said.

"Does Lynn know about this?"

"Which," he asked. "That Celia and I are splitting, or that I'm gay?"

"Well—both."

"No to both. I'd like her to know before she goes," he mused. "This isn't quite the right moment, though."

"No," I agreed softly, taking his hand which was breaking shreds of bark into tiny pieces. He pulled my fingers to his cheek, and held them there while we both continued to gaze out toward the Sierras.

"I pray, for every reason, that she survives the operation," I commented after awhile.

"You and me both," he agreed, and until the winds started up we stayed there in companionable silence sitting very, very still.

When the sun began to sink toward the western horizon, we made a ceremony of scattering the stones and wildflowers in four directions, intoning our wishes for Lynn aloud, and bowing solemnly to each other. Shouldering our day packs we started back down the trail, Jim in the lead.

"I'm glad you felt you could trust me enough to tell me," I declared, feeling for my footing down a steep place.

"I do," he replied simply, turning to look back at me. "Actually, I'm looking forward to our getting to know each other better now."

"Me too," I said.

"I've always felt an inherent bond between us. Do you know what I mean?"

"Yes, I do. From that day we first met walking in these hills with everyone. Remember?"

"Of course I do. I wanted, at the time, to get to know you but it was hard with Celia."

"It was—why?" He gazed thoughtfully out at the hills before answering.

"It's a bit hard to explain. Celia's a scientist, and you're a...ah..."

"Mystic?" I offered.

"Something like that," he laughed. "Anyhow, she's not very receptive to things that smack of spirituality."

"And I smack of spirituality, is that it?" I challenged, feeling stung. I had been blithely unaware of criticism coming from her.

"I smack of spirituality, too," he confessed, "which is part of the problem between us, of course."

"Are you saying that it's OK to be married to a man who you sort of know is gay but it's not OK if he or your friends have spiritual inclinations?" I demanded irritably. He shook his head ruefully.

"This is not terribly rational, I agree," he responded. "But the whole thing isn't very rational."

"Scientists…" I muttered still stinging from Celia's rejection.

"You mustn't presume that just because we're scientists we have any more sense than anybody else does," he teased.

"Oh, really?" I retorted ironically, my hands on my hips. I stopped on the trail and glared after him. He hopped nimbly down the trail, a mountain goat at heart, and waited for me at the bottom.

"I agree, it's strange," he shrugged, grinning, "but that's the way it is."

"You know," I countered, "I don't understand a single thing—why Lynn has cancer, why you're changing your life now but didn't before this, and why I was nutty enough to think that outdoorsy people had uncomplicated lives!"

"That'll teach you to jump to conclusions," he teased, starting down the trail again toward the road and a public telephone where we could call the hospital to learn the results of Lynn's operation.

Lynn writes, probably before the long agony of the operation itself:
I wonder about the passivity the medical world breeds in its patients. Despite all my participation, my questioning, my active role at least in wanting to understand and know—I feel it, too. In the hospital you're passed from specialist to specialist each with his or her particular task to do. Tho each may be pleasant and friendly, the contact is so brief that it's inevitably impersonal. Soon my reaction is simply to withdraw and endure: "Here's my body. Do with it what you must. Meanwhile I'll make my mind a blank or perhaps wrap myself in a dream of mountains, and return when you're done." I wonder about the harm this does—certainly to the Doctor, who must then bear all the impetus for action and deal with the potential of moving people like pawns, the blindness of unjustified personal power. Certainly to Patients. Some of it is self-protective, a saving of energies. But

there's a subtle blurring of self, a loss. Where does passivity slide into resignation? And when does resignation begin to interfere with speed of, or hope of cure? So little is known of this. I wonder if all this is not in some way antithetical to health?

Like the incredible trouper she was, Lynn did indeed pull through the heroic surgery and rehabilitation. We had a quiet celebration after her release from the hospital—with Jim there, but not Celia—and off she went back to Washington, to her husband, teenagers and dogs, and the etching studio in her green backyard.

Almost immediately she was back at her artwork, experimenting with raised embossing, with new printing techniques, with color. We discussed collaborating on a children's book about seeds, and she did some initial drawings. She began incorporating natural objects into her compositions: feathers, grasses, leaves. There seemed no limits to her creativity, and her output, especially considering the technical difficulty of her medium, was prodigious. Once each week we would check in by phone and she would tell me of the new piece she was working on, and her plans for yet the next. Her intensity was remarkable. It was as if she was racing against time.

For my birthday I received the latest of her etchings, a piece she called "Offering." It was an illusion of a conifer forest, or upside-down feathers, etched delicately in shades of buff and brown. A lit open space to one side held the pure down of a young hawk's feather, and hidden amongst the feather/trees were the embossed claws of a bird. Unwrapping the gift, I held it before me and wept.

I had to do something to celebrate this woman, to draw a sword against the coming darkness, to be active rather than passive. I was blessedly unaware, at the time, that "Offering" would be her last piece or that the copy that she gave to Jim would be bequeathed to me, in turn, when he died a decade later. I *was* aware, though, that at that moment I had to do something grand. So I telephoned her right away with a proposal.

"Lynnish!" I began, after giving my profuse compliments and thanks, "I've got an idea!"

"I'm all ears," she said.

"Would you consider having a show of your photographs and etchings down here?"

"A show?"

"Yes, in a gallery, with an opening and famous people coming, and music and food—you know, a *show!* I'll be the impresario, and you be the star, and your work will be the talk of the town."

"Really?" she asked in a little voice.

"Your work is stunning," I exclaimed, "and it should be seen. If you think you are strong enough to make the trip, the rest of us will do all the work."

What I really meant was that *I* would do all the work....

There was a moment's silence on her end, and then she asked again, "Really? Whew! You'd really do that?"

"Yes I would," I stated firmly.

"Well then—um—listen, let me try this out on Skip. Skip!" she called out to him, "what do you say we go back down to San Francisco for a show of my work?" I heard some fumbling in the background, and a somewhat querulous voice asking, "Who are you talking to?"

Lynn giggled, and told him. Before we hung up, we had discussed matting and framing, talked about gallery space and who absolutely *had* to be invited. We were both gleeful.

"Let's pick a date," she declared with excitement.

I went into a frenzy of activity, booking a friend's gallery, designing announcements, making up a mailing list. I contacted every artist I knew and insisted that this show was not to be missed. Lynn's brother and sister-in-law in Pennsylvania offered to come and provide live music. We arranged for framing, and set a date for hanging. I planned menus and borrowed tablecloths and invited her whole clan to a pre-opening dinner at my house, and cooked the most delicious meal I could dream up. I was trying to make up for the fact that Lynn was probably dying—and that I couldn't fix it.

From the moment she arrived, she was the star of our firmament. The event was orchestrated to deliver delight at every stage, from the excitement of hanging the show the day before, to getting dressed up and being presented to an admiring public.

She looked gorgeous—delicate and gamin-like with her short-cropped hair. The off-center gait of her tilted body looked like a gesture, a leaning toward, and a smile of pleasure never left her face. The crowd swirled about her, properly impressed by her work and many, inevitably, were moved to tears. She was so young, so gifted, so beautiful. One well-known nature photographer, with whom I stood regarding her photograph of sand dunes in Death Valley confided to me,

"I think this is better than Ansel Adams' sand dunes. Look at the way she's caught the shadows…"

"Tell her!" I cried, bustling him over to where Lynn leaned against a wall, supporting her back and surveying the scene. I all but pushed them together before I excused myself to check on the buffet's supply of cheese and bread.

Celia arrived alone and then shortly afterward Jim came in with a male friend. I introduced Celia to people on one side of the room, making sure she had a glass of wine, and then greeted Jim and his friend on the other side of the room, making sure they had wine as well. I blew up balloons for the children, popping my eardrums, and reminded my teenagers to keep the table stocked with dips. When someone new arrived I was the greeter; when someone looked uncomfortable, I provided them company. I was everywhere at once, Maitre D' and Jewish mother rolled into one, and I had no idea when to stop.

And at the end of the day, after the effort and the triumph and the glory, the fact was still the same: Lynn was going to die. Pushing myself to my limits had not changed her diagnosis one whit.

I lay in bed after that for days—weeks—depressed and exhausted. My body would not move. Depleted emotionally and physically, I did not have the energy to care about anything; not my family, not Lynn, not the rest of the world. I was suffering from burn-out.

Inevitably, it was only a matter of weeks before Lynn had to come back again for another surgery. Her bones, riddled with cancer, were crumbling around the hard-won steel bar. The doctors would again perform a similar operation to the last, which meant more pain and weeks of rehabilitation and medical horrors beyond belief.

I couldn't face it—neither for her nor for me. I was still exhausted. Even if Lynn was able to keep a sense of hope, I wasn't sure I could. From where I stood, this was the time to begin preparing realistically for death. Straight dealing was in order, as far as I was concerned, not more medical heroics. But my attempts to speak with her candidly were a disaster. Her eyes clouded with mistrust, and she turned away.

Still too weary to move much, I came to the hospital less frequently—once each week, or at most, twice. During the last surgery, I had visited every other day.

The first week she was there, Jim and I visited together one evening. A spring rain was falling lightly, more mist than rain, and it shrouded the soft air with the particular perfume of newly-wet city streets. I breathed it in deeply before gagging on the hospital odors, letting Jim lead me through the corridors like a dog on a leash. If I could have, I would have turned tail and fled in the other direction—*any* other direction.

As it happened, she was in the same room as last time, with the same windowless walls, the same nurses on duty. My sense of *deja vu* was overwhelming; I was certain that time was running backward.

It was the evening just before her surgery and we sat on either side of her bed, Jim holding her left hand and I holding her right. Beneath the sheet her body made not much impression, there was so little left of her. Her face, however, was pure Lynn, somewhat puffy with drugs, but otherwise eloquent with her full gamut of expressions. Between us, she lay clenched in outrage, her now-meager body tight with frustration.

"I want to see the spring!" she lamented, clutching each of our hands hard. "I'm stuck in this sterile place, with four horrid blank walls, and outside I know spring is happening and I'm not there in it!" She clenched her teeth tight to keep from crying. "I want to go to Austria this summer. What if I don't get out of here in time to see Austria again?" I cupped her tensed hand in both of mine, trying to keep my thoughts to myself. Her skin was dry and scaly. She wept soundlessly for awhile, and I felt impatient, wanting her to scream. And then with tightened lips she moaned,

"Oh, I'm sorry I'm being so selfish…"

I all but lost my temper.

"You can holler and piss and moan, and it won't mean you're selfish," Jim assured her gently. "Try and get it out, if you can. It's quite all right to be angry." I nodded in agreement, unable to remember ever having seen Lynn cry.

"Get it out," I repeated, hearing the impatience in my voice. Turning it into a joke, I added, "I think it's about time you did a little whining." For a moment, we all shared a giggle. Then she took me up on it and whined loudly, at first in jest and then in earnest,

"Why can't they make me better? Why is this happening? Why me? I never did anything bad to anybody. Why can't I just go home and live my life—my boring old life—with my doggies and my garden and my…." Here she finally broke down, screaming and sobbing and shaking. Jim and I, still attached to her on either side, joined our free arms across her body and created a kind of cradle for her, rocking her between us, crying and crooning comfort to her until she fell asleep.

We finally left her, spent and sleeping, when the late-shift nurse came on duty. Leaving her in that hated, sterile room—she of the mountain air and green hillsides—was like leaving a lamb in the slaughterhouse. But, I kept reminding myself, this was an operation that she herself endorsed.

Would I have done the same, I wondered? Would I, in fact, have had the guts to face my death straight on at this point? Was it just easy to be brave because it wasn't me who was in the hot seat?

Or would I, like Lynn, be holding out for time, for the medical miracle?

"I just can't stand it!" I complained to Jim as we strode down the nighttime corridor arm-in-arm. "If it were up to me, she'd never be put through this butchery." I was convinced, at that moment, that I meant it. The leathery smell of his jacket made me want to burrow my nose in his shoulder. When I did, the tears came again.

"Why can't she just come to acceptance, and have some peace for the time she has left?" I bawled. He held me expertly, having spent many a night as a hospice volunteer for men dying with AIDS.

I was still very much a beginner.

"Because she's Lynn," he said simply after awhile. "She's not ready to give in to it."

"But when will she be? Does she *have* to go through all this pain first?" We left the glare of the hospital lobby and emerged onto the city night streets, and the soft spring rain.

"It's not for us to say. This is her choice."

We wandered until we found an open café, and slumped down at a table with our two beers.

"I can't stand pretending to her," I admitted. "It's making me crazy." He sat quiet, musing.

"I don't know that there's anything we can do but accept however she chooses to go through this. It's her life."

"But it's her *death*, too, and I'm a friend who's losing her!" I persisted. "And I feel like a liar when I have to keep up my end of these absurd conversations about plans for new trips, and when she gets better we'll do such and such. Did you hear that bit about Austria? Hiking in the Alps, for God's sake!" I was almost crying again, thinking, but not saying, "And what about *me?*"

He smiled sadly, picked up his beer and drank it halfway down. The foam lingered on his lips, and he wiped it off with the back of his hand.

"We had a long talk last night," he informed me, changing the subject. He rubbed his face wearily. He had been with her late, after the shift change. Lynn had been sleepless and asked him to stay.

"She said she had a confession to make." I waited while he played absentmindedly with his glass. Looking up, he went on. "She told me she was in love with me in Grad school!" After my surprise—not that she had loved him, but that she told him so—I remarked,

"Well, of course. Who wouldn't be?"

He wrinkled his nose at me and went on. "She said she only told me now because I was no longer with Celia." The tears brimmed in my eyes again. His too. He swallowed and went on, "So I told her about being gay, and she nearly choked." We both laughed a bit hysterically, and the laughter turned to tears. He continued,

"So she stared at me for the longest time, and then burst into giggles. You know how Lynn can giggle! Then she says, 'You mean I couldn't have had you anyway? After all?'" We chuckled softly and then gazed at each other with nostalgia. After a few moments I said,

"She has told me a bit about you and Celia in graduate school, and that she was surprised—those were the words she used—that you chose to marry Celia. But she never once said straight out that she wanted you for herself." I added, "But I guessed it."

"You did? I never had any idea."

"You didn't?" I asked archly. "Well, you should have." For awhile we sipped on our beers, each in our own thoughts. Then Jim turned to me, and went on,

"She did confess that most of the men she's ever been attracted to have turned out to be gay. And she asked me, very confidentially, if I thought that maybe there was something wrong with her because of it."

He guffawed and we both blurted into teary laughter, releasing the tension with a contagious hilarity that led the other patrons in the café to laugh along with us, sharing the joke.

"Oh God," he sobbed at last, laying his head on his arms, "I miss her already."

Her entry, written in a somewhat weaker hand, after the surgery and during the rehab, before she was pronounced well enough to leave the hospital:

Journey to a Strange Land—*That seems a fitting way to look at this whole experience. It's actually longer—7 weeks or 3 months if you count the entire siege—than any of our previous trips away from home. (Only Sierra summers, Europe with Margie and the Galápagos were longer, all of them life-changing experiences.) Hospitals are a different world, with a language and rhythm all their own. It's a world of white—sheets, uniforms, walls— and of long hallways. It's a world of pain and numb endurance—IV's, tubes down throats and noses, needles digging into arms, more IV's, wires and tubes all over the body, the hallucinogenic nightmare of Intensive care. Morphine…fuzziness…helplessness…having to ask for a toothbrush, for help to the bathroom, for another blanket, and please move the phone/nurse button/book/light/water within my reach. A world of sensory deprivation. Like a bad film, the dominant colors are white, black, neon-yellow—no green. When I escaped, after 6 weeks, for a day with my parents, I was daz-*

zled by colors and smells and the songs of birds. I lay and watched the rustling leaves dance silver and green in the sun, moved by flower-fragrant air. Flowers in a hospital room are more than merely pretty. They're a healing reminder of another life. In an ideal world, patients would be put not in sterile cubicles, but in untamed gardens (I want geckos and bright beetles in mine, tho that's probably a minority view!) Surely the clang of institutions can't be good for <u>anyone</u>.

In this world emotions are stretched thin, so that small frustrations bring unexpected tears. And because of the thinning of protective layers, the peeling away of ordinary busy-ness and activities and distractions, the seeing of any human pain becomes almost unbearable. The thought of "Man's inhumanity to man"—of concentration camps, of war, of any voluntary cruelty—sears vividly and deeply. A hospitalized child crying in terror for his mother, a newspaper account of tragedy evoke empathy from your own pain and fear with raw immediacy.

But it's also a world of people—numberless encounters with nurse after nurse, doctors, technicians, therapists—and so many of them are patient and warm and caring. Remember the confident optimism of Dr. Harrington, the calm of Drs Brown and Bohannon, the warmth of Dr. Yarnell...encouraging Randi, ministering-angel Mary, all important Ann and Wing, Lesley, and so many, many others—a succession of different faces and personalities and styles and cultured roots. It <u>Is</u> a cultural experience to be in a hospital in SF—Orientals, Latins, Indians, a world mixture. In trust you turn over the details of your body's care to stranger after stranger.

Through it all the people who matter most of all are the ones who are always there—family and friends. Skip—so steady throughout; even at my groggiest it gave strength to have him there. Mother, or Gertie, visiting <u>Every</u> day, Daddy and Denny when they could stand it—how could I have survived without them? Outpourings of letters and cards and flowers, the <u>Presence</u> of Carolyn, Jim, Carole, Truebloods, Kathy. A turning point in my acceptance of this particular 7-week piece of reality was the evening Carolyn held one hand and Jim the other as I choked out my frustrations and impatience at so much time ahead in the hospital in place of recuperation under the TLC of Mother and Daddy, my fear and anger at the horridly nasty things cancer can do—I'd naively, ostrich-like, assumed one simply lived along with assorted annoyances and reduced strength til something vital got *clogged up and one died. Despite warnings, I didn't really understand about the possibilities of complex, prolonged pain.*

I learned, or relearned, valuable lessons:

Be always gentle with people and don't leap to quick judgment—remember the nurse who seemed simply overweight and not too competent and who turned out to be very caring and with her own incredible cancer story—and the social worker who once seemed to be prying into my feelings and whose limp turned out to be due to a false leg from cancer at age 14—and the huge male nurse whose size and scarred face frightened me at first appearance and who turned out to be enormously gentle. In Carolyn's words, "Everyone has his own story." Wait for it.'

Be slow to judge and quick to listen.

Be careful of people.

Be patient. Now is the moment you have—don't spoil it with the tension and impatience of waiting for the <u>Next</u> thing to happen. When time is out of your control and you must wait passively, relax, enjoy "watching the parade."

Remember how much kindness people have—For example, Tom the retired fireman with his own back problem who came up to me as I lay frustrated and a little scared on a gurney in the hall: "Can I help you with that blanket?"—who radiated soothing calm—who actually came all the way to my room later to wish me well.

Learn to be alert to offer your calm to others.

The surgical horrors past, a rehab center is itself an incredible experience. The first impression was a terror at the basic assumption, "If you don't recover fully, we're here to teach you how to manage." It's THE necessary underlying precept of a rehab center, but everything in me shrieked in protest. "You don't mean Me. I'm going to get Well."

One of the oddest things about regaining mobility is to have to analyze movements you have always taken for granted. How do you stand up from a chair? Set the feet, lean forward, push off with the arms, tighten the quads and then the gluteals. Oouf! Is the strength there for each step? Today I can get off a lower seat than yesterday—progress! How do you roll over from your back onto your stomach? What do you do with that lower arm and how do you get momentum to get over? Suddenly one day it's possible again. What Are the moves you make to get up off the floor? Not the way the therapists showed—I've never done that in my life! I must rediscover the moves programmed into My bone and muscle.

And as movement returns, so do memories of times of ease and strength of those movements. I think of Margie and me shouldering our packs and confidently striding off across Norwegian tundra toward a road we'd been told was over there somewhere. I think of innumerable Sierra boulders and granite slabs—moving across talus, arms out for balance—step, leap, pause and poise in a cautious and ecstatic dance. I feel the prickle of mountain meadow sedges as I rise smoothly to a stand from a cross-legged or sprawled-flat start. I think of a sunny grassy hill in Vinalhaven and rolling sideways over and over and over down it, laughing giddy and joyful with the dizziness and the gold grass and the sun.

I'll never again be so young and strong and totally free in motion. But it doesn't really matter; I did it when I could. And now I will again be mobile and strong, always more careful, to be sure, but again able to walk and hike and move with strength and freedom.

That's no small thing—that movement we take for granted. A month in a rehab center sears that indelibly. At one point I was feeling sorry for myself and envying the rich man in the end room, thinking, "He has a spacious room with a spectacular view, and his wife comes every day to visit him and sometimes takes him out and…" Suddenly, in appalled horror, I Heard what I was thinking and, shocked, realized, "But I'll walk out of here and he's in a wheelchair for life." There's no way in that setting that I could not see myself as incredibly lucky and blessed beyond belief. (On the other hand, he may live to 90 and I probably won't. It's fortunate we don't have the impossible responsibility of choosing our illnesses, but must simply deal with what we're given.)

The patients in a rehab center are so diverse. Each has his or her particular problem to overcome and reality to face. Usually it's an instant in time that has irrevocably changed their entire life—an accident, a stroke. In so *many cases it must be terribly hard to escape the "If only...." I'm awed at the constant hard work involved in making the transition from helpless immobility to successful life in a wheelchair. The therapy room is a place of triumphs and small victories, of failures and limitations. With the steady encouragement of the therapists, patients try and try and try again. Where do they get their courage? I could deal with paraplegia if I <u>Had</u> to—I once decided I could still be me with my head and its senses plus my right arm—but quadriplegia is another matter—Where do they ever get the courage to continue? I guess you simply deal with what you have to.*

There's occasional humor, too, and one conversation between a patient, an old man and his therapist was classic:
Patient: "Doctor, that's..."
Therapist: "The doctor's not here. That's a tricycle."
P: "You mean I've been talking to a tricycle?"
T: "Yes, sir."
P: "Well...is it talking back?"
T: "No."
P: "Well then, that's OK."

Finally, in this strange land, ostensibly so far removed from my reality and my roots, there happened a kind of crystallization of my life. As at Agape, while Margie and I chopped vegetables in the kitchen, memories of people and places floated up from all levels. I felt with joy the richness and variety of my experiences. I saw change—often so unpredictable—as a dominant pattern in my life and in others'. I saw—as lines meeting and crossing and interweaving in a never-to-be-duplicated pattern—the interaction of my life with others, the importance beyond words of all those friends who are forever a part of me—Mother and Daddy, Skip, more than I will list; they know themselves. Seeing so very clearly the coexistence of change and constancy was sharp and stunning.

At one point I saw myself in a corridor with frightening medical happenings behind and around me, a sharp turn in the corridor ahead. I didn't really have courage to look around that corner until Dr. H told me that my back, at least, was most likely solid and safe from further problems. Then the corridor around the bend was straight and open, and I was ready to move along it. And by then the direction was unequivocally clear: As I lay there all those weeks, it wasn't teaching I most missed, thoroughly tho I enjoy it. I missed Skip, the dogs, the green backyard, the small daily things of my life. It became easy to think of giving up my role of teacher-botanist and busy commuter and switch to home-person and growth as an etcher. It's a shift in emphasis, not direction, a decision that feels right in all ways.

So be it."

So be it. Again, to the amazement of family, friends and I daresay the whole medical establishment, she made it through the surgery and the rehabilitation.

I visited every other day now, and brought with me armloads of branches and ferns picked in a nearby park. Under her direction, we made the room look like a jungle. I brought mangoes to tempt her palate, and avocados like the ones we used to pick wild on Santiago. She forced herself to chew on steak, for protein, she said, and swallow down her jello, but it was clear her body was no longer interested in eating. Pumped full of drugs, her face became puffier but her eyes retained their shine and, as always, she did not seem to miss a trick.

At last, after more weeks, she was declared well enough to go home—"to get on with my life," she amended with determination. She left the hospital on Skip's arm, returning to Washington via Maine, of all places, where she spent a quiet two weeks on an island in the bosom of an East-Coast family. We spoke once by phone from there, and she complained of not being able to scramble around the sea rocks as she was used to doing. As usual, I was flabbergasted into silence. Who knew—maybe Lynn *would* be the one to beat the odds and make medical history?

Once she was back in Washington, when we spoke by phone, she was still speaking in terms of eventual recovery. She referred to going back to teaching possibly by "next quarter." She talked of soon being strong enough to run the dogs, of getting back out into her etching studio. I felt reduced to saying nothing, not to mention feeling guilty and confused.

Jim went to Washington for a weekend visit—to say his good-byes, he said—and when he returned he suggested that I make the trip as well. "Do it soon," he advised, convinced that the time was now short. He noted that the dogs, what with her disability and her absences from home, had transferred their allegiance to Skip and the children, and that this seemed to devastate her.

"Were you able to talk realistically about dying?" I asked. He shook his head sadly.

"I tried once or twice, but she wasn't having any."

"Then I don't think I can go," I snapped. Softening, I asked, "How could you bear it?" He shrugged and shook his head.

"I don't know—you just do. When I left, I broke down in front of her, but she wouldn't cry with me. And when I was just about at the gate she called out,

"See you at Christmas!"

On Thanksgiving, their clan gathered together in Washington. A group photo shows her smiling and surrounded by her whole extended family, the two dogs lying at her feet. She is sitting up as straight as her spine would let her, her eyes fierce with will.

Two weeks later, on the morning of her mother's birthday with her mother by her side, she sang in a thin voice, "Happy Birthday, dear mommy...." all the way through, and then lapsed into her final coma, her mother holding her hand and talking softly to her.

A few days after her death I received a package in the mail addressed in her hand, which contained the journal that she, unbeknownst to me, had been keeping throughout her illness. The last entry is a poem written in a very shaky hand.

ALTERNATE SONG

I don't know where I'm going,
And there's no one going with me.
I wander thru the world
To the song of wind and water.

And as I pass you by
I ask your joy and laughter,
For later on I'll cry
And wander ever after.

The gift you give to me
That, passing I may love you
Is golden tho I will be
Tomorrow's longing memory.

The air is filled with gold,
The light of green leaves dancing,
The river glides along
And never heeds my asking.

Talked to doctor yesterday—a grim talk to say the least. The most important message is how much I love you all.

Gazing at Mortality

If we want to
die well, we
have to learn to
live well.
THE DALAI LAMA

ynn's death was devastating to me. I had never had a friend die before, and it exhausted me to watch her undergo one painful treatment after another, and then not be able to grieve with her the loss that both of us were facing.

My father was the first person in my life to die, just eight years before Lynn, when I was twenty-seven and he was not yet fifty. His was a rather traumatic, premature death also, and like Lynn, he submitted to outrageous medical heroics up to the last ragged pulse of his failing heart. His final moments were spent surrounded by medics pounding on his chest to restart a heart they knew was finished. We could hear him, from outside the hospital door, as he cried out in agony,

"Don't let me die!" My ears will never, to the end of my life, forget that sound.

At my father's funeral, I could hardly bear to look into the open casket. He was lying there still as a stone, rouge-cheeked and puffy—my father but not my father—in his good suit, which I had only seen him wear once in life, to my wedding. I was too scared to breathe. I could see the spectre of my own death right around the bend, and it was like a dagger of ice aimed right at my heart. How could he be right there—with an expression I hardly recognized—and yet be totally gone at the same time? I didn't know what he was thinking, or whether I existed anywhere in his consciousness. I hadn't even had a chance to tell him good-bye!

I had recently given birth to my third child, and it seemed uncanny, this juxtaposition of a life beginning and a life ending at the same time. It was a bit as if my new baby were taking my father's place. There was, at the time, nobody to talk to about my swirling thoughts and feelings: the officiating Rabbi said something about God's will and eternal rest and looked frightened when I asked him for *meaning*, and my relatives urged me not to cry around the children.

In the following weeks, I felt a growing sense of helplessness as my mind went in-and-out of being numb, my body tensed with unresolved grief and my sleep was disrupted by starts of terror several times a night. My husband held me and tried to comfort me, but there were no easy words to describe the depth of my grief and confusion. What I really wanted to do was wail and scream and sob and kick things hard, but this kind of behavior would probably have disturbed everyone—including myself—and would have earned me crazy-lady status in the neighborhood.

So, bottling it all up, I went back to the daily busy-ness of raising three small children, although, not for a moment would my mind get unstuck from that single image of my father laid out in a coffin, unbreathing. Obsessed, I would push my daughter in the playground swing and imagine her sweet giggling face turn into a waxen death's head, knowing, with terrified certainty, that one day she would die. As I pushed the children's stroller down the street, my eyes would go in and out of focus and all the other pedestrians would appear to be joined in a line dance, like the characters on the ridge in the last scene of "The Seventh Seal," waving up and down in their dance of death.

I put great effort into distracting myself from these visions by holding parties and creating art projects involving all the neighborhood children, but with a steady, dark gaze Death seemed to follow me from the corners of every room. I was in serious avoidance, I see now, covering the traces with frenetic motion and color and talk, much as my society had taught me to do. It makes me wonder about our avoidance, as a culture, of the normal event of death which is the eventual portion of every one of us, while at the same time giving a great deal of attention to violent death, assisted suicide and abortion.

What I needed to do then, more than anything in the world, was to grieve. And to express openly my fears of being inexplicably erased from existence, as my father had been. Not being—that's what was so terrifying—the nothingness; the void.

When I think back to that dreadful, sometimes suicidal period of my life, I realize that the basis of my fear was a fathomless sense of loneliness at someday being separated from the world, from other people, especially ones I loved, from my own life, from my mind. Like my father, I feared I would simply vanish, become invisible to the universe, cease to exist. I couldn't take this impossibility in, so I shoved it far away below consciousness, exhausting myself with the effort. As I turned away from everything that evoked that fear, my world became smaller and smaller and safety became harder to assure.

Until one night, in a dream, I finally went over the edge.

I am walking along the rim of a steep sea cliff, tensely putting one foot in front of the other, determined not to lose my balance. One wrong move and I can plummet to the rocks below, and to certain death. My calves are tight, my thighs braced, my breath is held, my neck is tense. One wrong move... one wrong move....

And then it happens! I lose control for a moment, one foot slips off the edge and I feel myself hurtling off solid ground into space. My stomach lurches in terror such as I have never felt before. The end...seconds away... pain unimaginable...ohhh....

But I don't drop to my death. I float. I am fully conscious. The air supports me and instead of a freefall to extinction, I am surrounded by vast sunlit spaces. Air, ocean, sky forever and myself, all the same thing. I am shot through with Light, aloft and easy. I have indeed fallen to my death, but in death I am still alive

elsewhere.

I awoke the next morning in a state of grace. Out my window was the play of light and shadow in the branches of the incense cedar, and on the quilt the shape of my hands, wondrous. The soft, in-and-out breathing of my husband, still asleep next to me, brought tears of tenderness, and in the next room were the burbles of the children waking. Miracles. Color, form, sounds of the vivid world. I took a few shuddering breaths and my chest opened, the heaviness in my body giving way to effervescence, and joy filling the places where frozen fear had been. I hugged the cat hard until he hollered, and moved through the house barefoot, grateful for every little thing.

The epiphanies continued and my days were profound with meaning, every sight and encounter like a peephole into the workings of a grand Universe. The chatter and chirps of birds and children playing, rumbling trucks and shouted conversations entered my awareness like a kind of life-music. I would laugh out loud at the brilliant red of a sliced ripe tomato, and the smell of a fresh-picked lemon once made me cry. I remember being astonished by my children's legs, the way they bent at the knees and ankles and hips, the gleam of intelligence in their round baby eyes. I was riveted by the way smoke spiraled up, and the way water swirled down the drain. Garbage trucks clanking down our street made me think of how ocean tides served the same function to the land. And making love, at night, carried me right to the core of life and death itself: life was the foreplay, death the climax. Which did I prefer? Both. *Both!*

Death was not separate from life, it was glorious resolution.

Life had come bursting through the doors of my perception, waking me up again and again, hour after hour, showering me with ordinary miracles that had always been there, but never seen before. The air I breathed became dense and interesting, as if all the breaths ever taken by living beings were contained in it, now breathed by me. Listening to the rasping breaths of the cat in the quiet of the morning, I knew these would be stilled, and sooner than my own. And I began to accept that after my own breaths had stopped, I would dissolve back into the air, absorbed once again in the rich enormity of eternity.

For a full month, to the day, I experienced these epiphanies and then, like a volcano after a series of eruptions, I gradually simmered back down to something resembling normal existence. But not quite. Like the volcano, I had accreted an extra skin that had not been there before, which covered every surface of my being—mind, body and spirit.

And, it seemed, I was no longer afraid of dying.

Once before, when I was a child growing up in Brooklyn, I had a similar experience. It lasted a moment rather than a month, but for years I wondered what I had seen, and if other people saw it too. It happened during a game of roller-skate tag, right in the middle of East 7th Street, near Flatbush. I was chasing after Larry, a wiry Irish kid who was a much better skater than I, and suddenly I could see double: there he was, skating fast just out of my reach, but also, there we both were, as if

I were watching us from above; the colors of our jackets, the silvery, flashing wheels of our skates, the houses on either side of the street. At the same moment as I felt the wind in my face and my legs pumping after Larry, I also saw all of Brooklyn stretching out to the ocean and beyond. I saw our whole earth whirling through all of space, dark and clear.

Trying to catch up with him, swift-turning after his dodges, I felt the tick of each second, but also the stillness of all-of-time. Suddenly, I knew the feel of the slow evolutions of earth and plants and animals; I felt into a future containing the children of my children's children. And for just that tick of time, I knew that I belonged to the whole thing, whatever it was, and that right there at that moment on East 7th Street, with all the kids skating and laughing like mad, we contained everything in the universe that ever was or ever would be.

A second later, Larry got away and Helen caught me so that we fell down together, breathless, but in that dizzying time out of time, I understood that it was impossible *not* to exist, in one form or another. Whatever else happened, I could never not be.

These reassuring glimpses of our world as existing within a much larger, gorgeous reality have led me, over the years, to ask in every way I know how: Who am I? Where am I? What is going on here?

At this point in my life, I have an evolving sense of myself as an essential, conscious Self that has taken birth in a physical body on the earth to experience the lessons implied in matter. My basic identity, my soul, is like a spark of light from a greater Light, and it incarnates again and again as a different being in a new body. With each lifetime this soul responds to the particular challenges presented and, over eons, painstakingly acquires the knowledge that it (or me) is ultimately connected to the entire cosmos and all existence in the universe.

So when I ask myself, "Who will die when I die?," I understand that my body will surely eventually fall apart in one way or another—that's what bodies do—but the "I" who inhabits my body will remain whole, conscious and viable in some other form I cannot yet comprehend.

I love the words of Hermes Trismegistis, the sage whose wisdom was ancient even to the Egyptians. This is a fragment from his teachings:

The Soul passes from form to form
and the mansions of her pilgrimage are manifold;
you put off your bodies as raiment,
and your suit of clothes gets left behind.
You are from old, O Soul of Man,
yea, you are from Everlasting.

On the beach at Santiago Island, Lynn and I came upon the rotting carcass of a sea lion, dead, we estimated, for close to a week. The body stank, and it crawled with flies, ravenous maggots, mockingbirds, gulls and lava lizards. The sea lion was rapidly disappearing as sea lion as it entered the bodies of other creatures, being recycled as food. Within days nothing was left on the beach but bleaching bones which, in turn, would gradually wear down into sand.

But out in the surf the waves were filled with cavorting sea lions barking, sleek, alive.

We swam with some pups in the colony one day, Lynn and I, treading in the waves as they dove beneath us and swooshed around us, playing with us by popping up right in front of our noses and then speeding away. We tired of the game long before they did. Riding the waves toward the beach, we let the surf carry us back until it was shallow enough to stand, and then walked out against the pull of the water.

It was like changing mediums, going from the density of the ocean to the bright, open, sunlit spaces of air. I moved from the rich juice of silty sea to a more subtle frequency of vibration; my eyes could not quite see its edges, my ears could barely hear its winds. I wonder now if the experience of dying won't be similar to that of coming up out of water, moving from the three-dimensionality of physical being into an open, all-encompassing luminosity—infinite, ineffable, loving. I wish Lynn, who loved the physical world so dearly, was available to ask.

I expect she knows by now the nature of the new sea she swims in, and could help me try to describe, in three-dimensional language, the difference between the limits of what my mind is able to formulate about the world I live in, and what I am able to intuit about the infinite, ultimate source of my being. I suspect that the one fits inside the other like nesting dolls, the world of form a kind of crystal in its medium of the infinite, made of the same stuff but hardened, shaped—a world.

"But how do you know?" asks my husband, a down-to-earth scientist who requires verifiable proof from me much of the time. My inadequate response, even after all of our years together, is, "I know because I just know." What I mean is that I tend to perceive the world intuitively, through my imagination, dreams, flashes of insight. I feel my way toward knowledge, and trust this process of perception just as he trusts his mode of logical thinking.

I try bringing him *proof* from the texts of various wisdom traditions. But they tend to say, in one way or another, that intuitive understanding cannot be taught, but must be *caught*, meaning that language, which refers to a three-dimensional world, cannot describe a multi-dimensional cosmos.

"I haven't caught it yet," he shrugs meaningfully, unconvinced by my insistence that it is the direct, unmediated perception of the Wholeness of things that is called for, rather than the precise, objective examination of one thing at a time. We have, by now, reached a state of mutual respect, if not comprehension, but all the time I was growing up, my subtle feelings and subjective perceptions were dismissed as wishy-washy; my dreams, I was told, were not real. For a long time, I assumed I was stupid.

The kind of training I received in school encouraged us to disregard what I consider the best of what it means to be human: the dreams and the fleeting moments of insight; synchronicities that occur out of the blue and connect us to the larger universe; unexpected rushes of joy and revelation; the creative fire that emerges as art. I even wonder if it is not perilous to ignore this intuitive gift, for it is our way into a transcendent universe that includes, but is beyond time and space as we understand it. For there in the context of the glorious, multi-dimensioned Wholeness is where the cycle of life and death really takes place. Like water lilies floating upon the reflecting surface of a vast pond, we all have roots that go deep into the nourishing, unseen mud on the bottom from which blossom each season's flowers. The surface is beautiful, but it is not the whole thing by a long shot.

Within this unimaginable immensity everything cycles—now here, now gone, now here again. This year's flowers fade, fall to earth and become humus for the next generation of plants. The seasons turn; day darkens to night and night brightens again to day. Human beings and animals die and new generations are born, and through it all, the essence remains.

For me, there is nothing to fear, for there is nowhere to go but here. I keep learning, a little more each day, that life is a voluptuous adventure, that love is the basis of my existence and that the death I used to find so fearful, in reality has no sting.

THREE

Jim's Story

To die in life is to become
life. The wind stops skirting you
and enters. All the roses, suddenly,
are blooming in your skull.

RUMI

After Lynn's death, Jim and I met once for a walk in the hills, to the place we had scattered the wildflowers, and then not again until a year had passed. At first there was the occasional phone call to check in, but after that, nothing. It was as if he had entered the gay world of the city and been swallowed up, gone where I could not follow.

So it was with some surprise that I heard his voice on the other end of the phone suggesting we get together for a little reunion on the first anniversary of Lynn's death, to remember our friend and reconnect with each other. "Anyhow," he said rather mysteriously, "there's someone I'd like you to meet."

When he arrived hand-in-hand with a striking man in wire-rimmed spectacles and a reserved, serious air, I hardly recognized him. It wasn't especially the tight pink T-shirt or the black leather jacket—but he had permed his hair! A frizzle of tight curls replaced what had been an ordinary crop of short brown hair. The two men together, one tall, dark and impeccable; the other short and outrageously decked out, were like an illustration of the attraction of opposites. Jim's dark brown eyes watched me closely for a reaction, crinkling with amusement. I tried not to gape.

"I told you she'd be polite," he commented to Joe, grabbing me in a bear hug and swinging me back and forth. I laughed into his shoulder, breathing in leather and clean skin and some unrecognizable, exotic fragrance. "Joe was a bit worried about your reaction," he informed me, opening our embrace to introduce me to his new partner.

"You really *are* extraordinary to look at, Jim," I admitted. A look of intimate amusement passed between them, and then pain. Joe cleared his throat and shot me an uneasy look, lowering his eyes when I turned in his direction. Jim gave his hand a reassuring squeeze.

"I *love* being extraordinary-looking after all those years of being a little brown mouse," he announced, doing a quirky two-step through the kitchen as I led them out to the studio in the garden where I had set up a small altar for Lynn.

In the center of a ring of cushions on the floor I had placed a photograph of Lynn at the flamingo lagoon on Santiago Island, her arms outstretched, her hair blowing and a wide grin for the camera. A lit candle burned steadily before her picture, and her etching "Offering" was set up alongside her bright, open face. Jim crouched down, pulling Joe with him and picked up the photo of Lynn, cradling it to his cheek for a moment. Then he held it up for Joe to see. Tears brimmed in his eyes, gleaming in the candlelight, and he reached for me. For awhile we just rocked together, not speaking.

"Missed you, honey," he finally crooned softly. "Missed *us*—all three of us!"

"Me too," I sniffled, rummaging in my pocket for a tissue. "It was like you disappeared down a rabbit hole. I thought I'd never see you again."

"No way," he objected, wiping his tears and mine with the palm of his hand. "I've been rather preoccupied with my new life lately, but you're my sister, no matter what."

I hugged him again and we both smiled through our tears, blew our noses and settled down onto the cushions around the little altar. I struck a match and lit a stick of incense. A curl of smoke spiraled into the candlelit room and spread. Joe crossed his legs somewhat stiffly, but sat straight and still, waiting. Jim, it was clear, was the extrovert of the two.

"Well, I've spent this year learning how to breathe," he confessed, leaning toward Joe for a touch of the shoulders. "It's such a relief to just be who the heck I am." He lifted his eyebrows for emphasis. "It seems like every day I find another way to come out. Sometimes I feel like an adolescent discovering the world. I didn't do this when I was seventeen. I'm having a blast!"

Joe nodded ironic assent, and they exchanged a private look. Jim caught me staring at his new hair-do and raked his fingers through his curls.

"Like it? Not to worry," he reassured me, "it's just a phase. I'm trying out everything and believe me, it gets worse—or better, depending on how you look at it."

"Worse, mostly," remarked Joe wryly, speaking in a soft-spoken twang.

"Too bad Lynn didn't get to know this side of you. Can you imagine how she would have reacted to curly hair?" I declared. We burst into laughter at the thought of her polite expressions of dismay, Jim miming her perfectly and reminiscing about the past.

"Remember the time when…?" Each sentence began that way, interruptions and laughter and tears flowing as we remembered our friend. We recalled the good times—nights and days in deserts and forests, clambering high mountain peaks and crossing lava beds; and we remembered the hard times—the stages of her decline and her fierce attachment to life. Joe listened quietly to our animated talk, his reserve gradually melting into fascination for the life Jim had led before they met.

"Hey, Lynn!" cried Jim, rousing the dark corners of my studio into motion, the flickering candle throwing moving shadows upon the walls with the wind of his voice, "We miss you madly. Don't forget that!" He beat out a rhythm with his hands on the wood floor.

"No," I repeated more softly, "don't forget that. But," I went on wistfully, "I wish to God we knew where you were."

We sat in silence for awhile, our breaths intermingling. The candle burnt lower, spilling tears of hot wax into the saucer holding it. The incense by now had smoked down, leaving a lingering fragrance of sandalwood in the air, and I sank into the peace of the quiet room and the presence of a well-loved friend.

"So," I sighed finally, "how are your colleagues reacting to all this? Have you come out at work?"

"I can hardly hide my perm from them," he replied reasonably, turning to Joe with a private wink. "Yes, I'm out at work, but it's not easy for them and it's not easy for me." He let out a deep, shuddering sigh. "But I'm committed both personally and politically to making it happen. All this secrecy doesn't do anybody any good." His voice took on an edge of vehemence. I could hear a fierce anger just on the other side of the words. The conservatism of university academics was legion, and as Jim tended to be academically as innovative as he was personally, this would not be the first time he had come under attack from certain members of the Establishment.

"This new stuff is only partly about sexual politics," he declared, shifting himself on the cushion as if to gain leverage for what he was about to say, "but it's much bigger than that." His eyes had that deep shine I remembered, reflecting the dancing flame of the candle. I leaned forward with anticipation, realizing all over again how much I loved this vast spirit, this playful genius.

"Tell me," I demanded, all ears for what he was about to come up with.

"Remember when Norm and I were in the North Coast range last year working on the floristic survey?" I nodded. Norm was a like-minded colleague with whom Jim worked closely, a man whose sexual orientation I had always wondered about. "Well, we realized that the standard *Manual* of native plants is out of date, and really not very useful in this part of the state anyway, so we've decided to revise it." He rubbed his palms on his knees as if he were petting a cat.

"You don't mess around, do you?" I remarked, shaking my head. The task of revising a standard botanical handbook of hundreds of pages had to be monumental, a lifetime's work, at least. "How do you propose to do this?"

"Good question," he declared, hauling in a deep breath as you do before the start of a race. "We want to approach it entirely differently than has been done before...."

"I'm not too surprised," I murmured, smiling sidelong at Joe.

"...and to make it accessible to everyone who is interested in plants, not only professional botanists. We want to use everyday English as well as botanical terms so that it's available to lay people as well as scientists. We figure we can get the job done in about ten years."

"Does that mean that someone like me, who's never taken a botany course, could go for a walk in the hills and look up the wildflowers I see?" I asked. He hesitated for a moment.

"With a little experience, I'd say yes," he replied. "That's the idea, anyhow." For a moment in the semi-darkness, his silhouette looked unfamiliar as if there was someone new in the room with me. He went on, his voice full of excitement. "It will be a big book and much more concise than an ordinary Field Guide, but the answer is yes, anybody who speaks the English language can easily learn to use it."

"It's a superb idea! I love it! Will you have trouble finding support, do you think?" Joe pulled uneasily at the tops of his socks, smoothing out the creases over his ankles. For a moment Jim distractedly watched the gesture, and then turned back to me.

"We may well have trouble finding all the support and acceptance we need but we are convinced it will happen anyway, because it's supposed to happen." He said this all on a single breath and when he was finished, the silence in the room fairly pulsed. His eyes dared me to challenge him.

"Bravo," I declared. He softened and shook his head.

"Believe me, I have no desire to always be the warrior. All I really want to do is teach and run up and down the mountains looking at plants. I get no joy from all this controversy."

"I know you don't purposely play the renegade, but you *do* have a tendency to challenge the conventional wisdom. Some people must think you make a career of it."

"Well, they're wrong, that's all," he snapped. "And when I think the conventional wisdom is off base, I've got to say so, whatever it takes. It's like staying in the closet and pretending you're somebody you're not. I won't do it professionally, and I won't do it personally!"

"Bravo and bravo again," I declared softly.

Jim's work in the past had indeed been controversial. He was researching a network of fungi which connected the root systems of plants from the largest trees to the tiniest grasses. This meant that beneath the ground an invisible system of nourishment, energy and "information" formed a living skin that spread through the soil.

"So these so-called individual plants," Jim was saying now, as we spoke again about his current work, "are really not separate from each other, but are more like projections from a living web."

"It seems so obvious, actually," I commented.

"From your philosophical point of view perhaps, and mine, but not from the standpoint of classical biology. The scientific model tends to be based upon specific differences rather than on how things fit together." He sighed somewhat wearily. "It'll change...in time...," he mused, cracking his knuckles, first one hand, then the other and then ran a caressing finger across the feather in "Offering."

"What's been hard to take," he confessed slowly, glancing at Joe before he spoke, "is that some of my colleagues have been characterizing this kind of scientific thinking as 'gay.' The mean rumor around the department is that my work is 'queer,' which they mean as an insult. '*Queer Ideas*' is a term I've heard bandied about when nobody thought I was listening. It's not everyone, by any means, but the insults are coming from a small group that holds the power, and the others sort of back off when the nastiness gets going. That hurts."

Joe, who had been silent all evening, now spoke up.

"Your ideas *are* gay," he insisted. "They've got a different quality from, say, what the zoologists do, or even the systemacists in botany do. Right?"

"Go on," said Jim gently, placing a light hand on Joe's knee.

"OK. So, the animal guys basically go out hunting, and they skin the animal and dissect it and describe it—dead. That's not what you're doing; you're searching for the unity in living things, which is a much more gentle approach. As far as I'm concerned, that's a gay characteristic. I mean, it's got soul."

"Thanks honey," Jim agreed, "but what about folks like our friend here? She's not gay and she's got soul."

"Neither am I a scientist," I chimed in. "But I take Joe's point, and happen to agree."

"Furthermore," continued Joe, warming to the subject, "from what I've seen, lots of botanists are gay and certainly there are more gay botanists than zoologists. Have you noticed? I suspect it's because botany is basically a gentler science altogether."

"I had no idea that was true," I commented.

"Oh yes," they both retorted, Joe with a wry purse of the lips. "Mind you, most stay quite well hidden in the closet, though it's clear to anybody who's interested just who is and just who isn't." Jim nodded in confirmation, seeing my eyes widen with the news.

"Norm?" I asked tentatively. They both laughed out loud.

"Of course," said Jim with a knowing smile.

"So nobody knows?"

"*Everybody* knows," he corrected me, "and nobody says 'peep.'"

"That doesn't sound terribly healthy for you," I remarked darkly.

"You're right. It's not. In fact, it's a first-class bummer. But as far as I'm concerned, especially with so many of my friends dying of AIDS all around me, there's no time to speak anything but your best truth, and there's no time to do anything but the best work you know how to do. And if my colleagues have problems with what I have to offer as a scientist, or if they have problems with who I am or how I live my life, then it's their problem to deal with, not mine."

"I just pray," I said after awhile, when the candle had sputtered and gone out, and the nearly full moon had risen higher into the sky, "that they don't make their problem *your* problem."

Later, after hugs and promises to keep in touch, when I walked them out to their car, they were still spoofing the little ditty that had arisen spontaneously from our conversation.

My problem is your problem so please don't make it his problem; 'cause her problem became his problem when my problem became yours!

Jim and Norm's proposal for the revised *Manual* in fact *was* met with some scorn and resistance, especially from the group that wanted to ground the project, and battle lines were soon drawn. A few systemacists were even more hostile than Jim had anticipated, and although a large number of botanists across the country were sympathetic to the project and interested in writing chapters on their own specialties, the detractors were vehemently vocal and, to Jim's dismay, covertly homophobic. The result was that many closeted gay botanists drew ever more tightly into their burrows of silence.

In an article written at the time about his research, he makes a plea for understanding:

What I see when I look at the non-human world around me is sets of absolute and very complex interdependencies. In all kinds of ways, at any level you want to approach it, organisms are interdependent, and the inanimate world is interdependent with the living natural world. And you can take that to a more cosmic level. My perception as a scientist is that the universe is all one piece. And I see humans as simply a part of that, as not separate from that piece. We are all interdependent in ways that are so subtle and so complex that we haven't begun to think about them. And maybe can't ever think about them.

His life, as he described it to me at the time, was often like slogging uphill in mud. He was sometimes depressed, and began to meditate in an attempt to maintain equilibrium in the storm. For every positive step of the process there were a series of hostile forces to overcome—from blatant mockery to undercover sabotage. More than once he faltered, heartbroken, and swore to step down and return to undergraduate teaching, either letting the *Manual* project die on the vine, or hand it over to his detractors to "do on a twenty-year timetable—which means never," as he mournfully told me. But each time—even after once handing in his resignation notice, and then retracting it—he somehow found the extra ounce of strength, and determined to carry on despite the obstacles. The heroic battle he waged in the open was being fought with equal valor in the privacy of his own heart.

We got together for a picnic lunch in my garden in the middle of a working day, at his request. He had news, he said. I spread a blanket in the dappled green shade of the apple tree and we sat down cross-legged, side by side over tunafish-salad sandwiches. For awhile we just looked at each other softly, eye-gazing. His eyes, as always those dark, bright wells, reflected more than the sky. In silence we took bites of our sandwiches.

"More juice?" I murmured.

"Please," he replied, holding out his mug. It was like the peace before the storm, and at last hauling in a big breath, he said,

"I've got good news and bad news. Which would you like first?"

"Good news," I responded immediately, holding off the bad for as long as possible and praying it had nothing to do with his health.

"OK. The good news is that we're hiring someone at the *Manual* project who may be the find of the century. She was the brightest, most enthusiastic student in my class, and she wants to work with me!"

"I've always said you were irresistible, Jim."

"There's no accounting for taste, I guess," he tossed back. "But she's a Godsend, really. She's already organized the office to a fare-thee-well, she's fund-raising like mad and finding sources of money we never dreamed existed before, and the best thing of all is that she believes in the project the way Norm and I have always envisioned it. It's a miracle for us!"

"Remember when you said it would work out somehow because it was supposed to work?" I reminded him.

"Right. I'd forgotten that. You've got to meet her. Susan. I think you'll like each other. And there's another really strange thing about it. She reminds me of Lynn. Same coloring, same kind of personality. You'll see. They even have a similar laugh."

"Strange coincidence, huh?"

"Nothing's strange to me anymore," he sighed. "So—I've decided to go on half-time," he ended bluntly.

"Oh." A niggling fear buzzed sluggishly somewhere in my gut. "Is that the bad news?" I asked tentatively.

"No. It's just part of both the good news and the bad news. I'm going on half-time so I can be a volunteer for the Shanti Project. Joe and I are going to do it together. Everyone we know is getting sick and dying…" He spoke this last word almost in a whisper, "and when I realized I had stopped counting after thirty friends died, I panicked. I've got to be out there in the trenches." He took a breath as if to say more and it struck me that he hadn't mentioned the bad news yet. My feet ached with the fear that he was going to say he was HIV positive, and my whole being backed away from the possibility. My fingers tightened on my sandwich and my shoulders braced for the rest of his news. The tension between us was palpable. At last, staring at me for an endless few seconds, he slapped the ground hard with the flat of his palm and said,

"Norm is HIV positive."

Inevitably, after that day our paths diverged. When Jim was neither teaching nor working on the *Manual* he was either at Norm's bedside or attending to his sick compatriots in the city.

"I am closing the eyes of many," he told me sadly on the phone one day when I asked how it was going. But he wrote a letter addressed to his friends outside the gay community, describing his life now and explaining why many of us had not heard from him in awhile.

One of the things that really helped me come out all the way was working with the Shanti Project. For the first time I got to know, in an emotionally intimate way, gay people who were entirely different from me, with entirely different histories. People who had been drag queens from age fourteen. People who were into leather and S&M. Militant lesbians who, if it hadn't been for the Shanti context, might not have been willing to speak to me at all. My horizon, my sense of what the gay community was, just exploded. And the sense of support and love that came out of that just blew me away—I had never experienced that.

The thing that really hit me was what acceptance was all about. I'd never really accepted myself, so I hadn't accepted anybody else. It allowed me to accept myself, and in the process see other people for who they really were, rather than what they looked like on the surface from a block away. It just helped me to see what the judgments were and to back off from them and say, "Hey, you don't need to live like that!" That's really changed my whole life.

The years that followed, Jim was to say later, were the years we both became healers. While he walked the path with men—mostly men—who were dying of this dread immune-deficiency disease, I experimented in my studio with various techniques of movement and sound in an attempt to find ways of enhancing immune system function. What I was trying to understand was how the body in motion might help maintain balance of the subtle energies of mind, body and spirit, such that what resulted was resonance with the Source. Whatever *the Source* was....

My hunch was that, like Jim's idea that all living things were connected to and interdependent with each other and the cosmos, a healthy organism, such as a human being, had to be in interdependent balance with the whole environment, both seen and unseen.

"I suspect we're doing the same research," I exclaimed to him one evening on the phone. "I start with the assumption of the interconnections you talk about, and try to bring them together in harmony in a person. It looks like I'm getting somewhere. I think some people are actually getting better as a result of dancing and singing once a week!"

"Working with any folks with AIDS?" he asked shortly.

"Two men," I answered. "One of them came in with a very low T-cell count, and after three months it's almost up to normal. I mean, of course this isn't the only treatment he's getting."

"How are you working with him?"

"Well, he's a special case because he's a classically trained singer—I couldn't do the same thing with everyone—but we're essentially doing improvisational opera, and he's working through his heavy emotional issues through drama and song. It's incredible to witness; and, the fact is that his T-cell count seems to have normalized." Jim whistled.

"Had any remissions yet?" he asked, half in jest. In fact, a few people with AIDS and cancer had been finding their way to my door lately. Some, like the singer Duncan, I used as guinea pigs, trying out one idea after another to see what worked; others I treated more gently, helping to alleviate pain, to reassure. I had not yet been called upon to prepare anyone for death.

"No-o," I admitted, not mentioning that in the secret spaces of my heart I had every intention of rescuing Jim if he became ill. I just had to work even more diligently, learn a little faster to find my way through this puzzle. I dared not say so out loud, not even to him.

"Not yet," I replied lightly, as if it were a joke.

Joe and Jim were married in a public ceremony along with two thousand other people in Washington, D.C., that year. The weekend demonstration was perhaps the largest gathering of gay people ever to have occurred in the world at that point. In a letter written to family and friends about the event, Jim writes:

Can you imagine half a million loving, joyous, angry, determined gay people on the front lawn of the U.S. Capitol? We stretched forever! Jesse Jackson, Eleanor Smeal, Whoopi Goldberg, Dan Bradley, and others had powerful things to say—but among all those people, we saw not a single negative or hostile interaction. Loving, proud, secure—and mellow!

He goes on to describe his experience of the demonstration and his arrest:

Early on Tuesday morning, our group of twelve gathered in the cold dawn near the Supreme Court, watching hundreds of riot and motorcycle police converge on the plaza where we were soon to confront them. They barricaded the Court plaza and lined up in solid ranks to keep us away from the area that is off-limits for all demonstrations. Before long, there were about 5,000 demonstrators on the east lawn of the Capitol, facing the Court.

Many of the women who organized the action were in the first wave to approach the steps. Our mixed group was, too, and by chance we were pushed right up against the barricades where we stopped, sang, chanted and waited. Demonstrators were being "allowed" onto the plaza in very small groups. When we realized that the police were controlling OUR action, our group decided to insist on being arrested now. The police responded dramatically with night sticks and barriers. We seemed stuck. But when the police began to drag a friend through the line, I cranked up my determination to squirm under the barricade and through four pairs of kicking riot boots.

It worked! I was hauled off, searched, handcuffed, photographed and loaded onto a bus. Over the next twelve hours, with about 850 others, I was in thirteen different holding units. At one point a policeman lost control, grabbed me because I was handy, and was pretty vicious. About 100 prisoners went wild. Joe heard the commotion OUTSIDE the jail and somehow knew I was involved! One result was that all the police were very cordial from then on. I wasn't seriously hurt, but did submit a statement that may be used in a class action suit to help control such things in the future. Eventually we made it to a courtroom, pleaded "proud to be guilty" to the charge of "parading on Supreme Court grounds," and paid a $50 fine.

The action was the most personally empowering thing I have ever done. It burned away much fear on many levels as I realized how strong I am, and how well I can stand up for truth and love in the face of daunting physical power. Joe had a harder time—he was on the outside with the responsibility of keeping track of us and making sure he was there when needed. I thanked him with a magnificent dinner at the stately Occidental—quite a contrast to jail!

Clearly, we are proud of ourselves and all others willing to stand up, be counted, and speak the truth. We send our love to you—and our pride in you as well—along with our hopes for a just and peace-filled world.

Love, Jim

After that we saw very little of each other for a long time. When he and Joe were not at work, they held vigil at the bedsides of friends and clients. Periodically, they traveled, getting as far away from the AIDS scene as they could. I would receive postcards from faraway places: China, Costa Rica, Paris.

During those years I continued to explore the use of dance and sound for healing, studying *Tai Chi Chuan* in Shanghai, joining the gospel choir of a local Black church, learning human anatomy. While Jim continued to work, despite the resistance, on his *Manual,* I wrote an allegory on the *chakra* system, using stories from my life to illustrate the subtle energies in the body. We each, in our own way, were renegades searching for an alternate way to perceive and describe the world.

When Norm died, we spent a sad afternoon walking in the hills together. Jim looked weary, a bit gray—not unexpected in someone deeply grieving. We talked of work, mine and his; we talked of our families, mine and his; but for a whole afternoon I could not ask whether he and Norm had ever been lovers. Of course, it was none of my business, but we both knew very well that the question of Jim's HIV status lay between us like a ticking bomb. Whenever the conversation veered anywhere close to the subject, a dense quiet would fall between us.

And then almost a year later, the other shoe dropped. There was his voice on my answering machine, breathy, exhausted.

"Hi honey," was the message. "I miss you. Call me, huh?"

I phoned him right away, and he answered groggily.

"I'm just up from a nap," he apologized, clearing his throat. "I don't always sound this out of it."

"I've missed you," I said.

"Sorry it's been so long. I've been a hermit lately. It's been a hard time—depression. I haven't been able to shake it."

"Jim...I wish I had known."

"I know...I just haven't wanted to lay it on anyone."

"But…"

"Listen, before you even ask one question, I have to tell you that the answer to every single one is 'Yes.'" That struck me dumb. "Gotcha!" he quipped.

"You got me, right. So, toss it to me." I was lying, of course, and he knew it. I would rather be doing anything else than listening to what he had to say to me. From across the telephone wires I could hear him hesitate. I closed my eyes, waiting.

"Yes, the *Manual* is almost finished. Yes, I'm officially retired from the University. Yes, Joe and I are still together. Yes, I would love to come and dance in your studio with you." With my eyes closed, I seemed to be sinking into a protective doze. I waited, my heart like a lump of lead in my chest. "And yes, I've got full-blown AIDS."

The words echoed, surreal, in my listening ear. My eyes were still closed and I slid toward sleep. The line between us went suddenly empty of sound, and then we both breathed again at the same time.

"That means you've been HIV positive for…how long?" I tried to keep the shock out of my voice, the hurt at not being thought a close-enough friend to have known, and my relief at having been spared grief before this moment.

"Seven years," he replied quietly. "And," he sighed, "you're wondering why I kept it from you all this time."

"Well, yes…but…you don't really have to explain…"

"Yes, I do. I didn't tell anybody because I didn't want to. Joe knew, and a support group—that's all."

"I guessed," I confessed.

"How could you not?"

"Oh, Jim…"

"So, when can I start this dance stuff with you? Finally, I've got some free time. Can I come?"

"When?"

"I'm a retired gent now," he informed me. "I've got all the time in the world! Pardon the pun." There was little I could do except laugh—a bit hysterically.

"How about tomorrow at one?"

"Tomorrow at one it is," he said.

By the time Jim drove up the next day, I had all but lost my nerve. I was in dread of what I would see. Would the Jim who came to the door be a cadaverous shadow of the man I knew, gray-skinned and covered with lesions? Would fear and horror show on my face? Could I, in fact, save him with my groundbreaking work? Was this a chance to make medical history…?"

I shook my head to dispel the workings of an overactive imagination and flung open the door. There Jim stood, a broad grin on his wonderfully familiar face and his quite sturdy arms open for a hug. His curls had long since given way to short-cropped brown hair, now speckled with gray, and his coming-out paraphernalia of bright colors and jewelry was replaced by the ordinary garb of a young, middle-aged professional man. He was a bit thinner, perhaps, but this was the Jim I knew.

As we embraced, pulled away to get a good look at each other and then embraced again, I found myself automatically doing the healer's intuitive intake: pallor; dryness of lips; tone of voice; light in eyes; quality of energy. Except for an undercurrent of strain and some withdrawal of energy compensated for by forced cheerfulness, his basic energy was good and much stronger than I had anticipated.

"I'm so relieved to actually see you!" I told him candidly. "It's been too awful wondering and not knowing, hoping that no news was good news."

"I'm sorry I put everyone through that, but I just couldn't handle having to deal with who knew and who didn't. If it had leaked out professionally, I would have been cooked goose. It's been hard enough as it is."

I put my arm around his waist and we silently walked through the house and out to the studio in the garden.

It was May and the roses had come into bloom and the jasmine was massed along the fence, just putting out clusters of its tiny magenta buds. On the fig tree, tender green leaves had begun unfurling from the tips of branches. The oxalis was bright green, and yellow and purple flowers dotted the sage and rosemarys' spiky stems.

"Paradise!" exclaimed Jim, his quick expert eyes taking in the panoply of plants on all sides. He drew in a deep breath, wheezing slightly as his chest expanded. A swift glance at me looked for my reaction, but I decided to ignore it and get right down to work.

"Let's start right here," I began. "Please close your eyes, and we'll start the session without further ado. We can talk later."

"This lady means business!" he observed archly.

"Yes, she does. We're going to take a 'smell tour' of the garden. No looking allowed." He grinned and scrunched his eyes closed. "I'm going to bring you various leaves and flowers to smell and to feel, and I want you to try and simply experience them in your body. So, although you'll no doubt know everything there is to know about what you're smelling, I'm asking you to bypass that and go straight for the immediate sensory experience of each thing I hand you. Do you think you can do that?"

"It'll probably take some doing," he confessed, "but I'm in your hands. This sounds like fun."

"It is," I promised, plucking a wand of wild sage, its early purple blooms stacked up along the stem. I crushed a few of the leaves between my fingers and held them up to his nose.

"Mm-m." He inhaled it in, coughing a bit at the end of his breath. "Strong stuff," he commented.

"Once again, and this time feel in your body for the sensation of the fragrance." For a moment he stood still, thinking, and then he bent again toward the strong-smelling sage. "Try not to *think* it as much as *feel* it," I suggested. He looked perplexed. "Have the sense of breathing the smell all the way into your body, and follow it."

Nodding, he took another big whiff, and smiled as he felt what I meant. "Got it," he said. "And it's different. You're right."

"Here's the next," I said, holding a sprig of rosemary just beneath his nose.

"Ah, my favorite," he smiled, sniffing it up and down and rubbing the tender needles between thumb and forefinger.

"Feel it in your body," I reminded him. "Pretend you don't know what it is, and experience it as if for the first time." For a long while he breathed in the rosemary, getting lost in it. I sensed it evoking memories of other times and places; other rosemaries. His face softened, and his shoulders began to relax. Good. Finally he took in a deep, releasing sigh. There was no wheeze at the end of this one. I felt my throat contract and, waiting until I could speak in a normal voice, I handed him a wand of lavender, suggesting that he smell and feel it at the same time. He responded to the lavender with a groan of pleasure, and sank cross-legged to the grass where he rubbed the flower all over his face. We both laughed.

"Spanish lavender," he couldn't help but say. "No Latin terminology, I promise."

"Better not!" I admonished, picking a stalk of marjoram and handing it to him. Again, he went into small raptures.

"In all my years as a botanist," he declared, "it has never occurred to me to do this. This is voluptuous!"

"It gets better and better," I promised. "Now, what I'd like you to do is sniff them one at a time and register how you feel *different* with each plant. It's pretty subtle, so you have to really concentrate on your body. Sensations, images, memories—whatever's there. Try and bypass your scientific expertise, if you can."

"You mean, try not to think."

"That's it. Stay in your body as much as possible."

"OK." Again he bent to the task, sniffing one after the other. While he focused on his internal experience of the plants in my garden, I focused upon him. The healer in me watched for signs of his body tuning in to the subtler energies. The me that loved this man just gazed at him with unabashed pleasure: his characteristic lithe stance; those perfect white teeth showing behind an easy smile; the asymmetry of his shoulders from a childhood condition of scoliosis. He breathed in the plants, and I breathed in Jim as if to fix him in my memory.

"OK," I said in a calm voice, "identify each of these out loud before you feel them. Ready?"

"Ready." First I placed a hybrid tea rose in his cupped hands and he lifted it to his face. "Rose," he said dreamily, dipping into it again and again. "Don't know which variety."

"No matter," I said, removing the tea rose and replacing it with a yellow climber which had a more spicy fragrance. He held it up to his nose and breathed deeply.

"Rose!" he exclaimed with a laugh.

"Here's the first again." I held the tea rose to his nostrils, then the climber and he smelled each in turn, concentrating. I could practically feel him dropping into a more subtle level of awareness. "And now this." I brought to his nose a cluster of wild rose petals from the vine that trellised up the studio wall. He buried his face in my cupped palms, and grasping the backs of my hands, cried,

"Oh! Rose!" Gulping, he took in draught after draught of the sweetness. A line of tears escaped from his closed eyelids and he sobbed out, "How I love this world!" The rose petals lay crushed between us as I wrapped him in my arms and rocked him like a child. We stood apart after awhile and solemnly wiped away each others' tears.

"I'm impressed," he declared at last. "I feel very different from the way I felt when I first got here, and I'm not sure what you've done."

"It's what *you've* done," I corrected him.

"What *we've* done," he allowed. "It's time to let me in on what you've been up to."

"C'mon into the studio." I led the way into the airy space of my studio and he gazed intently around him at the whitewashed cinder block walls and sprung wood floor. He was smiling. And breathing easily, I noticed.

"It feels so rich in here," he noted. "Something very good has gone on since I was last in here."

"I hope so." I placed two cushions side by side on the floor and we settled down, our backs against the wall.

"So tell me about what you've been doing," he asked.

"Well," I began, realizing that now he was not only friend and mentor, but perhaps student and client as well. I was not sure how to adjust my tone to this new configuration. "Basically, it's a pretty simple idea. As you saw, it's about learning how to recognize subtle energies in the body."

"It's amazing how quick and effective such a simple technique could be."

"I agree. The trick is to start with something very familiar to the person, and help them experience it in a whole new way."

"It sure worked for me," he affirmed with a grin.

"The point of the exercise is to feel your way into the level of awareness where you can directly experience your connectedness with the rest of the world." For a moment he stared at me and then whispered in wonderment,

"But that's the same thing as my infamous fungi, isn't it?" Excited and trying not to show it, I smiled at him like a satisfied cat.

"That's where I got the idea, silly. It was your work that inspired me." His eyes filled again with tears and he reached for me, lay his head on my shoulder and stroked my back over and over, very gently.

"I cry a lot these days," he remarked, blowing his nose with a great laughing honk.

"It's probably best to keep it all flowing."

"Rivers…" He lifted his head and faced me. "Thank you," he said gravely. "Thank you for being here and for receiving what I have had to offer. And for translating it into a usable form. You will never know what a gift this is to me."

"The gift is mutual," I whispered, placing my palms together as we bowed to one another. After some time he lowered his gaze, distractedly examining the wood grain in the floor.

"You know," he began slowly, "that you won't be able to cure me, don't you?" His voice carried a mixture of wistfulness and challenge, and I was not sure which to address. Very carefully I replied,

"That may well be so." In his face I detected a brief flicker of disappointment. "But what I think I *can* do," I went on, "is to help beef up your immune system. Depression lowers immune system function, we all know that, and I've found some effective ways of dealing with depression."

"You'd be pulling off a miracle, then," he countered wryly.

"What's wrong with miracles?" I shot back. "I have no reason not to believe in them. As far as I'm concerned, miracles are perfectly natural occurrences that scientists have no vocabulary for." He looked dubious and declared,

"OK, I'm willing to try just about anything you have to offer. Otherwise, I've considered ending it all right away, instead of hanging on being depressed until it happens anyway."

NO! NO! all the voices shrieked in my head. NO! With effort, I kept my face impassive and in as calm a voice as I could produce I heard myself say,

"There are better alternatives, I believe. Whatever the outcome, this is an opportunity to do important inner work..." my voice began to crack, "...and that every moment of life should be considered a precious gift..." Every unctuous word was making me feel sick, but I couldn't stop. "...and I think you would be making a tragic mistake..."

His eyes narrowed—in mistrust or concern for me, I couldn't tell which.

Embarrassed, I started again, taking a deep breath and smiling tremulously at him. For a few moments we regarded each other as if to reclaim our ground. Nothing but the truth, I decided on the instant.

"You can do whatever you want," I told him in a firmer voice, "but I love you and I just want you around for as long as I can have you."

His expression relaxed and I saw myself reflected in his eyes.

"Thanks," he replied. "I suspect you will."

We met again three days later, this time to actually begin the work. Wearing white drawstring pants and a bright yellow shirt, Jim, with his bare feet and slender physique, looked every bit the dancer.

"Let your eyes gently close," I instructed him, "and allow your body to softly unkink." I put on a tape of African rhythms and suggested that he let himself respond to the regular beats. "And breathe," I reminded him as he bent his knees and let the music take him over.

During the next half hour I guided him through his body, starting with the feet and working up to the head until his whole body was moving. As a dancer, Jim was a natural. He leapt and he twirled, twisting his torso easily and swinging his arms, bending over and rising in a single, graceful motion. He danced like a person starved for it, and I realized it had been awhile since he had been well enough to climb and scramble in his beloved hills.

By the end of the warm-up he was breathing deeply and evenly, and upon his lips was an unreadable smile. His head, tilted up, seemed to be listening to a music only he could hear and, rapt in his own visions, he waited for my direction.

"Let your spine move you," I said, replacing the African tape with the contemplative sounds of Medieval polyphony, "while the rest of your body follows it. Always breathing...." In his state of relaxed concentration, the goal of the extended warm-up, he moved easily, softly, his arms lifting with the music and his upper body arching backward until he formed a perfect half-circle. In one smooth, swift motion the arch straightened and the weight of his head pulled his whole torso forward. His fingers brushed the floor in front of him, and he sank slowly to his knees, rounding his back until he touched forehead to palms, as if in prayer.

With unbelievable grace he shifted smoothly from one shape to the next, filling the room with continuous form—sculptures brought to life by his body moving through space. To my knowledge Jim had never danced before. How did he know how to do this? A little smile of concentration hovered on his lips as he followed the will of his body into elegant extensions and minute, focused shifts. "Breathe," I reminded myself.

When the music modulated into a new key, it took him by surprise, and with a wide grin of delight he sank into the floor in a single motion, spreading himself luxuriously and rolling, like a child, first in one direction, then the other. He laughed out loud. I did too.

"Keep going," I said, keeping my voice soft enough not to break his concentration, "and drop your effort level in half." Immediately, he softened his body, relaxing more as the lighter motion gave him greater agility and strength. His eyebrows lifted with comprehension as his body, dancing with consummate ease now, registered the significance of the instruction. He was in touch with something ineffable—I could see it in his movement—and spreading his arms he danced full out, tasting it, embracing it, being shot through with the glorious light of it. As the music resolved into its final cadences, he brought the movement home to himself and came to rest in a perfect, balanced stillness.

The silence in the room pulsed. We stood facing each other quietly, and then sat down in meditation, our breathing even and synchronized. For how long we sat I do not know, but when he opened his eyes they were radiant. We gazed at each other for a long time, not speaking. There was nothing either of us needed to say.

Finally, he spoke. "I have two questions."

"Mm-m?"

"First, can we do this again…and again?"

"Of course."

"Thank you." He stalled, gazing at the floor beside him, swallowing as if to speak, and then holding back before he finally found his voice. "And second…will you be with me…at the end?"

The question caught me unprepared because I had no simple answer. Was I or was I not still committed to the possibility of a miracle cure through this work? My heart pounded in my throat loud enough to hear.

"You don't have to answer," he murmured, sensing my indecision. Quickly, I covered the breach.

"If you are the one to go first," I promised him, "it would be my privilege to be there."

"Thank you," he said simply, leaning forward so that our fingertips met in the space between us.

We met weekly after that—sometimes twice a week—and in each session we explored ever more deeply the subtle realms of consciousness. Jim, with his immense intelligence, was receptive to every hint I threw out, and loved the challenge of experiencing the world in novel ways.

"Use your body to transcend your body," I instructed him one day as memories of humiliation and self-hate from childhood began to emerge from his work on the floor. "Allow the feelings in. Live them again. Dance them out."

I watched as his face contorted and he bent over double, choking and howling with ancient rage. He stomped out tattoos with his feet, kicking and retching and sobbing. He bashed his fists against the walls, and then against himself, venting, releasing, despairing. Sitting there as witness, I made of myself a calm vessel to hold the enormity of the unbounded universe and held it as steadily as I could for him. Here in this larger world, I felt it was safe for him to let go and break down, to fling out the toxins of his conditioned history in order to emerge whole. Stuck emotions could become unstuck; the nervous system could find another point of balance and with the resulting freedom of internal energetic flow his immune system might conceivably kick in with renewed vigor.

This was my premise.

With a convulsive last shudder, he flopped onto the floor, spent. I continued to sit still as a stone, my attention held steady and open, my heart spreading as wide as I could spread it.

"Help us," I whispered soundlessly to whatever unseen presences were privy to our process. "Help. Please help us."

And as his breathing resumed a more normal, regular rhythm, he slowly pulled his knees up to his chest and extended one leg, testing. His foot braced solidly on the floor and shifting his weight he leaned into it, rising easily in a single motion. He rose to his toes, balanced effortlessly until, shifting almost imperceptibly forward he leaned into the air, which cushioned him until the critical second, and then broke into a run. It was more, really, like flying. Weightlessly, he danced into every corner of the room, landing with the lightness of a cat, taking up space, embodying grace.

"So, tell me," he remarked one day several weeks later, after a particularly inspiring session. Our conversations after dancing had become an integral part of the work itself, as we chewed our way closer and closer to the bone. "Is this a foretaste of what it's going to be like?"

I reflected for awhile and then replied,

"I think, rather, this is a taste of what it *is* like, right here, right now. We're just not used to looking at things quite this way."

"OK, let me be the devil's advocate: here I am an old biologist who has spent his life exploring the natural world, and I haven't begun to see a billionth of all there is to see. Why should I even be bothered with stuff that isn't even out there on the surface to see?"

"As Hillary said when asked why he climbed Everest: Because it's there." We both laughed. "Seriously, though, how could you not want to know everything there is to know?"

"But you can't!" he insisted. "That's just the point. If we didn't focus in, we'd be overwhelmed with facts and couldn't move!"

"That's true," I allowed, "but this isn't *facts*. It's not that it's more information to take in, it's just a whole other way of perceiving the world. It's about recognizing directly who you really are—that you're not an isolated being, but you're part of a vaster organism. It's like the trees and the grasses *knowing* that they're connected to each other by a network of fungi."

"And it's the fungi, too," he added, pensive. "But," he began slowly, his brow furrowed, "that still doesn't quite get to my question, which is: Is it really OK for me to be dying?"

It was my turn to gaze down at my hands, unable to speak. "I mean, there's nothing you need to say—there's nothing you *can* say. After all, *you're* not dying." There it was, a shot through the heart.

"No, I'm not, but yes, I am!" I cried. "Not this second, or even this year, but one of these days in the not-too-distant future. But how can I answer you? I don't know for sure about anything, but I do know that when I do certain things I get a glimpse of an expanded and glorious universe, and if that's the state we enter when we die then, goddamn it, it's got to be OK."

For a moment he looked contrite, and then with a mischievous grin he said, "I love it when you get so worked up."

"Oh, Jim," I breathed, throwing my arms around his neck and hugging him hard, "I'm going to miss you so much."

A few weeks later Jim brought Susan, his invaluable assistant at the *Manual* project, to his session with him. When they first walked in I thought it was Lynn by his side—the same windblown, sandy-colored hair, clear blue-green eyes and infectious laugh. I took to her right away.

"Jim thought I could use some help," she teased, turning to him with a deep laugh, "and I suppose he's right."

"Without you in good shape, I don't stand a chance out there," Jim teased back. Even though Jim still steered the course of the *Manual* project, Susan was responsible for the day-to-day work. It was now in the design and layout stage, and they both were showing signs of exhaustion. Susan changed from her neat office clothes into sweat pants while they told me of the latest glitches involving the typesetter who had only yesterday gotten his copy to them. "Just under the wire," said Susan wearily. "It wasn't the first time I've stayed up all night for this *Manual.*"

Jim gave a wan smile, breathing with effort. He closed his eyes and for a moment swayed on his feet.

"I'd like to start today's work with a rest," I announced quickly, laying pads onto the floor. "Sometimes," I explained to Susan, "movement has to begin with stillness." She looked grateful, and lowered herself tiredly onto the pad alongside Jim. In moments, they were both drowsing.

I let birdsong in the garden be the music, and taking a cushion I sat cross-legged alongside them, watching the rise and fall of their chests. Each inhalation was a struggle for Jim and I breathed with him, praying that his labored breaths were a sign of stress and fatigue, not a bout of pneumocystis. But as he relaxed his breathing grew calmer, more rhythmic, and I relaxed as well. I sat in quiet meditation while they slept, keeping my attention high on the crown of my head, steady, and letting a sense of airy expansion fill me with each breath. When anxieties tightened my chest, I noticed them and let them go.

For a long time they slept and I sat, until I felt a familiar tickling sensation in my throat, which I had come to recognize as a kind of signal from Jim. I listened—or rather *felt*—closely and sensed another presence, Susan's—not directly, but through Jim. These two knew each other well. I would try and communicate with them both as they rested.

Without speaking aloud, I placed my attention on the sensations in my own feet, suggesting in my mind that they do the same. When I sensed response, I moved my attention up to my ankles, and when I felt them react I went on to the lower legs, then knees and thighs. Gradually I worked my way up through the body; up through theirs via my own.

At the chest I paused and listened intently, physically as well as subliminally. I perceived no constriction, just the easy wash of free-flowing breath in and out, in and out. I gave a sigh of relief and in his sleep, Jim did so as well. When Susan sighed deeply also, I smiled to myself. They both stirred, shifting their positions for another few moments of sleep. "Please begin to awaken," I requested silently, enjoying with them those last few moments of delicious stillness. Shortly, they stretched, yawned and glanced around, surprised to have been so deeply asleep.

"Whenever you're ready, we'll sit facing each other in a close circle." I spoke softly, shifting my cushion closer to them and waiting until they were sitting upright, their legs crossed beneath them. "I'm going to hum," I told them quietly. "Join in when you're ready." I began on a low tone, more a voiced breath than a note and held the sound until my breath ran out. Again. I could feel it vibrating in my chest and I felt the vibration spread to include both of them. Jim sensed it and added his voice to mine, the tone growing in fullness the longer he held it.

For several breaths we intoned the same note, finally varying it with a simple beat, infusing it with rhythm. Susan joined now, singing the third above us in a pure, sweet voice.

This simple interval made its own beats in the air and we each adjusted our pitches ever so subtly until the harmony was perfect to our ears, perfect to our bodies. Into this I introduced a repeated riff, a melody of three notes sung in varying patterns. Jim began to slap one hand on his knee, adding a syncopated bass note and Susan, shaking out her hair, lifted into a soaring plainsong.

During our song I observed their shoulders relaxing, their necks loosening, their breathing rhythms lengthening. I noticed their spines give little cracks of release and heard their throats let go and open, allowing their sweet song through. Our sweet, sweet unrehearsed song. Which ended finally on a single note in unison—unforced, pure and held. When the sound died out, it continued to be heard in the silence of the room and Susan, dropping her face into her lap, burst into tears. Jim reached over and gently took her hand; I reached for her other hand and together we sat on in the stillness, bonded, ecstatic, complete.

All sounds in the forest were muted by the massive stillness of the towering redwoods, and the high canopy was obliterated by mist. Our feet sank into spongy mulch, leaving no sign of our passage and only our breathing—Jim's a bit more ragged than mine—betrayed our presence there.

Outdoors in wild country, Jim was in his element. His last project, now that the *Manual* was off to the printers and out of his hands, was to create guides of our bioregion to be made available to the general public. It was a project we created together as a way to utilize his immense store of knowledge during the time he had left—and as an antidote to depression. It was also the ideal excuse for me to go tromping in the woods, hills and seashore with him while he still had the strength to do so.

In the redwoods he seemed almost feral, stalking and sniffing, listening for the revealing movement at the edge of a leaf. While I gazed at panoramas, Jim focused in on minute bits of debris, root hairs, the tiniest life forms. Kneeling in close, he would hold a scrap of green between thumb and forefinger and tell me its complex history.

"Listen," he whispered, stopping and cocking his head—like a robin, I thought. At first I heard nothing but my own heart pounding in my ears, and then from far away the echo of a birdcall, in flight. The cry rose in pitch as the bird winged overhead and then diminished as it passed us by. "That's a great blue heron," he murmured, still listening, "following the river…"

When we perched, awhile later, on a decomposing log to eat our sandwiches, I reflected that if I were walking in these same woods alone, I wouldn't have noticed a fraction of what Jim, as a matter of course, pointed out to me. I told him so.

"That black bird up there, for example. To me it's just a black bird."

"Marbled murrelet," he informed me, "and on the endangered list. It's a little seabird that nests in the moss mats way up in the canopies of old-growth trees, and is the center of unimaginable controversies right now." As he spoke, telling me about habits and habitat, mating behavior and feeding patterns, I was suddenly overcome with the anticipation of loss. The world that he brought alive to me would sink back into obscurity when he was gone. I would walk through the woods and again be an ignorant stranger.

If Jim noticed my sudden drop of energy, he didn't let on. Hunkering down by the decaying log, he intently examined ears of creamy fungi sprouting from the crumbling, wet wood.

"Here, smell," he said as I kneeled down on the ground beside him. The musky scent of organic matter invaded my whole head, and I inhaled it until I was dizzy. "Close your eyes," he said, bringing me a variety of fungi and pinches of different mulches to smell, as we had once done in my garden with herbs and flowers. All at once I seemed to sense the presence of Lynn kneeling there in the brown-green shade of the forest with us, and the hairs on my arms stiffened. Jim must have felt something too, for he held up some leaves and bark in his cupped palm and glancing in all directions around him called,

"Smell it, Lynnish?" Above us a Stellar Jay dropped effortlessly from a high branch, sailed on a waft of wind and landed neatly on the twisted limb of a bay tree. It twittered at us fussily.

"I can't imagine never being in the redwoods again," he confessed in a hushed voice. The forest stirred and whispered around us, the deadwood decomposing into earth, the seeds burrowing and cracking, sending shoots of tender green up into the air of the world. At the root hairs of every plant the fungi spread silently, spores emerging and dying, connecting and dissolving, providing humus for the next generation, and the next and the next.

"If Lynn is here, then I suppose you'll be able to come back, too. Together," I ventured after awhile. He nodded thoughtfully, brushing dirt and leaves from the seat of his pants.

"Remember how pissed she was that she couldn't go hiking in the Austrian Alps again?" We laughed nostalgically. "Well, now I know how she felt." His voice held a trace of self-pity, which he immediately countered with,

"I have a feeling I'll come back from time to time, too—as a hummingbird. So when you see one, you'll know it's me."

A week later we went to his favorite beach, a wild stretch of sand and sea cliff at the end of a peninsula an hour's drive from the city. He napped most of the way there, waking only when I stopped the car and turned off the ignition. For a few minutes he sat motionless, as if to re-orient himself. Then he came to.

"I just had the strangest dream," he told me, removing his binoculars from their case and placing the strap around his neck. "Norm was there and his house was burning. He reminded me to spread myself out and feel the sea. What do you make of that?"

"Don't know," I replied, pulling a straw hat onto my head and reaching for the knapsack in the back seat, "but I like the idea of spreading out and feeling the sea."

The surf rose into rich blue wedges that crested into glistening cream before pounding down on the shore. Wave after wave lifted, raced toward us and broke into wild foam before being sucked back into the generating sea. Jim kicked off his shoes and lifted his face to the wind, unsteady on his feet. I linked my arm through his and we stood sucking in brine and sun and air and the traces of every creature that had ever passed this way.

"Spread myself out…" he mumbled.

"And feel the sea," I added. Felt…the crying of the seabirds, the thundering crash of sea against the land, the subtle shaking of our bodies, the taste of sea air, the life-giving heat of the sun. Felt. And merged.

Jim whooped and ran toward the water, but he didn't get very far. He collapsed, panting and laughing at himself, painstakingly rolling onto his back to squint up at the sun and grab fistsful of sand to dribble onto his chest, like a kid.

"You nut!" I teased, flopping down alongside him, stomach down and face toward the water.

That's where we spent most of the day, lying in the sand and watching the waves. The tideline came up closer and then moved away; pelicans sailed low above the water and gulls approached close, in alert anticipation of a handout.

We commented on everything, examining the broken shells of razor clams and sand dollars for evidence of the lives that had been lived within. Jim rubbed the bleached bits until they dissolved back into particles of sand and disappeared into the greater beach from whence they came.

"Transitions," he muttered thoughtfully. "Do you suppose I'm going to have much pain?" He asked this quite straightforwardly.

"I hope not," I replied. "Certainly less if you're prepared for what's to come, and don't resist the process too much."

"Will you help me?"

"Of course," I promised, mentally crossing my fingers that, when the time came, I would have the courage and wisdom to do right by him. "What's important to realize is that even if there is pain, it doesn't last very long—kind of like giving birth. Labor can be pretty excruciating, but once the baby is there, you forget all about the pain."

"I wouldn't know," he quipped.

"I would, though," I quipped back, not bothering to remind him that I had much more firsthand experience in birthing than in dying.

We spoke in detail about our understanding of the internal process of dying as the body shut down and released its separate elements. Having witnessed many deaths himself, he was able to concur on the signs, as the elements recycled back into the physical world—Earth, Water, Fire, Air. We talked about each stage of the passage, and what he could expect it to feel like: the weakness in the limbs; the growing coldness; the fearful noises; the sense of speeding up. I reminded him that at each stage he would have to remember that, as it said in the *Tibetan Book of the Dead*, his experiences would not be coming from outside himself, but would simply be his own internal process of release.

"You'll keep me on track if I panic?" he implored.

"I'll coach you at each stage to the best of my ability," I promised.

"You'll keep reminding me not to be scared?"

"Yes," I promised again.

" 'Cause I'm going to be scared."

"Of course," I said, adding under my breath, "I will too."

Interrupted only by catnaps and occasional snacks, we continued the conversation all day long. We went over and over the stages of dying, memorizing the process and planning our collaboration as we might rehearse a duet. We were just two friends hanging out at the beach, heads bent together, bodies stretched flat out facing a brilliant sea and could have been any two people gossiping about last night's movie or a new way to make lemon cookies. But our subject, approached from this angle and that, sometimes lightly and sometimes with pain, concerned the ultimate tryst. And in between, we threw bits of bread to the gulls.

"The trick, I think, is to remember that when it's all over, most likely nothing is over. You will have changed channels, so to speak. You're not supposed to even feel pain anymore."

"Sure," he laughed, "I won't feel a thing!"

"I think it's the other way around," I claimed, "and that feeling will be *everything*. What you won't have to worry about is physical pain, because that's the part you'll be shedding."

"Sounds better and better," he joked dryly. I regarded him silently for awhile. Then I said,

"For you, I think there's nothing to worry about. That may sound crass because it's not me going now, but I honestly believe it is so. The ones who have it the hardest are the rest of us who love you. You get to go home; we're left behind and have to live on without you. I swear, this is going to be harder on Joe than it is on you."

"Joe…," he cried, his face contorting with grief. "I can't stand it for Joe." I put my arm around him while he cried, handing him a sandy bunch of tissues. Wiping the last of his tears with the back of his wrist, he looked up with sorrow and said,

"That's what the burning house is about."

"I guess that's part of what the burning house is about," was all I was able to admit.

Some weeks later, when Jim and Susan arrived at the studio for their session, it was clear that Jim's condition had begun to visibly deteriorate. He had neither the wasting symptoms nor blotchy lesions so common with AIDS, but to anyone who knew and loved him the signs of deep fatigue and shortness of breath were immediately apparent. There was strain in his every smile and even the smallest laugh could end in a spasm of coughing.

"We've come bearing gifts!" Susan sang as they stepped through the lace curtain at the doorway, her tone a little *too* bright, her smile a little *too* perky. Jim sidled into the studio concealing something behind his back, his face a study in suppressed excitement. Still, his eyes betrayed something more weary. I crossed my arms over my chest and waited.

"Ta da!" he crowed—a bit weakly, I thought—and pulled out from behind his back an enormous book still smelling of the bindery. He hefted over to me with as much flourish as was possible with so heavy a book, the newly-published *Manual*. The effort cost him a fit of coughing. Susan and I, tense as steel rods, held our ground until the fit was over. Then we resumed the scene, re-animating like actors starting up again after stage directions. Susan giggled, Jim patted the cover picture and I held the *Manual* to me in a kind of delirium.

"Hot off the presses," he exclaimed, taking my face in both his hands and making me look straight at him. "Three copies came from the printer this morning: one for Susan, one for me and one for you."

I started crying and couldn't seem to stop. He nuzzled me into his shoulder and Susan joined the circle. And with the newly published *Botanical Manual* between us, we gripped each other close.

Our class that day was a quiet celebration. Jim was depleted emotionally as well as physically, and Susan seemed a bit manic. For her, this event was also the culmination of a decade of grueling effort, and could mean the loss of a job, not to mention the loss of her best friend and colleague. It was the end of an era. A life's work had been completed and sent out into the world; a life itself was on the wane. My dream of changing the course of an AIDS diagnosis had disappointingly not proved effective.

So be it.

There was nothing to do but carry on.

The warm-up was slow and easy. A restful beat helped entrain us to a shared rhythm, and gradually we found ourselves in a state of calm awareness, balanced and softly awake.

"Let your heart be the focus of your attention," I said, changing the music to the sounds of monks chanting in harmonics. I hoped this focus might relieve some of the constriction in Jim's lungs, as well as address the enormity of feelings that filled each of us.

I danced with them, cherishing every shape their bodies made and every interaction we had as we swirled slowly in and out of contact with each other. Jim's eyes were closed and his movements a bit cautious, but on his face was an expression of ineffable peace. I tried to memorize these moments, feel the air and friendship around me not only for right now, but to be called up in the future when this room would be empty of them. The tears came again and wetted my cheeks as I danced across the floor, embracing Susan and Jim with the breeze of my body and perceiving them in the timeless Now, my heart wide open in love.

"When I'm gone, would you like to have my stone collection?" Jim asked this one day over lunch. "And Lynn's prints?"

"Why, yes," I replied gratefully, as matter-of-fact as he. "I'd like that very much." I could picture the list in his mind being checked off item by item, the way we organize when we pack to go on a trip. I felt increasingly more uneasy as he went on, indomitable. Instinctively, I braced for what was to come.

"Joe is going to organize a party for close friends and family on the day after the memorial." He took a rasping breath and looked me straight in the eye. "Would you perform the memorial itself?"

I felt my head shaking wildly, and before he had finished the sentence I blurted out, "No!" A moment later, recovering, I implored,

"Please don't ask me to do that." My throat tightened with the pain of holding back tears and I hung my head, unable to take in the disappointment in his tired face. But this was a job I knew I couldn't do.

"Can I offer something else?" I asked with sudden insight. "Would you be willing to let me make a party for you now, and invite whoever you want, and we'll all plant a tree with you?" His eyes began to gleam with interest. "We'll plan it together, and I'll take care of all the this' and thats'. It can be anything you want."

"Anything I want," he drawled speculatively, warming to the idea. "Anything I want? Well then, why just a single tree? Why don't we plant a grove somewhere? Of natives. In the hills. Oh yes! I love the idea, you smarty-pants. I love it! Let's do it! "

That May was unusually rainy, and the hills were lush with green growth. Orange poppies polka-dotted the roadsides, and the slopes were bright with vivid yellow mustard and purple lupine.

Jim's cough worsened steadily, especially when he got excited, but he went about preparing for the tree-planting with gusto. He was determined to be well enough to do some of the work himself.

The site was in the hills, not far from the ridge where he and I had done our wildflower ritual for Lynn ten years earlier. The small grove of bay laurel and buckeye he had planned would rise where birds in the uppermost branches could look out over ocean on one side and mountains on the other, Jim said wistfully.

Most of us arrived long before Jim and Joe got there, and unloaded from our cars the saplings and spades, jugs of water, trowels, and party food and drink for afterward. Jim's friends from the city had come, Susan was there, and Lynn's parents. Old students came from out of state along with a number of colleagues—even his doctor arrived with her family.

When Jim and Joe finally got there and backed their car up to the trail head, we formed a semi-circle to welcome them into our midst. It was a perfect moment. Jim emerged from the car grinning, a floppy hat mashed onto his head and a trowel clutched in his hand.

"Yaay-yy!" everyone cheered, and each shouldering a tool or a knapsack to carry up to the site, we began to line up in a convoy.

"Will he be able to make it?" I asked Joe nervously, wondering about the steeper parts of the trail.

"He could handle it last week," Joe reminded me. Susan overheard my concern and joined us, saying,

"He's determined as Hell. And when Jim is determined to do something, there ain't nothin' gonna stop him. Look at him go, would you!"

Flanked front and back by people who adored him, Jim took off at the head of the line and climbed with measured steps, his face intent on placing one foot in front of the other and breathing evenly. Every few minutes he stopped to rest, and the whole line rested with him. Like some ceremonial dance—six steps and stop; six steps and stop—the file of friends wound its way upward, to the place where Jim's memorial grove would grow.

Cameras were already clicking like insects, whirring and snapping. Once we reached the site Jim, breathing hard, greeted everyone with a hug, posing with each of us in turn. He was giddy with enjoyment, mugging an American Gothic poker-face with an upturned pitchfork, and tossing out endless one-liners. He was the star of his show, and loving every minute of it.

When everyone had gathered, we formed a circle around the potted saplings and the group quieted down, waiting for the planting to begin.

First, a group of his students from past years stepped into the circle to speak. One by one they praised him as mentor, as inspirer, as friend.

"You were the one who taught me to see the diversity of the world, and I thank you," said one. "And to love the natural world and to make it my life," said another. They hugged him and cried on his shoulder, and we all wept with them. Jim gazed at them for a long while, receiving their praise and love. His eyes were shining when he bowed and placed his palms together, looking around the circle at his community.

"My beloved friends," he began, taking a big breath. His hand, in mine, was sweaty, gripping hard and loosening as he made his speech. "I don't think you'll ever know how much it means to me to have you all up here with me. Thank you for coming." He was controlling his breaths with great effort. Every eye was on him, and most faces registered fear, perhaps for themselves as well as for him.

"These trees that we're planting will be here long after I'm gone..."

He looked around the circle—I noted that most of the people were able to meet his gaze— and his mouth twisted wryly into a teasing grin as he continued, "…and they'll be here long after you're gone, too." Everyone laughed a little nervously.

"I'll miss you so much." He began to cough and, miraculously, controlled it. "I love you all, more than you can imagine! You'll never know how much." His eyes brimmed with tears, along with everyone else's. "Thank you for being with me today, but more than that, thank you for every minute we've spent together over the years. Thank you."

By this time everyone was crying and we pulled the circle in, gathering into a group hug, sobbing and snuffling into the warm darkness at the center. After a few minutes of this, Jim laughed and gently shook us all off, announcing in a tone of mock scolding,

"But I'm still alive, folks, so we'd better get those trees planted!" And in a flurry of giggles and the blowing of noses, we dug five deep pits, lowered the young trees one-by-one into position, spread their roots to encourage growth and packed them safely into the earth. Jim supervised the process, going from hole to hole and enlarging one here, tamping the soil more tightly there.

When each tree was in place he explained to us why this site had been chosen, how these species were suited to this environment, and which birds and insects would benefit from their presence. And then he poured, onto each young tree, the life-giving water from the jugs we had carried up the hill, like a sacred libation.

The following week Jim called to say he wouldn't make it to class that afternoon. "I'm in the hospital," he announced bluntly. The background hiss, I realized, was not the sound of traffic outside a phone booth, it was an oxygen pump. "My temp shot up yesterday," he said, "and when Joe took me to Emergency, they shoved me right upstairs." He sucked in several breaths before continuing. "It's PCP."

Pneumocystis carnii pneumonia. "Three strikes and you're out," was what I'd heard the last time he had been hospitalized. This was number two. I breathed into the phone almost as hard as he.

"I'll pull out of this one like I did the last one," he reassured me in a rasping voice. "I'm not ready to go yet." He chuckled, then coughed.

"Would you come see me? I'm in Room 319."

"Yes." Mentally I made lists of people to tell. "Tonight?"

"Please," he responded wistfully, audibly running out of steam.

"I love you, Jim."

"I love you, love you…," he whispered, making kissing sounds in syncopation with the oxygen pump.

When I got off the phone, I was unable to move. In any direction. My mouth was dry down to the gullet, and my brain was like a train that had slipped off its track. Then I remembered that I had a tool for grief, and willing my legs and arms to move, I put my recording of the "Brahms Requiem" on the turntable, took out the ironing board and iron, and plunked a basket of wrinkled laundry at my feet. Then I turned up the volume as loud as it would go and began to iron furiously.

Behold, all flesh is as the grass…
For lo, the grass withereth…

I cried with the full chorus as background, giving vent with full voice. My tears sizzled beneath the hot iron in a hiss of steam. Anticipation of loss filled me with a heavy, dark ache from foot to crown.

Blessed, blessed are they that mourn…
For they shall have comfort
They shall have comfort…

Singing at full voice along with the chorus, I did not at first hear the persistent ringing of the doorbell.

"Damn!" I spit out, almost deciding to ignore it. But then I wiped my eyes with the back of my hand and stomped across the room to answer it, an angry speech on my lips for the door-to-door sales pitch. Waiting on the porch, however, was not a stranger but a long-lost, well-loved friend who had dropped by to say hello.

"My goodness," she exclaimed as I bustled her inside and immediately fell apart in her arms. In between sobs I told her what was happening, flinging myself out of her lap to tune down the over-loud choral music.

"Hi, Judy," I laughed somewhat hysterically, apologizing for my chaotic welcome. "Believe it or not, you may be the only person I *really* wanted to see right now." She just shook her head, looking concerned. Judy was a no-nonsense nurse from Brooklyn who had, in her time, seen everything and kept a sense of humor about the whole human scene. In the past we had been good friends and had spent many fine hours together, but she had been gone for the past two years working in Egypt. "I want to hear all about Egypt!"

"I'll tell you anything you want to know," she informed me, "over ice cream sodas." Then she gave me her wide, reassuring smile and taking me by the arm, led me out of the house and up the street to the neighborhood spa—the ice cream parlor.

She did the ordering, and the serving. From the counter she brought back several dishes of ice cream, a flask of carbonated water, little jugs of syrup and a bowl filled with whipped cream. We each had a tall glass with a long-handled spoon and a handful of straws.

Mystified, I watched as she plopped into each glass two flavors of ice cream and a dribble of syrup, mixing madly with a spoon as she poured in the soda water.

"Quick! Drink it!" she shrieked as the frothy mess threatened to fizz right over the top. We both slurped madly, just seconds ahead of the spillage and then, with a deft motion, she added whipped cream to the whole concoction. I leaned back away from it, feeling out of control. "There," she sighed, satisfied, poking straws into each of our glasses. "Now I'll tell you about myself."

For the next hour we told our stories, adding ice cream and syrup whenever the sodas ran low, roaring with laughter the whole time and sticky up to our elbows. By the time all the ingredients were gone, the little round table was a disaster of melted ice cream and brownish bubbles, and the clotted remains of several flavors of syrup dripped heedlessly onto the floor.

And even though I had a severe bout of hiccoughs which lasted for the next two hours, I felt more relaxed than I had in weeks.

That evening I brought with me to the hospital a carton of strawberry ice cream, a jar of *Fox's U-Bet* chocolate syrup, a bottle of soda water and an aerosol can of whipped cream. The grocery bag was freezing against my chest, which already was cold with fear.

Jim lay with his face to the opposite wall, eyes open, nostril tubes attached to a canister of oxygen hissing alongside his bed. I stepped into the room and stood still by the door, waiting for him to respond to my presence. I could tell he was aware of me by a small shift of expression on his lips, but not quite ready for company. I shifted the brown bag to my other arm. Slowly turning his head on the pillow, his eyes found me and crinkled in a smile.

"Howdy, honey," he whispered hoarsely through dry lips. Like a sick child his gaze followed my every gesture as I moved forward toward his bed, leaned over to kiss him on the forehead, placed the brown paper bag on his tray table and pulled a chair up close to him.

"Howdy, honey," I whispered back. Our eyes met and locked. Between us was a deep-sea silence, where love was the water. Finally, he took in a ragged sigh, nodded toward the brown bag and asked,

"What'cha got there?"

"Surprise party," I replied. He raised his eyebrows skeptically. "You up for a party?"

"Maybe I am...depends," he replied, sucking in air. His face, with the tubes hooked in his nostrils, was partly a stranger's face and I found myself shifting my gaze continually to find the Jim I knew in it. "Normally, I love surprises."

"Then I'll need some paper cups, and some bendable straws," I declared, bustling about to create as much suspense as possible, "and lots of towels—*lots*—and, let's see, any plastic spoons?"

"More and more mysterious," he rasped, attempting a laugh. But it led to a spasm of coughing, and he turned again to the wall, helpless. In a fit of rage he ripped the offending tubes from his nostrils only to struggle, in moments, for breath. With trembling fingers he hooked them back in and lay still, exhausted.

I stood there, frozen. "Take a couple days for drugs...kick in," he explained, breathing on every other word.

All the queasiness of the afternoon's indulgence mingling with the hospital odors of illness and antisepsis caused my gorge to rise precipitously into my throat, and for a moment I thought I might faint. I steadied myself against the wall, closed my eyes and concentrated on breathing, finally regaining equilibrium. I turned again to the brown paper bag with meticulous concentration. The crisis had passed for both of us. Jim turned his attention to the bag, too.

"What the...?"

"Why, ice cream sodas, of course," I declared mildly, matching my dramatic aplomb to that of Judy's just a few hours earlier. "You ready for this?"

"You're too much," he breathed, unaware that it was not me, but a wise woman he'd never met who was too much. Scooping some ice cream into each cup with flair, I dribbled in the chocolate syrup, stopping the flow with a finger which I placed to his lips for a lick.

"Mmmmm," he hummed appreciatively, lying back with eyes closed to savor the taste of both chocolate and sweet memories. Then I filled his cup with the soda water, which fizzed into foam just as it was supposed to do. He leaned over to watch the proceedings, lifting himself onto one elbow. Giving the performance of my life, I pulled out the aerosol can of whipped cream and shook it like a *mariachi*, dancing around his bed with great ceremony. A smile hovered on his lips, and I aimed the can, cried *en garde!* and lunged, spurting cream onto the fizzing concoction. It made a spattery mess—just as it was supposed to do.

"You're totally nuts," he commented dryly.

"Yes, I am," I grinned.

"How'd you know...straw...berry chocolate...was my...favorite... flavor?"

"I'm psychic, of course." I sipped quickly at his overrunning cup and handed it over to him. *"Pour toi,"* I announced, deliberately letting some spill onto the sheets. While he slurped sloppily, I made one for myself and created the required mess on every surface. A nurse looked in once and, blocking the scene with outstretched arms, I assured her everything was fine. Behind me, Jim snorted with repressed laughter.

It was our last party, and we made it a good one. After two messy sodas apiece, I read to him while he rested and then gently massaged his feet. The feeling between us was vast, calm, complete. The very air was shot through with love, which was life itself.

My cup runneth over.

Jim was indeed out of the hospital later that week, along with his canister of oxygen. I could hear it hissing in the background whenever we spoke on the phone.

"The noise is driving Joe crazy," he admitted, as it gave one of its rhythmic thunks. Not only the noise, I thought. "But basically we're having a fine time."

The burgeoning shift from spring into summer enthralled him as every garden within sight of his window burst into color, and he found wonder in the tiny weeds sprouting from cracks in the city streets "flowering for all they're worth!"

He even found his changing body a source of interest, noting how one muscle after another was losing its tensile strength. "I tried opening the window this morning," he told me, "and my elbows didn't work."

But still, he and Joe took a short walk each day, eating lunch in some outdoor café or meeting with friends in the park. "Every little thing," he told me, "every little thing."

"I'm happy," he said frankly one day sitting across from me in a vinyl-and-Formica booth at his neighborhood diner. He had requested a lunch of 'merican food—pronounced with a midwestern twang—with all the trimmings for our last outing together. We deliberated for a long time over the menu before solemnly ordering two hamburgers, two orders of French fries and two cokes. My tongue will never forget the epiphany of biting into the first hot, crisp fried potato dipped in ketchup, nor the soggy mouthfuls of meat and onion and tomato and lettuce, juice dripping down my wrist, of that meal. He ate with one-hundred-percent of himself, joyously. We were feasting upon ambrosia! Watching him, I tasted with all my senses the textures and flavors, smells and colors of those hamburgers. Through him, I got an hour's glimpse of what it meant to be absolutely, uninhibitedly, totally alive in a physical body.

We walked home slowly and then sat resting on the terrace. Recorded sounds of Schubert leider filled the air, along with the hum of the freeway. A hummingbird darted, hovered above the feeder, took a sip and flew off. Below on the street one neighbor greeted another and they stood for a few moments, talking.

"I've never felt so alive in my life," Jim confessed after the final, quiet chords of one song. He gazed out over the city, taking in the skyline greedily. "Funny that I had to get this sick before I really *got* just how delicious this whole, insane world is."

He touched my hand as the tenor's voice soared into a high, held note. Jim's lips parted in wonder, his eyes gleaming as if in recognition of the grandeur hidden within the sound.

"Listen," he whispered intently. "Listen!"

Two weeks later he was back in the hospital.

"The adventure continues," he greeted me, gasping out the words from behind an oxygen mask that covered everything but his eyes. They gazed at me warmly, with confidence—even with humor.

"You ready for this?" I asked bluntly, trying to match my humor with his. His eyes never left my face.

"For the death part, sure. For the dying, I'm not so sure. I didn't know it would be so gruesome." This speech cost him, and he lay deeper into his pillow, panting. I lay my hand, palm up, against his and his fingers, one by one, twined into mine.

"I love you," he said simply.

"I love you," I echoed, pressing his fingers against mine.

After several labored breaths, he gathered his strength and asked,

"Are you all right with all this?" His eyes above the mask crinkled with concern, and shocked into awareness of what kind of friend I was losing, I broke down into uncontrollable sobs. Weakly he opened his arms and, gathering me down onto his heaving chest, he held me there against his warmth while I cried.

Joe and Susan and I each took turns round the clock in his hospital room. We were his advocate with the staff; we screened his phone calls; we monitored the stream of visitors, in general helping to prepare him, and ourselves, for the next stage. Actually, I suspect each of us wanted every last minute of him we could have.

He emerged, after one long nap during my shift, with a description of where he had been. "Very light…not dark at all…song…birdsong? Air is sound…the sounds…" The territory was familiar to him, somehow, and he let me know that. "It's like…it's like…in studio…dancing…" He drifted off again, his eyes moving behind closed eyelids.

The next time he awoke, he had several moments of disorientation and didn't know where he was, who I was. Then he remembered, and his eyes widened in recognition.

"You want to know…," he slurred, continuing in a syntax I could not understand. Realizing he had slipped into another place and language, he reoriented himself, bridging the gap between two worlds with his shifting consciousness.

Often he was completely lucid, right there—Jim. And then he would drift, disappearing to where I could not follow, sending back tantalizing images to me standing on the shore he was leaving.

"Fewer birds here…," he mumbled, waving an arm weakly toward the wall. "That was…botany lesson. I'm teaching…stones around sacred trees…" Again, he drifted off, peaceful.

All three of us were there together on what we expected could be his last night. Joe worked on needlepoint, I handstitched a purple-blue quilt and Susan sat at the foot of the bed massaging Jim's feet. The hospital was hushed as TVs were turned off and phones stopped ringing. Only the hiss and thunk of the oxygen pump broke the stillness. We sat around him, the three of us, like an intimate little family and between us, like the child, he slept. Life was stripped to its essentials; what was left was the reality of death, life itself and love.

Just before eleven, when the staff changed shifts, Jim's nurse came in to check his IV drips and vital signs before leaving for the night.

"You've got a wonderful friend," she whispered to us, leaning over Jim to say goodnight.

"We know," snapped Joe, unexpectedly gruff.

"Thanks, Kathie," Jim murmured, recognizing this nurse amongst the many, and remembering her name as well.

"You are one extraordinary man," I commented beneath my breath. But Jim heard me, for he responded,

"Thank you kindly too, ma'am."

Again he slept, and again opened his eyes to gaze at length upon each of us in turn. Joe leaned over and swabbed his dry lips with an ice-cube. They exchanged a long, wordless gaze.

"Please go home," Jim then said, kindly but firmly.

"But...but...," we sputtered in collective protest. He shook his head wanly against the pillows.

"I need this night alone."

"But...," we all blurted again.

"I've got...private reckoning...to do." His voice was muffled through the mask as well as through the worlds. "I'll have them...call you in time...if necessary..." He seemed to drop again into sleep. "I promise...," he continued, his voice very far away. "Please leave me..."

The telephone jolted my husband and me awake a little after three in the morning, and I lurched, heart pounding, to answer it, already staggered by the message I knew I would receive. My clothes were laid out, ready to put on, and my keys to the car were on a ledge by the door. The nurse had a professionally pleasant, daytime voice.

"Your friend asked me to call you." She hesitated. "He gave me your phone number from memory," she whispered, awed. "Your two other friends, too."

Jim. Jim! "How close is he?" I asked, already dragging on my socks.

"I'd get here as soon as you can," she said quietly. "He told me you'd get here first because you live the nearest."

Mine was the only car in the nighttime streets and turning corners at speed, I followed the route like a well-rehearsed maneuver for which I already knew the outcome. Observing myself the way I might watch a movie, I pulled into a parking space outside the Emergency Room, slammed on the brake and flung myself out the door in a single motion. Then I ran.

The hospital lobby was empty except for a single, pacing man who, as soon as he saw me, came forward with a pink-banded cigar. Impulsively, I congratulated him with a hug and, brandishing my cigar all the way to the bank of elevators, called back to him,

"Isn't birth a miracle?"

He would never know that the woman who greeted him in the middle of the night was on her way to a death.

Jim was wide awake, waiting for us. The pump clunked and wheezed behind him, sending air into his rapidly-failing lungs with more pressure than even a few hours earlier. I bent over and kissed his forehead, keeping my lips there against the downy warmth. Jim was still very much alive.

"Hi," he rasped, his eyes glowing with humor. I sat down on the edge of his bed and we held hands. His pulses throbbed into my palm, and I lifted his hand and kissed each knuckle as I used to do with the children when they were small.

"How you doing?" Our eyes met while he worked to maintain an even breathing rhythm.

"Smiley on the inside," he panted after awhile, "outside, not so hot." His head sank deeper into the pillows. "I want...to do this...well."

"You are already."

"'S...not over...'til fat lady...sings," he quipped. I laughed and gently massaged his thighs. Despite the course of his disease, they were still well fleshed out and firm. These are still the thighs of a man who climbs mountains, I thought with sudden anger, not one who is about to die! He must have felt my energy change, for he pressed my hand and said,

"You know what...makes God smile?"

"What?"

"When you give Her a big list of alternatives." He watched for my surprised reaction, and straining to gather breath for his next words, went on, "I never thought it would go like this...but, you know...it's perfect!"

A bit later when Joe entered, Jim and I were sputtering with laughter. Joe's face, already gray, got grayer.

"He's magnificent," I told Joe, standing up to hug him. Jim watched with luminous eyes as we held each other. Then Joe dropped to his knees alongside the bed and buried his face in Jim's thighs. Delicately, Jim ran caressing fingers across Joe's head.

"Tell him what you said…about me," Jim demanded, his eyes fairly sparkling with fun. His chest heaved with each breath.

"You mean that I'm awed by how you are doing—that?" Jim nodded, relishing the moment. "You mean, that your calm and humor and peace are rare and inspiring—that?" He nodded again, his eyes full and fixed on Joe. "That I feel in the presence of Grace, watching you, and that I feel privileged to be able to share this experience with you—that?"

He nodded and nodded, the smile on his lips hidden by his oxygen mask.

"Hear that…Joe? Tell everyone…who asks…what she…said…"

When Susan arrived, she brought face masks for each of us against contamination—doctor's orders—and we put them on. Now all four of us were hidden, except for the eyes. Feeling distanced from the others by the mask, I took mine off impatiently, but Jim said calmly,

"I could have…TB…please wear it…" I snapped it back over my face and took my place by the bed, Susan alongside me and Joe on the other side. Again, we sat in a circle around our friend like doting family around a precious child.

"Guess I won't…need a nap…today," Jim joked, breathing hard. He looked at each of us in turn, his expression radiating peace. In some ways he was in much better shape than the rest of us.

"Do you need anything more…from…me?" he asked, again glancing at each of us as if to memorize our faces. This time I tore off my mask and left it off. Then Susan removed hers, and finally, Joe.

"I just need to know that you are comfortable," choked Susan. "Do you need anything more from us?" She leaned toward him and placed her hand gently on his above the bedclothes. His eyes crinkled in a smile as his mouth strained behind his mask.

"What I've got…is…perfect," he said, again taking us in one at a time. "You are…so…beautiful," he breathed, captivated first by Joe, then by Susan, then by me. "Your eyes…," he told me, "you have…no…idea…I love you," he told each of us individually, his eyes spilling, glowing.

Jim was right; the moment was perfect. Nothing more was needed. Even with the oxygen pumping at full strength, he was beginning to gasp with each breath. Susan and I held hands so hard our fingernails left white crescents in each others' skin.

"Tell me...a story...," he asked, "while we...wait. Each...of you..." He let his gaze rest on Joe. Joe cleared his throat with a rumble, and then related, in a quiet singsong, the story of the day they met. It had been at a bedside much like this one, where a mutual friend lay dying. With death as the backdrop—both in the past and in the present—he told a story of romance and desire, awkwardness and triumph. Jim watched his lover tell their story, his eyes intent on the tilt of Joe's chin, the lift of his eyebrows, the smile on his lips. They grasped hands and Joe bent to the bed, sobbing into Jim's heaving chest. "I love you...to...pieces...," Jim gasped out, before turning his gaze to Susan.

In a mesmerizing, soft lullaby of a voice, Susan told the story of when she and Jim had climbed to the High Sierra Camp at Vogelsang, the highest mountain meadow in the Sierra Range. She recalled the rare wildflowers and the soaring hawks; the freezing brooks just released, for those brief weeks, from winter's ice. He watched her with shining eyes, remembering. She reminded him of blisters and late-night laughter, of jagged ridges and alpine hikes. "Do you remember?" she asked, tears brimming. He nodded weakly.

"I...remem...ber..."

Outside, the dark night was beginning to give way to a faint hint of gray at the eastern horizon, over the hills. Jim's body grew restless and he attempted to change his position. We leapt to help him turn, but it did no good. His breathing became more choked, more panicked. His eyes above the mask, for the first time, looked afraid. For a moment he regarded me with a faint air of apology. There would not be time for one more story. Then he glanced at the clock on the wall. Outside, the stars were gradually giving way to a misty dawn.

He spoke again. "In a...minute...I will...take off...the mask..." He lay back, panting. "I may...panic..." He closed his eyes, concentrating. "If I...panic...don't...give it...back...to me. Just hold...me." Again, he waited for strength to continue. "Agreed...?"

We each nodded.

"My spirit...is packed...I'm ready...to go!" He smiled at his own joke like a comedian warming up for the finest performance of his life, and went on, "Tell anybody...who wants to know...that I had...no fear...but only...joy..." My grip on the bedrail was so tight I had to release my hand finger by finger. Again, he gazed at each of us in turn.

"Joe?" he said. Joe leaned over close to him. "Make my...favorite...cake...butter frosting...for the...memorial?"

Tears blurred my vision, and I had to continually wipe them away to keep him in view.

"Remember...," he said, his gaze toward me, "look for me...in...the hummingbirds..."

I nodded my head yes, openly weeping now. Susan and I clung together, hovering over him like midwives at a birth.

"Are you comfy?" he asked us. The only thing we could do was laugh through our tears, and then he reached deliberately for the bottom of the mask and pulled it up and away from his face.

"Well, that's better!" he said in a much more normal voice. For a moment, seeing his whole face and hearing his real voice, I thought all of this had been a bad dream and we would all share a laugh and walk out of this antiseptic room together. "I can see you...much better...this way."

He glanced again at the clock. In the silence of my mind I sensed him gathering his forces for the take-off. "Jim!" I cried aloud.

"It's time to go," he responded, his body seeming to sink more heavily into the mattress. "I love you...I love you..."

His fingers curled, as if the strength were draining from them, and his pallor grew more and more waxen. Although I don't think he could have moved a muscle at this point, even if he wanted to, I could feel him still energetically very much with us and, as we had planned to do, I spoke to him mind to mind.

First stage, I reminded him, silently. *Stay with it. Keep steady and don't panic. Keep moving on through whatever you feel...Stay steady...*

His open eyes were fixed ahead of him, bright with purpose. Like a thoroughbred horse galloping toward the finish line he panted hard, snorting the air out of his mouth and sucking it in with great, hard gulps.

When his lips became dry and bloodless, spittle began to form in the corners of his mouth. Some tears escaped from the corners of his wide-open eyes as the fluids of his body shut down.

Stay calm, I urged in my mind. *You're doing it! The water element is leaving. Keep moving steady. Stay calm. You're gorgeous!*

The faintest hint of a grin at one corner of his mouth told me we were in communication. Silently, I cheered him on.

His nostrils caved in slightly and he began missing breaths, the rhythm that had sustained him for fifty-two years slowing down, entraining now to a new rhythm. I breathed with him, deep when his breaths were deep, stopping when they stopped.

Stay with it...stay with it...yes....Air element now. Keep calm...

It struck me with sudden remorse that with each breath I came closer to losing my friend, and for just a moment my intention to assist the process met with resistance. It was just a tick of hesitation, but he picked it up and I felt myself being grabbed back.

"Sorry," I whispered, leaning over to actually say it within his hearing. If he could still hear.

The air coming from his nose and mouth was turning cool as his body heat—the element of fire—was dissolving. I sensed something akin to a firestorm taking place within him as all the warmth left his extremities and centered around his heart.

Stay easy...go with it...this is the fire part...let it burn without fear...you are spectacular...I love you...

The intervals between breaths grew longer. Each inhalation now sucked air in convulsively, held it and finally let it out with a shuddering sigh. The air was leaving him, the air of this world! Despite myself, I let out a sob as a sharp exhalation was followed by nothing. But then he drew in breath again as his connection with the physical world broke down, breath by breath.

I could sense blowing winds coming from all directions, buffeting him like a storm in the wilds.

Stay focused...keep moving on through...stay calm...that's it...that's it, Jim! You're doing it...oh, magnificent! Oh, magnificent! Oh, yes, yes, magnificent!

"That's it," I heard myself whisper hoarsely as I felt him break through some barrier of chaos—like flying through the center of a cyclone—into a calm, restful place, and pass over. In the space of a breath, the storm gave way to stillness as, at the eastern horizon outside the hospital window, the sun emerged in a glow of red and orange and rose over the hills to claim the sky for the day.

"He did it!" I kept crying, "oh, he did it!"

Susan and Joe and I held onto each other and wept together, the man who had been Jim lying peacefully between us, his wide-open eyes calm with grace and still strangely bright.

When Joe leaned over, looking into his friend's eyes for the last time before closing them forever, they appeared to widen with wonder as if, at exactly that moment, he had crossed the first barrier, moved into the Light and been taken with rapture.

FOUR

A Brief History of Death

EVERYTHING
PASSES AWAY
BUT THE FACE
OF GOD. THE KORAN

bout a week before he died, Jim had a remarkable dream which he related to me:

I'm swimming in a kind of lake, or ocean, maybe. But it's a body of clouds rather than a body of water, and it funnels into a very narrow place, like a tunnel. I have to suck myself in to get through this tight channel, and then I come out into a bright, endless ocean of light. And the light is so wonderful! Sort of warm and translucent and very safe. So I'm swimming along in this stuff, filled with happiness, and suddenly someone says to me very gently, "You don't have to swim with your bottom up in the air. Here, let me show you how to do it." And he gives my bottom a little push and then I dive right into the ocean of God.

The dream felt familiar to both of us, from images that had come through during our work together in the studio, and from accounts we had read in spiritual texts as well as accounts of "near-death survivors," people who had officially died before being medically resuscitated.

Technological advances in the past two decades have made it possible to bring back some people who have been clinically pronounced dead, such that by the 1980's there were some eight million near-death experiencers in the United States alone. The stories they tell afterward tend to be variations on Jim's dream: they float weightlessly through space; they pass through a narrow tunnel; they emerge into a vast, luminous place; they are greeted by a helpful, kind being. Unlike Jim, instead of actually diving into the "ocean" they get sucked back into the world and their physical bodies—not always willingly.

Most near-death survivors describe their experience of dying as a kind of *coming-home* to a place of abundant love and belonging, where they were free from pain. They describe themselves as having been profoundly changed by *dying*, even if it occurred decades earlier. They claim to have lost their fear of death, and wish to commit their lives to the service of others. I spoke to a woman, now in her eighties, who confessed that for years she dared not speak to anyone of her experience, not even her doctor.

"They wouldn't have understood," she confided, declaring that the scene was as clear to her now as it had been sixty years ago when she *died* in a car crash. "I watched the whole thing from above and, my dear, I could have told them afterward exactly what happened, and how everyone was running about, and how the policeman carried my body away." Leaning toward me with a little twinkle, she added, "And ever since then, I help people across."

"Across?"

"Yes, across. You see, many people get lost after they die. They don't know they are dead or where they are, so I help them—in my mind, of course. I go to a certain town—of course, I only see the town in my mind, but I've been going there for many, many years. And I go up and down the streets until I find another poor soul who is lost, and I bring him or her to the threshold. I know how to get there. I should—I've been doing it for sixty years!"

The evidence continues to come in, in fact, not only from near-death survivors but others who, either through trauma or by design, have somehow transcended their bodies and *seen* further than eyes can normally see. I believe my experience as a child roller skating in Brooklyn was an instance of this.

Cultures all over the world have techniques for entering expanded states of awareness through drumming, chanting, dancing, meditation, sensory deprivation, and mind-altering plants, ingested or smoked. In the resulting ecstatic trances, the mind is transcended, the musculature is relaxed, the heart is opened, and the experience is of rising above the bounds of the physical body and bonding joyfully with others in the community and with all Creation.

My own work with movement and sound is designed to create a similar profound balance of the body, mind and spirit, and I have often experienced this magical shift of consciousness while dancing and singing improvisationally. I slip into a state of calm, effortless awareness in which I appear to be loosed from the constraints of my moving body. I feel connected to a *something* greater than myself in which I have utter trust. In this quite ecstatic state, I seem to have access to knowledge not otherwise available to me: the state of health of a client's body; collective memories; the significance of hieroglyphics. I frequently have precognitive awareness of events happening elsewhere, and sometimes feel that I could see through walls if I tried. It is a bit like dreaming while awake, or shifting into a different frequency from that of my waking consciousness. This is not a one-time fluke; I have experienced this shift hundreds of times, and shown others how to experience it, and it makes me wonder if human awareness might not have an existence independent of the body, a consciousness which uses the body as a vehicle.

And if so, what does that mean about death? When my body dies, will all of me die with it, or am "I" simply inhabiting this body for the span of a human lifetime?

Everything I have read from other traditions refers to an all-encompassing, indescribable universe or *being* which holds our physical world within it. This is a mysterious, immeasurable realm where the ancestors reside and guardian spirits roam. It is too vast and unknowable to name and is both feared and revered, approachable by shamans and witches but not by ordinary mortals—until we die. It is understood to be everywhere and nowhere at once; as invisible and ineffable as God. Like the water is to the fish swimming in it, this *ether* is the very medium of our being, without which our perceived world would not exist. If it is a realm of Light, we are dense manifestations of that Light.

It fascinates me that a number of contemporary scientists, physicians and philosophers have been exploring this same, elusive territory through their own disciplines. I like it that terms such as non-local reality, frozen light, energy fields, expanded universe and multi-dimensionality are being used to try and describe a very slippery concept, as if the hard, physical separateness of things is softening around the edges, allowing the world to press against its too-tight boundaries and expand into a larger description of reality.

If the physical world is the totality of all there is, then the death of my body would mean total oblivion for me. This, I find too horrible to contemplate. I prefer trusting what I understand of the ancient wisdom traditions, and comparing the knowledge of generations of people before our era with what my own body, mind and spirit tell me right now, every time I work in the studio.

On one of our long walks in the country together, during the period when Jim and I talked a lot about dying, he told me that every day the body loses about 500,000 million skin cells.

"But for every 500,000 million that die," he claimed, "another 500,000 million are born. In fact, did you know that every seven years the human body renews itself completely, down to the last molecule?"

This was encouraging. Apparently, it is the natural fate of cells to die, and millions die every hour of every day of our lives, and are even programmed to do so.

"It keeps our bodies functioning," he explained, trying to reassure himself, I think, as well as me. "So it's not a tragedy to be avoided. Cell death is really crucial for the growth and development of all multi-celled organisms. Like us. So death, then," he quipped with a grin of bravado, "is just a habit of the body and, from a biological point of view, is completely safe!" We both laughed.

"So could you conclude," I had asked, "that death can be seen as a habit of the whole physical world?"

"Yup. Just another irritating habit," he had jested, lifting his binoculars to follow the flight of a red-tailed hawk above us.

I wonder what it would be like to have clairvoyant vision and watch the world from a hawk's-eye view, way above it all. I imagine I'd see a constant brilliant pulsation as cells, insects, plants, birds—all the creatures, including us—came and went, were born and died, each in its own cycle of time. It would look something like a sparkle of sunlight dappled on the moving surface of water—bright, dazzling, alive!

Both Jim and Lynn, showing me the natural world they loved so much, pointed out to me again and again that plants and animals— even the rocks and waters of the earth—eventually lose vigor and become worn out. Everything has its season and sooner or later gets reabsorbed back into the earth and ultimately, I would like to believe, into the fundamental web of energy from which it came. The flowers outside my window wither and drop their seeds back down to ground at the end of every summer and their dried leaves and petals become humus for next year's flowers. And each new spring I see the soil grow moist and watch as new plants push tender shoots up into the air as pulsing life emerges yet again, like clockwork. (In fact, didn't the Miwok peoples gauge time by the flowering and fruiting cycles of their native plants?)

I expect it would be tragic for us if the cycle of growth, flowering and decay didn't exist in our world. Without death and decline to set limits, I could see the profligate earth getting overrun and, within a season, life choking itself out. Fortunately, though, there seems to be a balance between the terminating forces of death and the unlimited, creative potential of not-yet-born energies, a process that appears to be necessary, purposeful and ultimately benign. Wherever I look on the planet, life and death are occurring simultaneously. Seeing it around me everywhere, I trust that the process is a sacred one, and that it is perfectly safe for me to be part of it.

I have wondered if this natural cycle of life, death and rebirth might not be reflected in the mythology of different cultural traditions as well, and from what I have read, it is. Some version of the story of eternal return appears in every religion I researched, from animism to monotheism, and it basic elements are that before coming into physical incarnation a human soul is considered "not-yet-born," and after birth, the soul incarnates on earth for a lifespan of trial, learning and initiation which often involves pain, loss and suffering, as well as joy. At the end of a lifetime the soul leaves the physical body and returns to its source, or ultimate Home, to absorb the lessons that have been learned during its sojourn on earth. (In Aramaic, the word for death literally translates as "not here, present elsewhere.") The essential self, or soul, incarnates on earth again and again for as many lifetimes as it takes to accumulate spiritual wisdom, or consciousness of the Divine aspect of existence. (The Mohaves refer to reincarnation as an unending circle; to one West African people, the word is the same as that for a vine which spirals up a stalk.)

According to everything I have read on the subject, the accumulation of spiritual wisdom involves becoming aware that we are responsible for our actions, and that for every choice we make there is an inevitable consequence. The Hindus refer to this as the universal law of *karma* which in Sanskrit means *action*. From the retribution we receive for our acts of ignorance, greed or anger, we gradually awaken to the fact that we are all ultimately and inextricably connected to one another and to the universe, and that harm to another necessarily means harm to ourselves.

It was interesting to discover that the basic principle of reincarnation is implicit in the early scriptures of the Judeo-Christian tradition, from the *Kabbala* to the New Testament. I never learned that in Bible class as a child. In the ancient secret doctrines of the Jewish faith received by Moses on Mount Sinai, the transmigration of souls is an essential part of the system. From the first century Jewish historian Josephus, we are told, "The bodies of all men are indeed mortal, but souls are ever immortal...obtaining a most holy place in heaven from where, in the revolution of ages, they are again sent into pure bodies...."

Reading from the Essenes and the Gnostics, I was amazed to discover that the notion was implicit in early Christianity as well. It got lost, however, after the Council of Constantinople of 553 AD, a Council to which neither the Pope nor churchmen from the Western church were invited. At this Council of only five churchmen, the doctrine of reincarnation was declared *anathema* by a vote of three to two. One now unknown cleric made the difference! This caused a major schism between the Eastern and Western church which lasted almost one hundred years, and effectively silenced all discussion of reincarnation in orthodox Christendom for fourteen centuries! *Fourteen centuries!*

My understanding of the diverse ways the basic myth is expressed in different cultures is that when a life cycle is completed, the soul loses interest in its current body and, as if hearing a summons from its source, slips out like a snake shedding its old, worn skin and prepares to leave it behind. What the body experiences as death, the soul experiences as birth. During the process of physical death, the personal consciousness shifts to the universal consciousness where time and space have no meaning, and *here* and *now* become the same. Internal and external, then, become one and the same, and the illusion of all separateness is eradicated.

Several years ago I traveled to England on a personal pilgrimage to visit a number of healers and writers whose work I admired. One remarkable woman named Mary Scott, whose book *Kundalini in the Physical World* had become a beacon for me, invited me to visit her in her tiny Wiltshire hamlet.

"I'm rather old, you see," she informed me on the telephone, "so I can't ask you to stay, but there's a lovely inn just one village over where they'll put you up." I arrived planning to be there for one or two nights, and ended up staying a week. In the True Heart Pub.

We had a wonderful time, Mary and I. She was indeed elderly—almost eighty-five—and by the second day we were both so pleased to find someone so empathic to "chin wag" with about the subjects that interested us most, that we spent hours curled up on her bed talking and dozing. On about the fifth day she regarded me curiously and asked,

"Is your father still alive?"

"No, he died almost thirty years ago—rather horribly, actually," I admitted.

"I take it he didn't believe in the afterlife?"

"He was pretty much a non-believer in anything. Why do you ask?"

"Because," she intoned mysteriously, "I would say he does not know he is dead."

"What?" I sat up with a start. She was regarding me with a steady, serious gaze.

"I feel him here, right here." She pointed to her own midriff. "I've been sensing something all week, and I believe he has been hanging onto you since his death—when did you say it was—thirty years ago?" Suddenly, I felt sick to my stomach, and my throat crowded with tears. "Would you like to help him cross over?" she asked gently. "His people are waiting for him; I can sense them waiting."

"Of course. If I can."

"Lie down on your back," she breathed, placing her hands lightly upon my body, "and visualize somebody who loved him very much, someone who has passed." Immediately his mother, my grandmother, appeared in my mind's eye.

"Now, in your imagination bring him where she can see him." I did so, and behind my eyes my father immediately shrank into a small boy and reached for his mother's hand. She grasped it and led him away, without a backward glance, until they were no longer in view.

Mary's hands began to tremble, and soon her whole body was shaking uncontrollably. She had to grab onto the bedpost to keep from falling over, but I couldn't help her because I had begun to heave with crashing sobs which shook the whole bed. We were like two women at sea in a storm!

For the rest of the day, once we had both regained calm after what had been, after all, an exorcism, I lay with my head in her lap, alternately weeping and rushing to the bathroom to expel bile from my every orifice. Mary explained that some people literally don't realize they have died and therefore are unable to make the full transition, so they latch onto the body of a willing host. "Thirty years," she mused. "My, my. That's a long time. You'll be better off now, my dear."

In the evening she sent me back to the True Heart, advising me to spend the evening quietly and to get to bed early. I was completely drained, exhausted, and had little intention of doing anything else, but when I arrived at the pub the local farmers, engaged in their nightly game of darts, invited the American lady to play.

"C'mon, you be on my team," said a ruddy fellow, "you'll give me luck." So I joined him, with everyone watching as he showed me how to hold the dart and where to aim it. "Hit us a bull's eye!" he cried as I raised my arm for my first throw. Everybody laughed and watched expectantly.

I hit a bull's eye. Right in the perfect center of the middle ring. The pub went quiet, and then erupted in a roar of cheers. Everyone wanted to buy me a drink; everyone wanted to touch me. Nobody had hit a bull's eye in that pub for years, and here's this American lady who's never played before and, look!

"Phone call for you, missus," said the innkeeper, a look of curious dismay on his face. What was going on here? The crowd gathered expectantly as I took the phone. It was Mary Scott on the line.

"I told you, a quiet evening," she remonstrated from her thatch-roofed cottage a mile away. How in the world could she have known? "You're to be still and quiet. Take a bath, and then go to sleep, I tell you."

"Mary, I hit a bull's eye!" I told her, laughing and promising that I would forgo the next round of darts.

"Bully for you," she punned, "but you won't hit another, so quit while you're ahead, and off to bed with you."

The fact is that my life changed quite radically after that incident. I had actually *seen* my grandmother—not imagined her—and I actually *saw*, and felt, my father leave my body. Ever since then, I have searched the literature to try to understand what happens after we die, and whatever I have read, be it anthropological accounts of Siberian shamans, aboriginal Australians, Amerindian seers; ancient texts from all over the Asian continent; African spirit-based cultures, or contemporary channeled accounts of the after-death experience from the English-speaking countries of the world, the information is nearly identical. No matter what kind of language used, be it symbolic, mythical or scientific, the content is all of a piece from all over the world.

All of it, however, requires from us a basic acceptance of the world as having a vaster, more dimensioned spectrum than just the physical one we witness. Or just the willingness to suspend, for a few moments, whatever disbelief we may have of the reality of the unseen, and entertain new possibilities. Or perhaps just one experience—once—of the ineffable, when looking up at the ceiling, we saw the sky.

I was in my favorite local bookstore one day, during the time I was searching out whatever I could find on the subject of the afterlife, and the proprietor, my friend Richard Cook, handed me a long out-of-print book called *The Return of Arthur Conan-Doyle*.

"Take a look at this," he said, "and tell me what you think." It claimed to be Conan-Doyle's account of his own experiences after death, channeled through a trance medium some two years after he died! Dubious, but open-minded, I took it home and devoured it in a single sitting. Not only did I find the information personally convincing, but it corresponded to and enlarged upon everything I had been reading from the world's wisdom traditions. I went back to the bookstore at a run and asked Richard if he knew of any other contemporary channeled accounts. Together we did a book search that turned up another nine books channeled through trance mediums between the years

1909 and 1978, from England, Scotland, South Africa and the United States. Each spoke in a different voice and used a different mode of describing the experience, but the basic content of each book was identical to the others, as well as to the information I had already gathered from mythology. To me, this constituted a mandate to take the information seriously.

In brief outline, here is a summary of the essential information I have gleaned from my researches:

HOW DOES OUR WORLD FIT INTO THE LARGER PICTURE?

It's as if the universe were a many-dimensioned dart board, like the one in True Heart Pub, with infinity as the outer ring; the earth, then, would be the bull's eye. The immanent spirit and intelligence of the Whole Unity, sometimes called God, permeates the Whole Thing, not only all the inner rings, but every being, every atom, every thought within them. The rings encompass one another in layers of decreasing density (or increasing subtlety) as they expand farther outward, toward the finer and finer vibrations of the Ultimate Principle, which is Love. Since our language is based upon our familiar, earthly reality, words cannot explain the intricacies of this multi-dimensional and abstract universe, so we give it many names and descriptions and stories which can do no more than hint at the ineffable reality. In some cultures, respecting its ungraspable nature, we even insist it remain unnamed.

Souls are shards of light from the ultimate Light, and descend into embodiment on the earth to experience matter in its most dense manifestations. Ultimately, all souls are connected to each other and to the Whole from which they emerged. At death, each soul returns to the source, being pulled to the level of frequency which resonates with its particular level of development. In the dart-board image, the souls would retreat from the bull's eye and be absorbed by the outer rings until such time as they were ready for the next stint of earth life and experience.

WHAT IS THE PURPOSE OF LIFE ON EARTH?

Human beings incarnate on the physical plane to experience the limitations of matter as a means of evolving the soul, raising the denser vibrations of the earth's vibration to a higher frequency. Another way of saying this is that we are learning to illuminate matter with spirit; or we are, lifetime by lifetime, expanding into Divine consciousness.

WHAT IS IT LIKE TO DIE?

It is a peaceful letting go, or shifting into another mode of being which feels freer than the constraints of the physical body, especially if there was sickness or trauma before the passing. You wake up recognizing that you are still yourself, still in the world, still amongst other beings, often your own relatives. This is the transition phase, before going on to your rightful sphere of vibration.

WHAT IS IT LIKE ONCE YOU GET THERE?

Since the soul has simply shifted to a more subtle frequency of vibration, it appears very similar to the earthly world, except that matter is finer, more tenuous. You still look like a human person, not an angel. Being on the level of *thought,* you perceive your surroundings in whatever way you think of them. If you died in anger and despair, you will find yourself in what has been called *Hell,* but it is not a place so much as a creation of your own state of unhappiness. You may create whatever you desire; the very thought brings it instantly to existence, and so you may lift yourself from the *Hell* of your own making simply by your desire for change. Thoughts, however, cannot be hidden from other souls, with the result that you eventually choose to clean up your inner act, which can now be read like a book. Sooner or later every soul's impulse is to move on, either back into incarnation for further lessons, or into the next realm of finer vibration.

WHAT HAPPENS THEN? WHO IS THERE? WHAT DO YOU DO?

The first thing you do, is die again. Passage from one ring to the next always involves the transition of death, as the soul shifts to a higher frequency. By resonance, you are drawn to those other souls of a similar frequency, or your soul group. These have been your long-term companions on a journey that has been ongoing for millennia. At this stage, you continue the process of assimilating the lessons learned from your previous earth-plane existence, and you may assume a number of tasks: teaching, assisting the newly arrived to make the transition; preparing souls for coming incarnations; guiding those currently on the physical plane; waiting for those in self-imposed Hell to awaken.

THEN WHAT?

At some very advanced point in the soul's evolution, you have attained the pure, high vibration of absolute Love. Willingly, you give up form, however tenuous, and merge with the immanent, Divine Source from which you originally sprang, thus assisting the Whole toward yet greater evolutions.

Like the dart board, there are circles within circles and the widest circle and the inner, bull's eye circle, are reflections of each other—a microcosm and a macrocosm. Life is a continuum on a multitude of levels, and death is simply a part of it. Nothing more, nothing less.

All of this information, as I found it repeated in text after text, culture after culture, rang true to me. I know these shifts of awareness in my own body and recognize that I am capable of more than just my everyday state of consciousness. I am not a stranger to transitional states, however painful they might be. And I will never forget—along with the other patrons of the True Heart Pub, I daresay—standing in front of the dart board after having been purged of horrors, my whole body relaxed and my mind clear and without expectations—in an altered state, as it were—and, from the center of an unencumbered awareness, simply lifting an arm, taking aim and sending the dart quivering straight into the center of the bull's eye.

In the zone.

FIVE

Alice's Story

Be it life or death, I crave only reality.
If I am really dying, let me hear the rattle
in my throat and feel cold in the extremities;
if I am alive, let me go about my business.
HENRY DAVID THOREAU

lice was brought to my studio one gray, rainy afternoon just after the turn of the new year, less than six months before her death. It was the same last six months of Jim's life as well, and had I known at the time that they were to die within two weeks of each other, I might have thought twice about bonding to Alice as strongly as I did. But then, had I been more cautious—or less passionate—about this seventy-five year old woman in the terminal stages of bone cancer, I would have missed the chance to meet one of the most memorable characters I had ever known in my life.

More than memorable, as it turned out—as essential to me as air! Already in those first moments of helping her out of the car—this little sparrow of a lady with disheveled gray hair and a wizened, wrinkled face, her legs no more than bones encased in black stockings—I found myself smitten. She gave me a sharp look out of jet black eyes set deep above flaring cheekbones and sized me up in a second. Then a hint of a secret smile. Who was she—a pixie, an elder shaman? Her smile confirmed my wildest thoughts, which she acknowledged by taking my supporting arm.

"She's here," I kept thinking as I led her slowly through the garden to the studio. Actually, it was as if she were the one leading *me* there, that we had a destined tryst and since it had taken us so long to find each other, we had to work quickly now. "Thank God, thank God she's here," my heart kept saying.

At the door to the studio, with the rain misting down on us, she turned and faced me for a suspended moment, her clear, dark eyes intense. I sensed then that I had waited all my life for her, that I loved her unconditionally and that I would be there for her no matter what, no matter why. She pursed her thin lips into a mischievous grimace of approval before she turned her head and stepped painfully across the threshold of the studio. In that single glance I understood that our recognition was mutual.

Inside, I lay her down on raised cushions like a queen, wrapping her warmly in woven shawls and quilts. She restlessly fingered the sateen binding of the quilt, her papery skin waxen against the vivid blues, purples and oranges of the patchwork design. In moments, she was asleep and snoring.

I prepared myself to lay my hands on her, settling down cross-legged by her side, but immediately I sensed her making subtle contact with me, like a restless bird fluttering against the constraints of its cage.

"Dance!" was what I seemed to hear. "Dance for two."

Oh! Of course that was how to start our relationship—by dancing, she fast asleep on the floor and me moving through space, vibrating the floorboards beneath her and gathering warmth and energy from the atmosphere for both of us. I would start slowly, letting my whole body soften and breathe until I found the internal rhythm we shared, and then I would dance it full out.

When at last I felt it, I caught the beat and spread it into the space, twirling it into the air and the corners and pounding it into the sprung wood floor. With my voice I searched the scale until I found the note that was resonant between us and I scrubbed away at it, like bunched wet cloth on a washboard, until I felt the pain in the marrow of her bones begin to ease. Then, smoothing out both my voice and movements, I washed the pain away in clear water, rinsing and rinsing until the very air was cleansed. Faintly, she smiled in her sleep.

Still pulsing with energy, I at last settled down beside her to meditate until my hands, of their own accord, lifted and were held suspended above her torso. Healing heat coursed through me and into her, invisibly, irrevocably joining us.

For me it was a homecoming. I had finally located my elder mentor, the mother warrior whom I had always sought. To have found her just in time to lose her took my breath away, and my hands above her body trembled as the tears crowded up in my throat. In her sleep her eyelids twitched, and then again grew calm. I lay my hands gently on her body, feeling her birdbreaths lightly expand and contract her fragile ribcage. I let my eyes gently close, and the two of us entered the same sleep for most of an hour.

When at last I opened my eyes I saw that her sleep remained unbroken, and it occurred to me that she might be in a coma. I whispered, with heart-pounding apprehension,

"Are you there?"

"Of course," she responded immediately. Startled, I jumped. I had not yet heard her speak and her voice was strong and clear, the last thing I had expected to come out of that weakened husk of a body. She laughed, studying my face with intense interest and then said,

"It's you."

I nodded, tears welling with relief at her confirmation of our connection. If this was some kind of strange fantasy, then at least we both shared it.

"It's me," I agreed quietly, my heart pounding so high in my throat that my ears could hear the beats.

"That's good," she replied simply. "Help me?" she asked, pulling her hands feebly from beneath the quilt and raising them with difficulty into the air.

"Of course," I murmured. "Whatever." She drew in a deep breath and began raking the air with expressive fingers, as if drawing in three-dimensions on an invisible canvas before her.

"In the center we'll have a waterfall—in oranges and yellows, I think—and it plummets to the base in great swirls of foam—these in whites and clears." I was mystified, and also astonished by the articulate clarity of her speech. Her words came through like well-enunciated poetry, composed and cultured. Of course, I had no idea what she was talking about, but I listened hard for clues.

"You really ought to take notes," she suggested. "I may not have the strength to repeat all of this again."

"Ye-es," I agreed, jumping up for a pencil and writing pad. As soon as I was again seated she continued,

"Flying birds in greens and purples against the variegated blue background sky—yes, the blues shall be only in the sky portions. Got that? Birds are shades of green, shades of purple." Her fingers drew life out of the air, coaxing color from invisible substance as she drew with her hands what she saw in her mind's eye. I wrote down every word she said, not knowing if this were a sick woman's hallucinations or the last words of a genius. Nor, if they had anything at all to do with me.

"Thank you," she breathed finally, still watching the lightshow behind her closed eyelids. "It was important I get that down."

Again she slept and I tried to relax, figuring I would consult later with the person who had referred her to me, and learn what I could about her condition and background. Stilling myself and listening closely for clues, I felt deeply into layers of myself where I connected with her, finding my heart softening with the contact. I loved her on sight and on touch, it seemed. I wanted to give myself to her one hundred percent without question, grateful for the chance to love anyone that much. It was like stepping into the shallows of a river and being dragged suddenly, unexpectedly on an irresistible, wild current. I gave into it and let it carry me off, not worrying about where it might eventually dump me.

"The two things I need your help for," she declared, right out of sleep in a firm voice, "are the completion of the triptych for the church, and resolving my insane relations with my family."

What? I bent attentively toward her to make sure I did not miss a word. I still had no idea what she was talking about. "The triptych...?" I began encouragingly.

"I want to finish three windows—stained glass," she added, no doubt finally realizing that I might not know what she did for a living, "that are in progress for a new church. I *must* do them for those people."

"How close are they to completion?"

"I'm still designing them," she replied shortly. "Three of them." Again she seemed to doze off, this time fitfully. I took a deep, steadying breath and she followed suit, sighing, "Ach, I just want to be left alone to do this, but they're at me like vultures."

"Who is at you like vultures?" Indignant, I was ready to slay dragons for her.

"My children," she answered in a weary voice. "They want to dismantle my studio, sell my tools, fire my assistant. They want me to stop working."

"Oh."

"You'll help me...?" she pleaded. I nodded even though I worried about what I might be getting myself into. For all I knew, she could be a madwoman who knew a softy when she saw one, and I had fallen right into her trap. For all I knew, she was making all of this up. For all I knew, her children were doing right by her, and I would be meddling where I did not belong. But again, with nary a tick of hesitation, I dove in without looking back, committing myself to this stranger-whom-my-heart-loved, and praying that I might help keep her alive for as long as possible.

Three days later I went to her small garden apartment in a hillside complex of working-class housing overlooking the Bay. A leggy rosebush by her doorway was still producing a few straggling blooms, which I bent over to sniff before letting myself in through the unlatched screen door. She was asleep in her armchair in a room filled with books and papers, her legs propped up on a tattered leather hassock. Only the ticking of the kitchen clock broke the silence.

My entry did not rouse her. Tiptoeing across the small room, I looked around at this place that was her home: large-format art books were stacked everywhere and the bookcases were filled to overflowing with esoterica, from the Mystics to treatises on light from every tradition in the world. Sketch pads, papers and letters graced every available surface, including the carpeted floor. On the tripod table next to her chair a large newsprint pad showed a charcoal sketch of the waterfall and bird design I had notated for her a few days earlier. I picked it up to examine it more closely, inadvertently rustling the paper, which woke her.

"Oh!" she exclaimed, startled by my presence in her room. She took a moment to make the transition between sleeping and waking. Then she said more softly, "You." I placed a steadying hand on her shoulder until her breathing settled down and then kneeled beside her.

"Do you remember I called yesterday about coming?" She stared ahead of her as if still in her dream and then she nodded.

"I lose track of the days," she said, scratching her head a bit feebly, huffing a sigh through her nose. "Yes, yes…"

Hiding my disappointment that she might not have any recollection of who I was, I picked up the newsprint again.

"The sketch is poor," she declared in a stronger voice, "but that's the idea of it that I asked you to write down on Tuesday." She gazed up at me archly, as if to let me know that she was not nearly as far gone as I might be thinking.

"You do remember," I said foolishly.

"Damn right I remember," she commented vigorously. "Help me to the bathroom, would you, and then shall we get right down to work again?"

All afternoon we alternated between short periods of dictation and brief naps, when she sank into the tattered cushions of the armchair and went limp. After a catnap, she would awaken and continue as if there had been no break between her last sentence before sleep and this one.

"I want the birds swooping up—like this," she would indicate with an upturned palm, "and the water swooping down—like this," and her frail body followed her palm toward the floor. "Then the tree rises, rises—like this!" Again her arm rose into the air. "So the three panels together form a kind of sine wave between the birds, the waterfall and the redwood tree. Do you see?"

"I see," I murmured, trying to write all this down, copying the motions of her hands as well as I could with a pencil on paper. When every new idea had been duly transcribed, she fell again into a doze and I sat on the hassock at her feet and watched her sleep. I had not felt such profound peace in years.

"Thank you," she acknowledged graciously when she awoke. "Now, what can I do for *you?*"

"Tell me about yourself," I said simply, hugging my knees to my chest like a pupil at the feet of the teacher.

"There's not too much to tell," she confessed. "I make art—stained glass. That's my passion and my life. I'm not very good for much else."

"You've been doing it for a long time?"

"Over fifty years," she smiled, with the knowing look of one who has had experiences for longer than her listener has been alive. "Sacrificed two husbands in the process, and totally alienated one son and one daughter." She raised her eyebrows ironically and shook her head from side to side, chuckling. "All in the cause of my one true love—bits of colored glass and the light that comes through them. I have been married to light all these years," she mused, "and wouldn't have it any other way."

"I just love you!" I cried, crawling over and pressing my head against her arm. She stroked my hair gently and when I lifted my face to look at her, her dark eyes were moist.

"It's a good thing you weren't born to me, that's all. Then you would have had to play second fiddle to a soldering gun, just as they did." She stared grimly at the family photographs on the bookcase across the room and then, with a deep sigh, remarked, "But I'm not sure I would want to live with someone obsessed like me, either." Wincing with pain, she tried to elevate one leg in front of her. Gently, I lifted both of her feet up onto my lap. Covering them with an afghan, I removed her slippers and began softly to massage her cold toes, breathing in her clean leathery smell.

"Intense might be the better word," I corrected her. She considered the revision.

"Selectively intense, perhaps," she allowed. "My family never received much of that intensity, I'm afraid. It was reserved, always, for my work, for the way the setting sun might come through bits of red glass so that they would be as brilliant as fire. For blues so liquid in the morning light that they would reflect like pools onto the tiled floors. No, my dear, I was an obsessive. Still am."

"I'll bet I could have handled being your child, 'cause I'm the same way," I insisted, smoothing the knots out of her arches with my thumbs.

"There's some truth in that," she allowed, "because it is clear we are from the same tribe, and they, unfortunately, are not." Her recognition of me again melted my heart.

"Say more," I urged, hoping she would expand eloquently upon our connection, so I could hold onto it when she was gone. For awhile she didn't speak, staring off into the middle distance with a stony expression. Then she grunted.

"Ach, they're a couple of dull, blonde burghers." She spit this out with venom, and in that moment I had some sympathy for what these children might be up against.

"How did you come by blondes?" was all I asked, regarding her deep-set eyes and exotic facial structure and imagining what must have been, in her prime, a braid of shining blue-black hair down her back.

"Blue-eyed, too," she observed. "Hard to believe, eh?"

"Can't see it at all," I admitted. "Was their father very light?"

"Two fathers," she corrected, "and both rather ordinary-looking Anglos. No, it comes from *my* family. *I'm* the alien in the crowd; they're the ones who are true to type." She regarded me with bright eyes, her chin rising ever-so-slightly in a gesture of challenge that looked like a habit of very long duration.

"You're going to have to tell me more," I declared, perplexed.

"How'd you get all this out of me so fast?" Her eyes narrowed and she squared off with me, her gaze never leaving my face. I matched her, gaze for gaze, and replied lightly,

"No time to waste."

"Touché," she acknowledged with a smile.

"So—you're the alien…?"

"You are looking at Black Alice, the only darky in a family of Mayflower descendants—Yankee bluebloods—and how did she get this way? No doubt by some Iroquois hanky-panky somewhere in the distant past that only pops up maybe once every other generation."

"But that's extraordinary!" I exclaimed, seeing her high color and flared cheekbones in an entirely different light now. "Does that mean you're the only artist in your family, too?"

"It does indeed mean that. I was a stranger in their midst," she confirmed. "Despis-ed and reject-ed and acquainted with grief. They would have hidden me in a back closet if they could. I was everyone's shame personified."

"Oh, no!"

"And my children, you see, are from their grandparents' line—not mine. Unfortunately, I seemed to know it as soon as they were born, and never could quite claim them as my own. For which I shall roast, surely, in Hell. And, my dear, am roasting now, even as we speak."

From then on I came as often as I could, alternating my time with her with my time with Jim. I told Jim about Alice, but never told Alice about Jim. I tried to reserve one day a week for walking by the sea alone as a way of maintaining some balance, but even so, the prospect of my upcoming double loss would sometimes sweep over me with the force of a typhoon. On those days I would cancel whatever else was up, put a Fred Astaire movie on the VCR, and stay in bed until ten.

I became something of a girl Friday for Alice—cooking delectables to tempt her to eat, fetching in her mail and tidying her bedroom. I read to her and became a confidante to her working-class neighbors, who adored her and mistrusted her children fiercely. They kept me informed by phone of everyone's comings and goings from the apartment, so I knew when the family hired a visiting nurse to come by daily, and that Alice had protested vehemently. As Alice's healer-friend from *outside,* I was identified as her official caregiver by the neighbors, who carefully guarded our secret from the family. I felt like a character in a whodunit, hiding out behind their drapes until the coast was clear and slipping through Alice's door only after we heard a car door slam on the street. It was a bizarre conspiracy, and I never did understand why such secrecy was necessary, but it was weeks before I ever crossed paths with her children.

Arriving one morning, I found an entirely changed Alice slumped half-asleep in her chair. Her eyes, drooping, were glazed and unfocused. For a few moments she slipped back into a doped sleep and then, with obvious effort, forced her eyes open.

"I'm drugged," she slurred slowly. "Help...me..." I kneeled quickly and felt her pulse, which was uneven and faint.

"Tell me," I whispered urgently, slapping softly on the palms of her hands and the soles of her feet. "What happened?" With a weak hand she tried to grab her opposite shoulder, lapsing again into sleep with her arm ineffectually raised. I lowered her arm and placed it in her lap, gently massaging the shoulder she had been trying to reach. Again, she roused and lifted her hand to her shoulder.

"Patch," she managed to articulate, scratching feebly at her clavicle.

"Patch?" I urged, trying to get more information before she conked out again. She nodded.

"Mor..."

"More what?"

"Mor...phine." Her lips had trouble with the "f" sound, but she worked on saying more, which I could not understand. Quickly, I reached through her nightgown and found, on the skin above her shoulder blade where she could not possibly remove it herself, a skin-patch. Morphine.

"Someone put this on you, and you think it's morphine? For pain? Was it the doctor?"

141

"Not doctor. It *is* morphine. Don't want it. Don't..." Again she drifted off. For a moment I stood beside the sleeping Alice undecided. I had no authority, nor enough medical know-how to make a decision based upon what, very likely, were doctor's orders. But she had been alert and present the day before, and now she was comatose. And the difference, apparently, was this patch on her shoulder, out of her reach. Had it been placed where she could easily have gotten to it herself, I might have let it stay, on the basis that I had no business meddling with a course of treatment prescribed by her doctor. But by its placement—and her obvious helplessness—I smelled a rat, and without another moment of hesitation, I reached in and ripped it off, stuffing it quickly into my pocket.

"Thank you," she mumbled faintly.

"You're very welcome," I mouthed, in a heartbroken whisper.

For about an hour she slept in her chair and I watched her sleep, studying the angles of what was already a beloved face, though ravaged by illness, and wondering what was happening behind her closed eyelids.

Leaving her to her rest, I scanned her bookcases, gathering a stack of books to borrow. The subjects she had spent her life studying were the ones that also impassioned me: sacred music, theories of sound and color; altered states of consciousness. If only I could have learned from her when there had been time! I almost willed her to wake up so I could ask questions. I was leafing through the pages of a book about harmonic proportions when she called to me.

"I'm coming back," she said slowly, enunciating as if trying out the workings of teeth and tongue and voice. Grimacing, she pulled her body into a straighter position and her feet slipped off the little hassock. "Help me...please," she grunted, searching for a comfortable way to sit. "You must...not let them...give me...that patch." She spoke haltingly through clenched teeth.

"I wish I had some authority here, my dear," I reminded her. "Your children and your doctor don't even know of my existence."

"So what?" she exclaimed with heat. "...um...would you...um...do what you did today anyway?"

"You mean take it off?" She held my eye, nodding craftily.

"Why?" I asked, playing the Devil's advocate. For several minutes there was silence as she gathered her thoughts, and then she explained, as if to a slow child,

"I realize it is for pain and I agree that I ache and it makes the ache go away. But it makes me go away, too." Her voice got stronger, her eyes fighting to glare at me. Despite her efforts, they swam. "It makes me stupid and sleepy," she said with an attempt at patience. "I don't have time for that. I would prefer to feel the pain. Can you understand?"

"I do," I replied, dropping to a kneel by her side, "and I also am concerned about your having pain. Too much pain can make you dopey as well. Won't you compromise?"

"Of course I would compromise," she retorted, "but my family is out to get me—they're the ones who administer the drugs."

"Out to get you?" I asked skeptically. "You are pretty sick, after all." She waved me away impatiently, mumbling to herself. "You can count on me to help you through this," I told her, "but I reserve the right to make my own judgment calls." Tilting her head almost coyly, she regarded me critically for a few minutes. Then she remarked,

"You're going to have to tell me again, who are you and how did you get here?"

"And why didn't we meet twenty years ago when it might have done us both some good?" I finished for her, laying my head in her narrow lap while she stroked and stroked my hair dreamily.

When I arrived the next day the door was opened by a nurse, a stoutish woman with graying hair, who was on her way out of the apartment. Behind her back Alice was making faces, like a kid who has just been punished by a humiliating teacher. I would not have been surprised if she had put fingers in her ears and stuck out her tongue.

"I'll be back tomorrow at ten." The nurse had a high-pitched voice, and sounded like a little girl. "OK, dear?"

"OK, dear?" Alice mimicked as soon as she was out the door. "They've made me a prisoner in my own home!" she fumed. "I am mortified. *Mortified!*" I stood quietly by until she had blown herself out, and then asked,

"How often is she going to come?"

"Every damn day for two hours!"

"Who arranged it?"

"Christa."

"Your daughter?"

"None other," she intoned darkly. "This is violation! This is intrusion on my life and privacy! I resent it, resent it, *resent it!* I even suspect they are beginning to clean up my papers! I can't find things. My son has admitted they are 'tidying' up a bit! I could scream!"

"Why don't you?" I suggested. "One big one. You'll feel better." She made theater of hauling in a big breath, and emitted a tight little squeak. We both laughed and she put her face in her hands. I wondered if the nurse had fed her lunch before leaving, and glanced toward the sink for the telltale sign of dishes. Alice caught my furtive gesture and asked with exaggerated sweetness,

"Are you hungry?" This woman was much too quick for me. What must she have been like when she was young and strong?

"I'm not, thank you," I replied with equally exaggerated politeness, "but I wonder if you are?" She gave me an appraising look, but did not answer. "Well, have you eaten yet?" I asked more sternly.

"You don't think that biddy would let me get away with *not* eating, do you?" she retorted angrily. "Anyhow, it's none of your business!"

Her sharpness hurt, and I considered it for awhile, lowering my eyes. She pouted. Then I replied,

"Whether you eat or not isn't any of my business. But I take it as my business that I know the best *you* that I can know, and if that means making sure you're nourished, than that's what it means. That's all." I was breathing heavily, surprising myself by my outburst. I think she felt some dismay at my fervent pledge of loyalty and waved the back of her hand at me.

"All right, all right," she muttered impatiently, "come here and let's have our *quality time.*" The irony in her voice stung me again, but I ignored it and took my place—the devoted apprentice—at her side.

"Hand me that album, would you?" She pointed to a three-ring binder on the bookcase. I hauled it over and she reached for her glasses.

"Here," she said, turning the stiff pages, "this is work I was doing about ten years ago." She squinted appraisingly at the pictures of her compositions, pursing her lips with interest as if she were looking at another artist's work. "Here," she said, pushing the heavy album closer to me.

There, in colored glass, were seascapes with dark birds hovering in stormy skies; stylized forests with canopies of autumn leaves. Boats rocked in swirling bays, their gaily-striped sails billowing, and cattails sprung at the edges of a marsh beneath cloud-laden skies. Each piece was a study in the moods of light. Alice was as adept with shadows as she was with variegated brightness, and I was stunned by the beauty of her work.

"More," I breathed, impatient to turn the page. "Alice, these are extraordinary! I had no idea."

"You like them," she stated.

"I'm bamboozled," I declared. And here were birds: a peacock in full display; a soaring hawk with light shining through its tail feathers; a flock of flamingos in flight. I caught my breath. Suddenly, I was on a deserted beach on the other side of the world with Lynn. Alice had even gotten the wild fuchsia of the underwings.

"When did you do this one?" I asked, pointing to the flamingos. She counted out time on her fingers and stopped at the year Lynn and I had been in the Galápagos together.

"Why do you ask?"

"It's a long story," I replied, promising to tell it to her someday. I never did.

I turned the page. Here was a live oak tree the size of a whole wall, its dry-leafed branches spreading from a solid trunk represented in part by the door of the room it was in. Mountain ranges appeared, and an ice thaw in a mountain stream; three-dimensional sculpted glass abstracts seemed to rise right off the page, and there was a whole series which used mirrors instead of colored glass.

"You see," she told me, excitedly, "here the color and movement come from inside the room—from the people moving about."

"Alice, you're a genius!" I cried. "They're gorgeous. I'm totally astounded! Oh God, what I wouldn't give to have studied with you—I had no idea.

"Yes, you did," she said simply. "Why else do you think you latched onto me like a bulldog that day and haven't let me go since? Hunh?" I nuzzled my face in her fleshless shoulder and we both chortled.

"OK," I began, "I want to know what it's like to *be* you when you're working. I want to know how it feels when you get your ideas, and what your process is from when you first get your vision to when you bring it to form. I mean, does it change along the way, or do you design it once and then that's it? What do you see behind your eyes when you're dreaming up a design? Can I come to your studio sometime?" I said most of this on a single breath and she watched my face, amused.

"You mean it, don't you?" she half teased. But her eyes were soft and she placed a hand over mine, smiling, and for the next hour or so, with breaks for catnaps or water, we talked. Or rather, *she* talked and I listened, asking the occasional question.

She spoke glowingly of the "joyous concentration"of creating something of beauty from bits of shattered glass. She tried to convey to me her image of light as it appeared in her mind's eye, and her obsessive need to try and approximate it in physical form. She lamented that no matter how vivid or "prismatic" she was able to make a piece of work, it never lived up to the "ecstatic wash" of her inner experience. She expressed the joys and frustrations of accomplishing a piece that was sometimes fairly decent, objectively, but rarely matched what she saw in her mind's eye.

"There are always a dozen more ideas waiting to be done," she complained. "I'm like a faucet that won't turn off, but this body has gotten too weak."

Her eyes filled, and I put both arms around the frail vessel of her precious body, and holding her, I rocked her and comforted both of us.

Alice's neighbor Marva phoned the next morning. I was sipping tea in the garden, still in my nightgown, and looking forward to a morning of doing nothing before my afternoon session with Jim.

"You'd better come," she said. "There's a crowd in there. Relatives from all over the place—I think one of them's a lawyer." She sounded scared. "I bet they found out Alice has made her own will and they're gonna try and get her to change it. I don't like the looks of it in there.

You better come." I broke my rule of "only one a day" immediately, left a message on Jim's phone machine saying we'd have to meet later in the afternoon, threw on some clothes and drove over to Alice's place.

The door was open when I arrived, and the screen door latched. The small apartment buzzed like a hive before a swarm. An unhappy-faced woman of about my age met me at the threshold and demanded to know who I was.

"You're not the nurse," she declared suspiciously. This had to be Christa.

"I'm your mother's friend," I said quietly. "She's expecting me," I lied.

"I don't think so," she responded rudely. I glanced over her shoulder for a glimpse of Alice in the midst of the throng, but there was no sign of her. She would be in the bedroom, then, perhaps drugged with morphine. It took all my restraint not to push past this woman and take the bedroom by storm.

"Well, then," I stalled, still hoping someone would shift position and there would be Alice, "I can see you're all busy...um...I can come back later." And with that I backed away, waited out of sight around the corner for a discreet several minutes and then snuck back to slip into Marva's apartment from where we could watch Alice's door.

"Do you suppose what these morphine patches are about," I asked Marva, "is to make her incompetent?" We stared at each other, horrified.

Marva told me, "It's too late, anyway. She's put a copy of the will into our hands for safekeeping, all signed and notarized. She made it last year when she first got sick, our Alice did! She knew they'd kick and scream when they found out. It's not like she's leaving a bundle, either, but she figured it would be needed to pay back rents on the studio. The landlords have given her that studio for almost nothing for years and she wanted to thank them. She told me she thought the family'd be furious."

"Did she know they'd all be showing up today?" I asked, wondering why she had neglected mentioning it to me.

"She suspected something was going on," Marva said, "but not what. Family people have been around a lot lately, and suddenly it's like a fortress in there. We've always been in and out of each others' places, no problem, but now the screen door's locked and when you knock half the time you're told to go away. I don't like it."

Neither did I, but there was precious little I could do about it except wait.

I phoned Jim, explained the situation and rescheduled with him for the next day.

"Give Alice my love," he said before hanging up. The poignancy of those words suddenly overwhelmed me, and I broke down crying in Marva's lap. Then I ate the tunafish sandwich she put in my hands.

At last we saw a knot of people, including Christa, leave the apartment. Shortly after, her son Greg left alone. Like a spy in a Grade-B thriller, I slipped out Marva's door and into Alice's before they had a chance to latch it closed, barely nodding to the one person left sitting at Alice's kitchen table.

"I'm Alice's healer," I said briefly, with authority. "She is expecting me. Is she in bed?"

"She's sleeping, I think," the man said with a shrug.

"That's all right," I assured him, slipping through the kitchen and into Alice's bedroom before he could think of stopping me. Shutting the door quickly behind me, I leaned against it and took in the dark-as-night bedroom, my heart beating hard in my throat.

A regular, wheezing breath emerged from the narrow lump beneath the bedclothes, and the air was heavy and stagnant. Without raising the drawn shades, I opened the window to let in some air and then sat down at the edge of the bed. Alice didn't stir. Feeling beneath her shoulder for the patch, I found it in place but did not remove it. Fury rose in my chest, but I dared neither pull it off, nor fly in a rage at the poor man—obviously left behind as a baby sitter—hanging out at the kitchen table.

I tugged off my shoes and climbed onto the bed with her, crossing my legs and placing my hands gently upon her back. For a long time I felt nothing but the actual in-and-out rhythm of her breathing—no sense of life-force, no sense of pain, no sense of Alice. But then, at last, I felt beneath my fingers a faint stirring of contact, and in a whisper I asked,

"Where are you, Alice?"

"Right the hell here," she slurred out, dopey but fully and feistily herself.

"Thank God," I choked out, half-sob, half-giggle. "What's going on?" I demanded.

"Where? Inside me or...out there?"

"Both." She slowly stretched her legs, groggily attempting to turn over. I reached out to help her. She groaned softly and for a moment, seemed to fall back asleep.

"Out there...mmm," she mumbled haltingly, "they're arguing about...my money. They're worried who's going to get...what... hmmm."

"Who *is?*" I challenged.

"That's *my* secret...hee hee." She drifted off again, but then came back. "It's all...taken care of."

"So I'm told."

"By whom?" she broke in quickly, aroused now. This was a woman who could awaken from a drugged sleep and say *whom* rather than *who*.

"Marva. Is it OK with you that I know?"

"Yes. But tell her...not to tell anyone...else."

"I'll relay that," I promised.

"You will not, under any...mmm...circumstances, relay this to my beloved family...I trust?"

"Of course not. Anyhow, they have no reason to suspect me of knowing any more than they know."

"Good," she murmured.

"I met your daughter," I informed her.

"Good," she repeated non-committally. "I think the morphine's wearing...off. Will you...get rid of this...damn patch?"

"No."

"No?" She opened her eyes for the first time and glared incredulously at me. "No?"

"No, I can't," I apologized. "Not while your whole family, including some lawyer, is around here. It could mean terrible trouble for me, and even more for you. They have the authority to deny me access to you, at the very least. I can't do it."

She lay back and closed her eyes again, breathing heavily. Her hands were balled into ineffectual fists. I stood by the bed, as ineffectual as she. "Sorry," I said. Finally, she relaxed.

"I haven't taken you…into much consideration…have I?" Her eyes opened, and in the darkened room she found me again. "You didn't know you were taking on…family politics along with me, did you?" She chuckled and heaved a sigh.

"Don't worry about that," I reassured her. "Anyhow, I can hear in your voice that the morphine is wearing off now. So, relax. I didn't bargain for your family, but I'm willing to put up with them if I can have you."

"Where were you years ago when I *really* needed you?" she teased, even through her fog.

"Probably in diapers," I retorted, grabbing hands with her as we heard the screen door squeaking open and banging shut as the troops returned. Like actors who knew their parts, we each took our places on the stage: she closed her eyes, playing possum, and I slipped into the shadows behind the door, perching onto a pile of her clothes strewn across a chair. Then, I think, we both stopped breathing. Her son came into the room and tried to gently shake her awake. No response. Then he exchanged places with her daughter. I went unnoticed by both of them. Christa leaned over her mother, who managed not to move a muscle, and muttered her frustration into the air. After awhile she gave up and left the room. Alice remained impassive, even through the strained, whispered conferences in the next room. I dared not leave my seat. An argument rose to a crescendo and faded out; a teakettle came to the boil and whistled; a toilet was flushed.

Again the door opened and her son with an older man—the lawyer, I think—attempted to rouse her again. To no avail. Alice would not be moved. They left the room again, letting the door slam this time. Finally, the conversations in the other room petered out, the screen door banged shut as people left, and the apartment was quiet except for the pad-pad of one person approaching the bedroom.

"Mom?" It was Christa, alone. I shrank deeper into the shadows. "Mom, you awake?"

No response. "Mom?" She reached over and gave her mother's arm a gentle shake. Nothing. "Mom…c'mon, Mom. You're doing this on purpose!" She stood there for a moment, her arms crossed on her chest, and gave a shuddering sigh. Tears rolled heedlessly down her cheeks and she shook her head with what looked to me like longing.

"Tough old bird, my mother," she murmured, acknowledging me for the first time. "Always did whatever she wanted to. Who did you say you were, again?" Her back was still toward me.

"I'm a healer and a friend of your mother's." I told her my name.

"Yeah," she sighed. "Well, are you going to be here for awhile?"

"I can be," I replied.

"Would you mind staying until I get back? I've got some errands, and I don't want to leave her alone."

"No problem," I assured her.

"If she wakes up, would you give her that drink that's in the fridge?"

"Sure."

"Thanks," she said, still not looking at me. She gave her mother one last, helpless shake and then left the room quickly. When we heard the screen door bang shut, Alice opened her eyes and said,

"See what I mean?"

"See what?" I asked.

"How impossible they are?"

"What do you mean, impossible?" I argued. "They're frightened, they're concerned. Your kids are losing their mother, for pity's sake! If you ask me…"

"Which I didn't," she broke in coldly.

"Too bad!" I was hot under the collar now, and there was no backing away. "I think you're being unreasonable!"

"Listen," she said wearily, "I was a stinking, lousy mother and they hate me—and I can't really blame them. They can hardly wait to obliterate every sign of me and carry off the spoils—of which they have a very inflated notion."

"I think you're being unfair," I insisted. "Nobody's *that* mean, I won't believe it. Especially if they come from your gene pool." That got her, and I felt her go very still, listening. "They're scared. Their mother's dying…"

"No I'm not!" she shouted, stubborn. I hauled in an exasperated breath. She gave a short bark of a laugh. "Stop being such a realist," she complained. "I've got work to do and I won't die until I'm good and ready!"

"I love you, you stubborn coot!" I exclaimed, bending down to kiss her on the forehead. "Maybe the most important work you still have to do is to make it up with your children."

"You asking me, or you telling me?" was her response as I left the room to fetch the drink Christa had left for her in the refrigerator.

The following day was the day I spent eating hamburgers and fries at a diner with Jim and listening to Schubert on his balcony. My senses were sharp and aware, every taste and sight like a gift of the body, poignant with life. I found myself savoring the living presence of Jim, of Alice, until I felt I could embrace every second of life—theirs and my own—with gratitude. No matter what was to come next, right now was filled with glory.

And the next day I took off, reading in bed until late in the morning and sewing on a patchwork quilt for most of the afternoon. It was a crazy quilt, in honor of the craziness of watching two beloved people decline rapidly, neck and neck, right before my eyes.

I had emptied my fabric drawers of all the scraps of reds, blues, browns and whites I had collected over the years. Nothing matched, everything clashed. I was putting them together in a Four Elements quilt, sort of like a stew made of leftovers.

My inspiration came from Alice and her shards of colored glass. I wanted to make a stained-glass window in cloth, an abstract design representing Earth, Air, Fire and Water. Eight squares of Earth were already done, a glorious hodge-podge of prints in rusts, maroons and shades of brown and deep green. The overall effect was of layered earth, subsoils and topsoils and rock pressed and tumbled into a fertile geology.

Onto my worktable I spilled scraps of reds and oranges and bright yellows for Fire and began matching them up. The strips of color shimmered, and with concentration I began arranging them in unlikely combinations. A sunburst in yellow I lined up with an orange paisley, ironing them smooth and then sewing them front to front on the sewing machine. My favorite moment—ironing the two fabrics open and seeing their combined effect—was an epiphany each time. My body responded first with anticipation, and then with a perceptible burst of pleasure.

I chose a brilliant bit of red brocade to go next to the paisley, lined it up and then sewed them together. Again, delight. I felt thankful for color, amazed that something so simple could produce such pleasure. It reminded me of the time I laid face-up on a lonely country road, watching a snapping turtle lay her eggs from beneath her. Staring straight up at her opening I waited, again and again, until her underbelly bulged, releasing the next perfect white egg to fall softly into the pile beneath her feet.

Ah!…and ah!…and ah!

A print of red and blue swirls came next and I laid it diagonally across the sunburst yellow. Already the pieced fabric was giving the impression of fire. Bright orange next, a bold strip across the red brocade. Yes!

I imagined Alice doing the same thing with glass—a slash of bright red cut in the shape of a flower, soldered carefully onto the adjoining section of clear glass. Cloth, in comparison, had to be a cinch to work with. I held my bit of patchwork up to the window, but the daylight shone through only faintly. Not like glass. But still, something in my chest softened and I felt the kinship between the two of us. It was something like singing in ensemble and hearing the tones beat together in harmony. I gazed with deep satisfaction at the patchwork, relaxing and balancing.

A bright yellow calico came next and then a red with yellow dots. Ah! Then a deeper red shot with gold thread, oh yes, then a bit more of the orange. I ironed them out. My first square was done, and it sparked like flames. Ah!

When I arrived the next day after the nurse's visit, I found Alice in the bedroom, leaning precariously against her bed as she struggled to pull on a pair of black stockings. She was dangerously off-center, the hose dangling from one hand as she tried to make contact between the flimsy nylon and her uplifted foot.

"Whoa!" I cried, dropping my packages and diving toward her before she fell. "What are you trying to do?" I righted her carefully, taking the stocking from her fingers. She was gasping with exertion and frustration.

"Get to my studio," she snorted.

"How?" I asked. She resisted, with a strength I would not have thought possible, my attempts to sit her down on the bed.

"With you," she informed me, "in your car."

Preparing for the outing was a macabre comedy of errors and quite beyond the abilities of both of us, as she was feeling a level of pain she was determined to ignore. My attempts to talk her out of it were futile; explaining that I would be held liable if anything were to happen to her cut no ice. She was determined to go, and despite all my arguments to the contrary, she insisted she was capable of making the trip.

"I won't fall, you'll see," she assured me as we worked at fitting her foot into a closed shoe, "and I will give you explicit directions to get there. I've already phoned my assistant, Benjamin, and he is expecting us."

I said silent prayers as we closed the screen door behind us and began the long trek, step by shaky step, her arm held tightly in mine, up the concrete path to where my car was parked.

We got lost going there—of course. The building which housed her studio was in a warehouse district; street after street of anonymous facades separated by parking lots.

"There!" she kept saying. "Turn right here." But the street would end at a barrier and we would have to turn around and start over. I felt trapped, wondering if I ought to just drive back to her place and live with her fury, but just then the right building appeared as if by magic, and she gave a cry of relief and directed me to pull up to the front steps.

"It's on the third floor," she mumbled as I helped her out of the car. Her body was trembling with anticipation.

"Where is the elevator?" I asked as she hauled herself, one step at a time, up the metal staircase to the wide front doors. I steadied her with an arm, guarding her body from behind with my own in case she fell backward. She pulled on the handrail with all her fragile might, never losing hold.

"There is…none," she gasped, finally achieving the top step of only the first stage of a third-floor walkup. Where was this Benjamin? I considered the possibility of carrying her; or leaning her against the wall while I ran to find her assistant; or banging on a door in the hallway for help. But she made her determined way toward the stairs, and I had no choice but to follow her, steadying her progress as best I could.

It was like climbing a mountain at altitude: step—pause—breathe; step—pause—breathe. With determination she kept taking the next step, and the next. Her whole body shuddered with the effort, but she never slackened her pace, never let go of her grip on my supporting arm. I prayed for Benjamin to appear and considered shouting out his name, but she achieved the summit of the third-floor landing on her own, her black eyes gleaming with triumph.

Benjamin, apparently recognizing the sound of her tread on the wooden stairs, rushed down the long hall to greet her and lifted her off her feet in a hug. Laying his cheek tenderly against her disheveled hair, he carried her like a beloved bride across the threshold of her studio. Over her shoulder he gave me a welcoming wink.

"Let me down!" she protested, half in pain and half in impatience until he placed her carefully back down onto her feet. Benjamin and I shook hands and introduced ourselves while she, all business, got her smock off the coat rack, put it on, and staggered headlong and unsteadily toward her desk.

With each step she became transformed into a different person. Expertly, she made her way around a soldering table, alongside a long workbench strewn with glass and knives, and across the minefield of glass shards on the floor. At her desk she climbed onto her tall stool, stuck a cigarette into a long holder and lit up, inhaling deeply before blowing out a firm stream of smoke which momentarily clouded the long, tall windows. For awhile she gazed out, as if remembering the scene of sky and sun that lit the studio like a blessing, feeling herself again in the seat of her power. It was from here that the finest creations of her imagination had come forth. Benjamin and I stood back and allowed her her moment.

"Ahh-h," she intoned with satisfaction, her cheeks taking on some color. Her eyes reflected the bright sun shining through the windows and her hands got busy, pulling a sketchbook toward her and reaching with practiced ease for her pencils from a chipped jug. I could no longer visualize the worn, gray husk of a woman I had, less than an hour earlier, helped into stockings in a darkened bedroom. Then she motioned Benjamin over to the desk, bent with him over a set of their drawings in progress, and for the next two hours while they worked, I was on my own.

I drank in every bit of the scene where her heart, for the last four decades, had lived and worked, and listened to every word that passed between them as they discussed this last piece she would design. Examining the art on the walls, the books and papers on the shelves, the postcards from friends tacked onto cork boards, I probed my way a little deeper into her life. I listened to their work-talk as I meandered, hearing how she wanted the shape and light to indicate movement, how the very up-and-down swoop of birds and waterfall and redwood tree would embody the cycles of water.

"Swirls," she insisted to him. "I want spirals in this, vortices, like at the bottom of a waterfall when it all splooshes and churns. But I want the light to do it—do you understand?" Benjamin nodded and offered a suggestion.

I longed to jump into the conversation, to be part of their creative process. I wanted to discuss how light and shape were interconvertible; about how we perceived color; about synesthesia. I still longed to study with her, even if it was only for the few weeks—the few *days* that might be left. She couldn't die yet!

Why was this happening? This was not fair! Oh God, *no fair!* I wanted time with her and there was so little of it! At least with Jim, we had a past with years of days for friendship—but now, with each so close to the end, I had to divide my time between them! I wanted all of myself for each of them, but even that was to be denied me. *No fair!*

Overcome with self-pity, I stumbled into her black and white sweater on the coat rack, caught its smell of her, and in an agony of anticipated loss, I leaned over and wept.

After awhile, I continued my slow circuit of the studio and uncovered a stash of framed windows stored beneath a workbench. I squatted down to leaf carefully through them.

"Pull them out," Benjamin called, noticing my awkward caution at the workbench. "You can handle them—they're not that fragile." He turned back to his work with Alice. With held breath I removed one window from the stack, and then another. They were part of a series on the theme of swans on rivers; peaceful windows in milky whites and blues, each highlighted by some splash of bright color, either in faraway mountains, or close-up flowers, or flying birds. Swans meandered along river bends, singly or in pairs. Stylized trees stood tall against azure skies; on some, green banks held jewel-like blossoms, red, yellow, violet.

Benjamin left Alice's side to hold one window up to the light for me, and the whole scene sprang into life—a swan swam in moving water beneath round-crowned trees while red flowers on the stream bank burst with light, exploding into my eyes. To my embarrassment, I started to cry again. Alice, at her desk on the other side of the room, laughed softly.

"It's yours, if you want it," she said. "Wrap it up for her, Ben. I think that one is hers."

How we reached home again after more than three hours at the studio, is something I may never understand. Benjamin helped us downstairs and into the car, but once we had turned the corner Alice collapsed like a deflated balloon and sagged against the door, ashen and spent. After one or two false starts, I found my way out of the warehouse complex and had her back home within a half hour, praying that nobody in the family had meanwhile discovered her absence. I realized that neither of us had thought to leave a note.

I parked illegally, as close as I could to her door, half-carrying her up the flight of concrete stairs and along the steep path to her apartment, not knowing at each step if this would be her last. Like survivors in a shipwreck we dragged each other against the tug of the surf onto the beach, in this case her small apartment, which mercifully was empty. I settled her into her chair where she fell immediately to snoring, and I flopped down beside her onto the floor, falling fast asleep with her.

During the next two weeks, the screws continued to tighten. Jim went into the hospital and came out again after a few days, with a portable oxygen pump; Alice's doctor put her into a neck brace for collapsing vertebrae. Her son and daughter had taken over the apartment, "cleaning up around her" as if she were already gone. Her greatest fear was that they would take over her studio and do the same. More than once I retrieved papers and magazines from the outside trash bin, refilling cupboards that had been emptied, against her wishes, of their stacks of art journals and old *National Geographics.*

She doggedly continued to work, rethinking her designs and phoning Benjamin at the studio several times a day to make corrections. I brought my camera with me, hoping to chronicle her during this intense period of creativity, concerned that, when this was all over, I might not believe that such indomitability of spirit was possible.

"Orange at the bottom of the waterfall," she enunciated into the telephone, outlining the swirling pattern in the air with her fingers. "No blues in the water at all. What? No. No greens either. Let it be all sun— falling and crashing sun." She nodded with intensity. "Do it!" she demanded, hanging up and staring, abstracted, into space.

She was a woman possessed, working against the clock. I scooped up the handful of pills the nurse had left for me to give her—I was now on the official caregiver schedule three afternoons a week—and brought them to her with a glass of water. She downed two of them before she took stock of what she was doing, and then pushed my hand away impatiently.

"Ach!" she complained. "I don't need drugs to make me sleepy. I'll sleep soon enough. Listen, I need you to protect me from them so I can finish this piece!" Discreetly, I put the pills down and handed her a high-protein drink.

"Why are you so sure anyone's out to keep you from doing that?" I asked mildly, holding the glass up to her lips. She took an awkward slurp and pushed that away too, glaring up at me as if I were a spy from the enemy camp.

"You don't know them," she muttered. "They hate everything about my art and they know they finally have the power to stop me. I can't let them. I've got to finish those windows despite them!"

I knelt down beside her and took both her hands in mine. "Alice, listen to me," I begged. "You're the one with the power to change this situation—you're the only one. And it's probably not even that difficult, if you're willing to give it a try. Would you, please?"

"Would I what? I don't know what you're talking about."

"Would you be willing to just consider—just for argument's sake—that maybe they're doing all of this not because they hate you, but because they love you?" I realized I was pleading with her, and gripping her fingers much too tightly.

"Never!" she expostulated even before the words were fully out of my mouth. But just at the edge of her eyes I saw some of her certainty crumble ever so slightly.

"Would you consider that just perhaps, maybe, you might be a bit mistaken on this?" She looked dubious, but was not so quick to argue. I rushed into the breach.

"Finishing the windows is essential, and I don't doubt that you and Ben will do it. And they will be gorgeous, I know it. But there's something else you've got to do while there's time…" There was the pleading note again. I steadied my voice with effort, and kept it as neutral as I could keep it.

"It has to do with your Christa and Greg. Alice, please—you've got to let them love you." My eyes filled with tears and hers did too. "Please Alice, just let them love you."

She turned her eyes, filled with her years of seeing, upon me. Her dry, thin lips turned up in an ironic smile and, poking a finger at my chest, she asked,

"Who did you say you were?"

Those were the last significant words Alice and I ever exchanged in this life. Two days later, when it was my turn to come and be with her, Jim was taken to the hospital for the last time and I had to cancel. Ben kept me informed and Marva called almost daily, but my focus, during Jim's final week, was on him. By the time I was ready to come back to Alice, her family had closed ranks around her and refused admittance to anybody, except for Benjamin, who was not a blood relative.

She died shortly after, leaving the night before Independence Day, as the fireworks shot bursts of color into the night. This most independent of women jumped right up into the sky!

Benjamin, who had been with her through the end, said she was calm, coherent and seemed to be at peace. The design of the windows was complete and he had all the instructions he needed for executing them. The last thing she said to him, he told me laughingly, was,

"Orange and yellow only. No blues in the water! Do you hear?"

Alice's memorial was held at a sunset service in a church overlooking the Bay, the late rays of the setting sun pouring through the prism of a rose window and four tall altar windows she had created a decade earlier. Her colors filled the sanctuary: rich golds and blues, royal reds and purples, and they bathed all of us in brilliant light.

A large crowd was there: colleagues and students, neighbors, friends, and family. I sat in the back with Benjamin and his pregnant wife while Greg played the guitar for his mother, and one by one, people from a life I had longed to know and take part in, told their stories about her. With each story I got a clearer picture of the Alice I never knew—the feisty, brilliant, determined artist always making art and fighting the good fight. Colleagues spoke of the range of her creative imagination; students spoke of her patience and care.

"She was one of the first women to break into an art form that had been male-dominated for centuries," said her agent, "but that never stopped Alice!" Everyone laughed and nodded knowingly. Marva, along with two other neighbors got up and spoke movingly about her sense of justice.

"To her it made no difference if you were Black or you were White. To her, people was people. And our Alice, she was people!" Again, everyone nodded, teary-eyed while her grandson, a tall young beauty of a man, swarthy with her dark eyes and hair, got up to speak. He must be the "one in every other generation!" Why had she never mentioned him to me?

"You never asked," I could faintly hear her saying.

"Grandma was more than a grandmother to me—she was like a fairy Godmother. All through my childhood she would send me postcards reminding me in a zillion ways that I had to look for the light in things. When I was a kid, I pretended I didn't understand, but she did it anyway. And now, Grandma," he said, choking up and gazing upward at her windows streaming with the sun's waning light, "I'll confess to you that I always knew just what you meant. I was just being stubborn 'cause it was a little embarrassing then. But not anymore, Grandma. I promise you I'll never, ever forget what you've shown me."

I cried into Ben's shoulder and held his hand hard. He put one arm around me and one around his wife, passing around his handkerchief. An organist played a contemplative piece and we all sat with our own remembrances of her, and then, as if as an afterthought, an elderly woman rose and, limping, made her way to the podium.

"I have one more story to tell," she said quietly. Gazing down at the front row where Alice's family sat, she addressed them and asked, "May I tell them?" I sat up quickly, wiped my eyes free of tears and listened hard.

"I'd like to tell you of a miracle," she began, adjusting the microphone to her height and smiling. "I've known Alice for forty-three years, and three days before she died she called me on the phone first thing in the morning. She was all excited. She told me she had spent the whole day with her children reminiscing about the past. She said, 'We laughed and we cried and we hugged. It was amazing!' As many of you may know, relations between them had been rather strained for a long time."

"To put it mildly," Greg piped up from the front row.

"Well, I was very pleased and I told her so and thought that was that, but then in the afternoon she called again! Now, any of you who knew Alice well, know how rare it was to get two calls a day from her—or even one!" There was a sprinkling of knowing laughter. "And again, she had to tell me about the morning they all had together, driving out to visit all their old haunts—the house over the hill, their old place in the city. She said they had such a good time, and that there was so much love between them all!"

My belly clamped with a shout I could not release. I wanted to raise my fist into the air and stomp on the ground. But I sat still as a stone and listened with all my ears to every word Alice's friend had to say.

"I thought to myself that a miracle had occurred. I certainly didn't expect there to be more, but there was! The next morning she called again to tell me that they had sat up a good part of the night, and had said to each other all the things they had been needing to say all these years, and she told me that she had begged for their forgiveness and that they had told her that they loved her. And she told them that she loved them! I just wanted to say that," she murmured, out of breath, before stepping down from the podium and being escorted, after long hugs with Greg and Christa, back to her seat in the congregation. There was a long, contemplative silence in the sanctuary, and then the organist began to play again.

The colors of Alice's rose window glinted and shimmered, the pattern alternately blurring and clearing through my tears, while the light shone luminous, rich and ecstatic in the early twilight.

SIX

Aging (is not for sissies)

BECAUSE I LOVE THIS
LIFE, I KNOW I WILL LOVE
DEATH AS WELL.

RABINDRANATH TAGORE

t struck me as ironic, during that time when both Jim and Alice were facing their deaths, that Jim, at 52, was so accepting and Alice, at 75, was fighting the idea tooth and nail. It was as if she still saw herself as a young woman who had decades of living ahead of her, and, indeed, had notes in her notebook for creative projects that represented many years' worth of work. Some days it made me impatient with her, and I wanted to tell her to cut it out and be reasonable; most of the time, however, I knew I would probably react exactly the same way when my time came.

While I was working on her story, I was spending the summer in rural Vermont in a house at the end of a long dirt road. I would write in solitude each morning, and then set out for a walk in the woods with lunch in my backpack. One day as I left the house, I caught my reflection in the glass panes of the door, and was shocked to see a middle-aged woman standing there. She was decked out in protective gear: wide-brimmed sunhat and dark glasses, baggy pants and stout walking shoes, her skin wrinkling about the eyes and lips, her black hair frizzing and running to gray. Me.

This took me by surprise as, despite all evidence to the contrary, I have tended to think of myself as still being the agile, dark-haired adventurer who braved the sun and sharp rocks of the Galápagos in little more than a blue workshirt and shorts, stripping down to bare skin for a swim in frigid waters with the sea lions. But the image of my well-covered self in that glass was indisputable—I was aging.

Until meeting Mary Scott and then Alice, I had virtually no elders in my life to look up to. While growing up in Brooklyn, the adults in my life were variously damaged by their experiences as Jewish refugees fleeing from pogroms in Russia. The men tended to be crude or taciturn; the women crippled or controlling. In my family they were a self-absorbed lot, more mean-spirited than not. Dignity, wisdom and loving kindness were not characteristic of the elders I knew and, as a result, I have been wary about growing old.

Until my fifties, I almost got away with it. My hair has remained dark, my body strong and my tastes eclectic. My friends tend to be adventurers like myself—of all ages—and my stamina has been generally reliable, if not even better than in the past.

But that is beginning to change. The years are taking their toll, and despite myself, my self-image is in chaos. I admit with a certain amount of dismay that while I believe I am reconciled to my eventual death, I still resist, like Alice, the idea that I am growing old.

I recognize myself, with a certain poignancy, in the words of the novelist Jean Rhys:

Age seldom arrives smoothly or quickly. It's more often a series of jerks. After the first, you slowly recover. You learn to live with the consequences. Then comes another and another. At last you realize that you'll never feel perfectly well again, never be able to move easily, or see or hear well.

When I went to the Galápagos at the age of thirty-five, I was pretty much in my prime. True, I had begun to find the occasional silver hair amongst the black and there were those wet mornings when my knees felt undeniably stiff, but after three months of rough outdoor living on the islands, I was gratified to discover that I was totally fit and supple, not a gray hair to be found on my head. I had drunk, unsuspectingly, at the fountain of youth.

It didn't last, of course, and time inexorably has had its way with me. In the twenty-five years since then, I must confess that I often find myself embarrassed not to be young, wishing I could hide all evidences that my body is being reduced by time. Even though I recognize that all my contemporaries—including those in the generation behind me—have, to a person, become middle-aged, I still would give a lot to be the exception. Even though nobody, however famous, beautiful or brilliant, has ever been able to do it, there is no reason for me not to be the first.

I was interested to read in Dr. Sherwin Nuland's *How We Die* that as we age, the vital force in our bodies peters out, and the walls of the arteries thicken and lose their elasticity, which restricts the flow of blood to the muscles and organs. And that nobody escapes this destiny.

Furthermore, he says, our brains lose two percent of their weight every ten years we live after sixty. Finally, he claims, the process of aging is an overwhelming strategy to achieve its ultimate objective of destruction.

This is sobering.

To what extent can we fiddle with the inevitable? Exercise and eating the right foods can perhaps prolong our allotted time somewhat, but in the end it seems that we have no choice but to get older and older and then dissolve.

So, given that this is the natural order of things, what is it that makes me, like so many others, uneasy about this spectre of aging? In his wonderful book on aging, *The View in Winter*, Ronald Blythe says, "To fall into purposelessness is to fall out of real consideration. Many old people reduce life to such trifling routines that they cause the rest of us to turn away in revulsion." Or as W.H. Auden puts it, "…via self-disgust, thinning blood and nipped vision, we find ourselves caring more and more about less and less."

My mother-in-law, a rather spectacular woman of eighty-six, who has survived the Holocaust and raised two sons to become prominent scientists, says periodically, "I'm just an *old lady!*" Her face assumes an expression of self-deprecation, projecting much of society's assumption of the purposelessness and shame of old age.

Despite myself, I know that deep down I also harbor the presumption that when I have passed my useful, vibrant prime, there is nothing more left. I don't think I'm alone in feeling this way. We worry about being left behind, feeling worthless, ashamed, mostly invisible. As we decline we fear being defined—and define ourselves—as boring, dependent and irrelevant. Certainly we are not lovable. Even Alice, who was still vital and creative at seventy-five, was convinced she was not lovable. The classic image of the elder mentoring with wisdom and kindness and self-confidence seems to be relatively rare. As Hans Christian Anderson in his old age advised his contemporaries sadly, "learn to be forgotten, and yet to live."

This is rather grim. It implies that we have few positive options as we age; that there are neither gains nor challenges nor qualities of experience worthy of the final phase of a lifetime. Even the ancient Hindu

practice of leaving home to end one's years in contemplation is cultural-
ly not available to most of us.

So it is not surprising that many people resist the inevitable, staving
off the signs of aging with agonizing diets, hair dyes and facelifts. (I still
remove my glasses in the company of young people because I think I
look like a granny with them on. And I *am* a granny!) As if, by being
older, I were somehow from a different species than the young ones, forever separate.

"These people do not love me!" The poignancy of Jean Jacques
Rousseau's *cri de coeur* of his old age rang with especial clarity for me the
other day as I rummaged through a box of old family photos. I found
two pictures of my grandmother, one taken when she was in her twen-
ties, the other many decades later. The young woman who gazed out at
me may also have been gazing out at my grandfather, for her expression
is seductive and teasing—full of life and promise. The old woman, barely lifting her face toward the camera, has long since been crippled with
multiple sclerosis, is heavy and dead-eyed, her useless body stuffed into
a wooden wheelchair in the Home for Incurables where she lived most
of her life. Looking from one picture to the other, I had difficulty recognizing that they were the same person.

The tragic circumstances of my grandmother's life—she contracted
MS before her thirtieth birthday and remained in a wheelchair until she
died thirty years later—may be seen as an extreme version of the disillu-
sion in many of our lives. For one reason or another we miss our opportunity to savor life when we are young, and then mourn our loss when
it is too late. The waste tastes sour in our mouths, and we worry that we
are unattractive and unlovable to those of the next generation who have
usurped our place in the center of the world.

My grandmother hardly had a chance. She was a female refugee from
Russia and her best hope was to find a husband and put down roots in a
new land. As her granddaughter, even though I have been blessed with
an infinitude of opportunities she could not have dreamed of, I recognize her basic dilemma, which may be the basic dilemma of all of us as
we age, and it has to do with expectations.

Older women, according to the popular culture, are expected to be
grandmotherly, nurturing and self-effacing, providing haven, good ad-

vice and chicken soup whenever it is needed. Older men are expected to be stalwart patriarchs, providers and protectors with wisdom gleaned from a lifetime of experience. Personally, I have met nobody who fits either simplistic standard, but I wonder how many of us feel like failures because we don't. We are inadequate, not good enough. Whatever causes this popular misconception, there seems to be an epidemic of self-hatred in our midst, and I suppose it is neither aging nor death that ultimately causes us so much grief as our appalling lack of self-acceptance.

My father deemed himself a failure, being of a rather poetic nature when men were supposed to be suave and tough, and suffered his first coronary before his fiftieth birthday. My mother, at eighty, finds herself so suspect that she trusts nobody else, especially those who have affection for her anyway, and her habit of self-betrayal gets passed on with her every encounter. Unfortunately, this is not unusual and, having drunk of this sense of unworthiness at our mothers' breasts, many of us carry it unconsciously with us, offering it to each new generation in turn like a curse.

Neither aging nor death are the enemy at all; self-hate is. For they are programmed into our cells, and while it may not be easy to stare directly at the stark realities, for me it is much harder not to. Unbearable, in fact. Ignoring it takes more energy than I can spare, and leaves me numb, unfeeling and afraid. Perhaps I am resisting the experience of "caring less and less about more and more." I prefer to stalk the beast, not knowing what I shall do when I find it but knowing that the alternative of avoidance has become unacceptable to me. This has proven to be a good thing because the adventure has brought me unexpected treasures, one after another.

Saint Catherine of Siena said, "All the way to Heaven is Heaven," which is to say that each step of life lived intensely—the pain as well as the pleasure, the youthful as well as the aging—is the gift. Heaven may be hidden from us at times, but right beneath the surface, there it is. I find a poignant paradox in that, as my body begins to wear down, growing stiff where it used to be soft, and flaccid where it used to be firm, something else begins to emerge. The underground stream which has been concealed by its covering of vigorous muscle and bone, the Self that is inhabiting this body, has started to daylight more and more. As the stream bubbles closer to the surface I recognize it as the part of myself connected to the universe, the ageless part that never runs out but keeps up its strong, steady coursing. Even this, the gazing at my own mortality, is a fascination.

I take another look at this lady reflected in the glass panes of the door and examine her a little more closely, a little less harshly the way, perhaps, somebody else might look at me. With devotion, say, or with fond memories. Those eyes, though ringed with dark lines on drying skin, have looked upon much in fifty-nine years of living and have responded with laughter, with tears, with love. That body, sagging here and there and everywhere has birthed three children, has worked hard and has been scarred by years of taking risks. She has lived well, this woman, and has little to be ashamed of. Every day she learns a little bit more about what it means to be human, and she never takes a break.

I am amazed by her persistence, and grateful. I turned on the radio yesterday and there was Beethoven's "Missa Solemnis," the glory of it bursting into my kitchen where I was making a melted cheese sandwich for lunch, and I began to sob, stomping across the kitchen in time with the music and waving my knife in the air like a conductor's baton. My heart was too big for my chest and I sang along at top voice, ecstatic. Had anybody come by, I would surely have been branded as a crazy lady, but I didn't care. After weeks, months of being vulnerable enough to examine my worst fears, I was ready to be cracked open, accessible to the stream and the joy that passeth all understanding. And there was Beethoven, right when I needed him.

As I move toward my sixties—a short time, really, in the scheme of things—I sense the accumulation of my experiences alchemically transmuting into something like human gold: gladness, acceptance, love. This may be what the Medieval alchemists were really after, this gold.

I am becoming a conjurer of joy, grateful for the privilege of having survived this long, (so many have not), and ready to regard the varieties of my hard-won experience as refiner's fire. All the dross—the regrets and the humiliations and the shame—may be neutralized in the intense heat of that fire, leaving behind the nuggets of wisdom—pure, precious, essential.

Here I am, a bit unsteady on my feet and somewhat more wrinkled than I was before this, but tested, tried. True.

Like Alice, I still hope to design my own ways of letting in the Light—as many as I can possibly create in the time allotted to me—and to keep opening my heart.

And to let them love me.

SEVEN

Duncan's Story

Jump into experience while you are alive!

What you call "salvation" belongs to the time before death.

KABIR

uncan.

He was a man who could fill a room with his presence. A colleague brought him to the studio one day, a woman who worked as a nurse-midwife at the County Hospital. Arisika and I had been exploring movement and sound to improve immune system function, and she thought we might be able to help him. This attractive, charismatic fellow in his late thirties had recently received a positive HIV diagnosis and his T-cell count was dropping rapidly.

When they appeared together at the door I was struck by the beauty of them together: Arisika dark and dramatic in a long batik dress and dangling earrings, and Duncan like a Scots Paul Bunyan, tall, fair and raw-boned. Honey-blond hair curled at the nape of his neck, and his large green-blue eyes scrutinized me frankly, as if testing for trust. Then they softened as he relaxed into a warm, generous smile. He fairly sizzled with intensity. It was hard to imagine that he was ill.

Generous, that was the word to describe him. Even his body was generous—large trunk and long limbs—as if he had a heart that needed a lot of space to beat in. But he also had a winningly vulnerable quality, the melancholy of a person who intimately knew pain. I got the impression of a gentle giant who was more beautiful in the eyes of others than to himself. I offered him my hand and felt an unexpected rush of warmth as he eagerly grasped it in both of his, feeling for who I was.

"I'm so glad to finally meet you," he said in a voice so resonant I felt it vibrate in my chest. I wanted to hear that voice speak again. Arisika had told me he was unusual, but I hadn't expected to be so charmed. She grinned broadly, enjoying the scene she had apparently predicted would take place. "Arisika has told me about the work you do here, and I feel privileged to be invited to join you," he said.

Oh, my. That voice!

"It's more than my pleasure," I replied sincerely, bringing them into the studio. He gazed up at the clerestory, and around at the white-washed cinder-block walls, breathing in deeply.

"It smells good here. I'm going to love this," he announced with quiet certainty, removing his shoes and shrugging out of his plaid woolen shirt. He made a neat pile of his things by the side of the room and placed his wristwatch carefully on top. I took his willingness to take off the ticking watch as a propitious sign.

As we dressed for dancing, I explained that the work was improvisatory and that it began with a half-hour, full-body warm-up, after which we would move right into an impromptu ensemble *sounding*.

"By the end of the warm-up, the song simply comes on its own," I said. "I won't even try to describe the experience, but we find it magical. You'll see." He looked willing to be mystified, his legs twitching to move.

"Arisika tells me you've sung professionally," I remarked, doing some deep knee-bends before the warm-up. "Opera?"

"Some," he responded briefly. "A little bit of everything."

"I feel a bit presumptuous to be teaching this stuff to a trained singer," I confessed, feeling a bit shy. He laughed a deep baritone bark of a laugh.

"Don't worry," he reassured me. "I'm in your hands." His voice, as before, was resonant as a finely tuned harp-string; I could hardly wait to hear him sing.

After a few moments of reticence he relaxed into the warm-up, vigorously shaking his arms and legs and twisting his torso, and by the end of the tape of African drums, all three of us were breathing freely and moving with ease. Then, in the calm that always follows satisfying movement, we met in the center of the room and felt for the beat that continued to hover in the air around us. Swaying, we waited for the first sound to emerge and Arisika provided it with a two-note chant, like a babe calling for its mother. I came in, syncopating a three-note riff against her two notes and then Duncan joined with a long, low tone, grounding us with his rich baritone before varying it with rhythm.

We were off! The song picked up interest as we felt for each others' pitches, staying at first in a narrow range of notes before one of us tested the waters with an unexpected dissonance. We carried the phrase from key to key, flipping it on its head, rolling it inside out and shaping it into new forms as we sang. Duncan's voice still had a listening quality, as if he were testing his footing in new territory, but after one humorous phrase he responded with a burst of laughter and then let his voice rip!

It was huge! The whole room shook with his sound. Following his lead we let go and poured into the song. Whole operas emerged from the three of us, oratorios! Duncan broke into a melody which roared up the scale, and I followed hot on his heels. At the top we both turned, a beat away from each other, and chromatically raced back down the scale. He charged ahead, and I broke away with a new riff, which he grabbed on the upbeat and twirled into glory. Arisika and I teased his rhythm, adding new dynamics to the beat he was pacing, and together we drummed it until we were like a single organism with three voices.

We flipped about the scale like dolphins leaping in the sea. Each foray was a challenge to be matched. Inspired by his brilliance, I heard my voice enter a place it had never been before, and there we met. Encouraged to be matched, Duncan took even greater risks until we were the song itself, nothing but instruments for the music. The song went from sublimity to noise and back again and we used everything—tongues and teeth and lips, smacking and sighing and clicking—to create harmonies and rhythms I had never heard before.

We were ecstatic, all three of us. The song went on for almost an hour, and ended only when we were too exhausted to sing another note. It ended gradually, the variegated sounds giving way to deep, rich humming which melted into barely voiced whispers. But the air now contained our sound; our harmony now was part of the studio, bonding the three of us inextricably.

For a long while we stood in the silence, still hearing the music we had made, still caught in the rapture of filled stillness. Gradually, we joined hands—warm, alive hands—and moved closer together, our breaths mingling and our hearts open. And then Duncan drew in a great breath, gulped noisily and broke, sobbing, into our arms.

That was the beginning of a weekly collaboration that lasted several years and which focused on the question of how to use the arts to raise immune system function. Sometimes we invited Jessica, an actress friend of Duncan's, to add a fourth. By combining our skills, we explored how the arts might enhance health, and in the process we formed deep, intimate friendships based upon mutual exposure and trust. It was a time of exciting experimentation and we became each others' teachers as well as students, trying to understand the true nature of healing.

Duncan's T-cell count gradually rose to normal during the first few months we worked together, and it remained stable for a few years. I dared not conclude that we had found a way into the immune-deficiency dilemma, but each week that Duncan continued to feel fit I crossed my fingers and said a silent prayer.

Meanwhile, we continued to try out every technique we could think of to induce states of relaxation and focus which, we found, led to a profound sense of well-being. We practiced expanding the peripheral vision, and we taught ourselves how to concentrate on two body parts simultaneously. We tricked our senses to see sounds and hear color, and we wrote down our dreams and acted them out for each other. Mostly, we told each other about our lives, our childhoods, our fears, our relationships. From all this exploration emerged a technique in which we performed improvised pieces for each other based upon stream of consciousness images as we danced. We called it "talk-story," and the experience was not unlike dreaming aloud, in front of witnesses. Over time it evolved into a new genre of improvisational theater in which Arisika, Duncan and Jessica were all brilliant.

Duncan's abilities as a performer were stunning, and it seemed there was no limit to his creative imagination. In a single session he could convincingly go from child to derelict to the last overripe cherry in a bowl. As the months went by, he began to explore his personal stories: the mama's boy; the youth with unacceptable yearnings; the self-rejected adult alcoholic. With astonishing persistence he probed for the truth of his life, working his way closer and closer to the bone, sometimes clenched tight in pain, sometimes shrieking in rage, often just comic.

For several sessions he delved into childhood memories of Mother, making the personal a metaphor for the universal, and then he moved on to Father. He would emerge from these pieces wide-eyed, as if barely knowing his way back from that territory. Sometimes he would collapse onto the floor between Arisika and me and curl up, shaking, and we would hold him tight. When his fury came bursting out—which with the volume of his voice was no small thing—we would worry about the neighbors, and when he at last took on his fears of dying, we could offer only our breaking hearts, our solemn witness and our love.

But then he would report back from his periodic check-ups at the hospital, and his T-cell counts would continue to be normal.

One crisp fall day—I remember that the fig tree outside the studio was dropping its leaves—he stepped out onto the floor to perform for us, his eyes closed in concentration and his expression intense. In the failing light of late afternoon the room held an air of enchantment, as if he had moved through a veil and been shape-shifted. I found myself blinking, not sure what I was seeing—his hair framed his face like a haze, his features wavered—or where he had gone that I could not follow. In that moment I knew I would one day lose him. My tears, which ran so freely these days anyway, were spilling even before he began to dance.

And hum. I could feel the vibrations of his voice from the other side of the studio, and my chest ached with the sensation. He circled the room slowly like a raptor in search of prey and then, beating his fists drumlike against his chest, he began to sing.

My father gave me a broken drum
I tried to dance, but my feet would stum-ble
It was his best gift, he too was numb,
For years I've been...my father's son.

As we watched, he enacted a lifetime of self-loathing, gazing at it with frank curiosity and the beginnings of detachment. Verse by verse he improvised a song that rhymed and scanned, like a bard, and the tale he told was about the King's youngest son who is left in the care of a de-vouring, dissatisfied Queen. As a composition it was seamless, and I had to keep reminding myself that he was making it up on the spot, because each line led perfectly and effortlessly to the next.

Deep in the dungeon I hear them scream
"There is no dungeon" replies the Queen
You're just high-strung and prone to dreams
You must resist vain imaginings.

Oh father please give to me the key
Please do not hide what I must see
Do not will me this legacy
Of dark despair and secrecy.

Playing all the parts, he was now the mesmerizing Queen, now the proud and silent King, now the desperate Prince, now the crazy Fool.

"Fool, am I crazy, or is there a dungeon in this castle?" the Prince cries out.

Then twisting onto the floor as the Fool, he cackles alarmingly and screeches,

Has the ruddy rose a thorn?
The unicorn a horn?
When we stand stock still at noon
Is there a shadow on the moon?

Arisika and I, seated side by side on a mat against the wall, held hands hard. The Fool cries out,

When the cage is broken
The bird can always fly.
Truth too long unspoken
Makes way for faithless lies.

He began throwing himself around the room, bashing against walls and groveling on the floor. Breathing heavily, the Fool rises to Duncan's full height and sings in furious pronouncement,

To come up one must go under.
To awaken, one must dream.

To ascend the throne of manhood
One descends the well of screams!

This was *tour de force* theater, immediate, true and universal. He took
the Prince on a journey of discovery, through madness and addiction,
through loss and the beginnings of healing. Then, returning to where he
began, he sang again sadly and in a higher key,

My father gave me a broken drum
I tried to dance, but my feet would stum-ble
It was his best gift, he too was numb
For years I've been, my father's son.

He blinked his eyes open and stared at us, speechless. He had been
somewhere, and was back, the piece having coursed through him, using
him to communicate itself to him. He stood in the center of the room
silent for a long time and then slowly walked to where we sat on the
mats, lowering himself into the space between us. We each took a hand
and sat quietly with him. For a long time, nobody spoke.

"I want to go home and talk to my father," he declared finally in a
low voice. Arisika and I nodded agreement. "And then I want to perform that piece."

Taking a week off from his work as a landscape gardener, Duncan left
for his parents' home in Oregon and had that talk with his father. They
had sat together on the porch one morning as his mother still lay asleep,
and they spoke about the past. Duncan confessed that he had no idea
who his father was—as a man, the boy he had been—and how he felt
about his son's homosexuality.

"Remember Jack?" his father had asked quietly, reminding him of the
man who had been a long-time friend of the family, and "uncle" to the
children.

"He was, too?" Duncan had cried, "Dad!" His father had nodded, a
small smile on his face.

"He was a good, good man," was all his father would say, but it was
enough, and for the next several hours they exchanged their stories,

acknowledging past fears and silences, asking for forgiveness, mending, mending. Duncan sang for his father the song of the broken drum, right there in the old neighborhood on the front porch, and for the first time in their lives they embraced and cried together.

I cried too when he told me, and he cried again, both of us knowing, but neither of us saying that this was one more task completed before the end—this despite the fact that, at forty-four, he was observably at the peak of his powers and his T-cell count was maintaining in the range of normal.

Without further ado, he and Arisika began planning their show.

In the late days of fall, the three of us took advantage of a four-day weekend and went to the country for a vacation-cum-intensive together. Our plan was to leave behind all the responsibilities of work and home for a few days, and to immerse ourselves without distraction in the four elements—Earth, Air, Water and Fire—experiencing in a natural setting each of their intrinsic healing qualities.

We went to the redwood forest where Jim and I had been a few months earlier, rented a three-room cabin with fireplace and kitchen and settled in. For the first day and night we did little more than rest, moving from the cushions around the fireplace, to bed, and then back again to the warming fire.

On the second day we awoke to the season's first gentle rain, and so we began our *Water* day, wrapping up in ponchos and going down to the river. We settled wetly on a sloping bank beneath the branches of a protecting buckeye tree and watched the rain come down and dimple the flowing river, musing. The raindrops pelted onto fall-dry leaves, hissing as it fell into the parched California soil and sending up fragrances of earth and musk. We sat very still, smelling and listening.

"I can't resist it," sighed Arisika after awhile. She pulled off her boots and, holding up her skirts, waded into the slow-flowing river, squealing at the shock of the cold. Duncan and I watched her as the current swirled around her calves, but we remained huddled beneath the overhanging branch, talking. He asked about Jim and Alice. I answered non-committally, reluctant to pour out my grief and frustration to him, although he, of all the people I knew, was the one who could most help me. But he was probably the next to go, so I felt that his shoulder was not available to me. What I longed to do was curl up in his ample lap and let all the anguish out, keening as Gypsies do, while he held me and smoothed my hair. Instead, I swallowed a surge of self-pity and tugged angrily at my boots, pulling them off and shoving them under the wings of his poncho. Running to the river, I splashed into the icy water, yelping with the cold and scooping up a handful of river water which I dribbled onto Arisika's head like a baptism.

The next morning dawned rainwashed and clear so we made it our *Earth* day, hiking to the grove of old-growth redwoods where Jim and I had seen the heron fly. The forest floor released its fragrance with every step we took, the air sharp and clear, and the autumn woods of brown and green and mulchy orange-yellow intensified by yesterday's rainfall. Fresh fungi were already pushing their way through needles and fallen branches making telltale mounds, and Duncan knelt to clear their upward path into the air. We knelt with him, carefully brushing needles away from the emerging mushrooms, and I scribbled down a few notes on their gills and stems and locations to pass on to Jim for his paper on these woods. The tenderness of Duncan's big hands, and the seriousness with which he greeted each wet little cap reminded me, with a pang, that I would soon be losing Jim, but I caught myself and shifted quickly to the present in which both men were still alive. Duncan was right here in the flesh and I was with him, sniffing the wet earth, hearing the rustling silence, uncovering brand new mushrooms to the air. He must have sensed my confusion for he looked over his shoulder and gave me a smile.

Continuing our stroll through the woods, we found a giant fallen redwood blocking the path. It must have been a recent fall, for the upturned, splayed roots were still matted with earth and stones. The hole made by the uprooting was a deep pit half-filled with yesterday's rain and the tree was so enormous that from where we stood at the roots, the other end was barely visible. Even on its side the trunk loomed in front of us like a high wall. We clambered through layers of peeling bark and tangled debris just to get to it, and then hoisted ourselves on.

Duncan scrambled up first, stomping on the downed tree as if it were a giant drum. Arisika and I followed him up, catching our breaths before adding our feet to his rhythm. The huge log shivered in response to us as we danced out the beginnings of a new song. Our feet made the beat and our laughter was the music until Arisika sang out a clear phrase, which was our invitation to enter the song. Duncan repeated her phrase adding owl-like hoots, his face raised to the treetops that stretched dizzyingly above. I followed his bird theme with warbles off the beat and we all chased each other like hawks in flight, teasing, perching unexpectedly on a single riff before plummeting toward the ground and landing softly on a hushed tone. The massive trees surrounding us caught our sounds and echoed them back, creating more music for us to respond to. Alone in the dense forest, our sounds could swell into the open air unrestricted. For Duncan it was second nature, but Arisika and I were neophytes in so much letting go, and at first our voices came out strained. He opened up with an enormous volume of sound and I tried to keep up, feeling the release first in my feet, then in my back and at last in my throat until I heard a voice emerge from me that I had not known was there. Arisika's voice, thin at first, also opened up to a new sound, which came through throaty and rich.

Duncan slapped his thighs in counterpoint, while our feet pounded a regular rhythm on the trunk. We sang with waves of longing; all my tears were in that song and I felt them pour out in a flood and circle back cleansed, as if they were filtered through my friends' voices. Soprano notes coming from a range higher than I had ever sung before went into the wind, leaving clear interior space where a dense wall had been. With each renewed breath I breathed in relief and gratitude, drinking in the music as the three of us created it. We sang and sang until our insides were softened to quivering, and then we let the song drop by degrees until it was sibilant whispers, and finally an almost imperceptible hum. Then, in voices lower than breaths, it was over.

The sun sent shafts of warmth through the canopy above, and after a long, quiet sit together we clambered off the log, dug out sandwiches from the day pack, and each went into a different patch of woods for an hour or so of solitude.

Like lovers in lust, we could not seem to get enough of singing in the forest. When we meandered back from our separate naps Duncan, with a mischievous smile on his face, began to slap the redwood log in a seductive rhythm that could not be ignored. He then climbed onto the fallen tree and kept the beat with his feet. He continued to play the tree until Arisika and I hoisted ourselves on, and then he sashayed up the trunk toward the first branches and sank into a cross-legged sit. Doing my own two-step along the trunk, I went to the other end and sat facing him, my back against the roots. Arisika remained between us, sitting where she could watch both of us for cues.

We could hear each other only if we drummed in relays, like tribespeople sending messages across the distances. It was a conversation in rhythm—call and response; question and then answer. Then we had rhythmic disputes, teasing and one-upmanship leading to wild, raucous laughter which bounced off the surrounding trees. My hands stung with all that pounding and slapping and I was breathless with laughing. And in the midst of all this, Duncan began to sing.

I could only hear him when I stopped drumming, so I rested my hands and listened. Like a mountain yodel, he threw out a pure, simple phrase which Arisika then repeated, adding a small variation. I repeated the whole melody and added a few more notes, singing as loud as I could. Duncan replied with a low rumbling phrase, and when Arisika came in her voice got stuck in her throat, so she shook her head and opted for her role as beat-keeper, thumping on the log and holding a simple, steady chant.

Duncan sang loud, then soft. I realized I could hear him either way, so I relaxed and let my voice come through without strain. The higher my notes, the more easily they carried across the distance so I opened my mouth and let them ring. He gave me increasingly more complicated riffs to respond to, and we tossed the song back and forth like a ball, hearing ourselves as separate voices and as a duet, unique individuals and bonded friends.

I was completely happy. I let myself go into the song without holding back, knowing that I was doing exactly, precisely what I wanted most to do in the world. Every second was perfection: the lowering sun through ancient trees; the growing chill in the clear and fragrant air; the solidity of the trunk and earth beneath me—and the ephemerality of our lives, this friendship, this moment that was passing.

Our song ended on a hum, resonant in the forest quiet. We sat for a long time relishing the stillness, and then we stretched our stiffening legs and got up, starting the walk slowly back toward the center of the log where Arisika waited for us, our gazes holding each other softly, our faces composed and our hearts wide open. Meeting in the center we spread our arms and gathered each other in with a great whoop, roaring with laughter and breathing in each others' smells, making a warm, tight circle of three.

Rehearsals for the show had begun in earnest. It was to be an evening of personal pieces which spoke to the universal issue of relationships: child to parent; man to woman; human to God. A few friends were invited to participate; a date was set four months away, and they went to work.

I watched their work in progress from time to time to give feedback, but other than that I was not involved in the show. Jim and Alice were now in serious decline and had become the focal points of my life, and since rehearsals were swallowing most of Duncan's and Arisika's free time, our weekly sessions in the studio began to peter out. And when, shortly thereafter, Duncan fell in love with a man who lived an hour's drive away, we knew the time for disbanding had come.

He and Alex met at a resort on the Russian River and had spent a weekend together there. Alex had only recently lost his partner of seventeen years to AIDS, and was still in the first flush of grief. Duncan had held him and listened to his story, expecting nothing more than friendship, but the alchemy was there and not to be denied. Alex, according to Duncan, was not ready for an involvement with anyone yet—least of all someone who was HIV positive, but, as Alex was to tell me much later,

"I would have had to be crazy to turn down someone like Duncan. I wanted to be friends with him in any case, and losing him would be just as hard, so why not be lovers? I mean…look at him!"

And indeed, as Duncan's interest in Alex became an all-consuming passion he became radiant, his green-blue eyes glowing like beacons and his great bark of a laugh ringing out with every excuse for laughter. He was gorgeous, irresistible! In the way of all lovers, he wanted to talk about his beloved and would invite himself over for tea between jobs just to tell me about Alex's latest love token, or bring me another picture of the two of them taken last week at the beach. He was downright giddy, awed that someone as fine as Alex loved him.

Always amazed that someone of his caliber doubted his own worth, I would tell him for the fiftieth time that it didn't surprise me at all, that to me he was totally magnificent, and for the fiftieth time he would listen intently to every word I said and then ask, "You really think so?"

"Yes, Duncan," I would reply, "I really think so."

On the first night of the performance, the hall was abuzz. The audience, mostly friends of the performers, was composed of Arisika's multi-ethnic colleagues from the hospital and Duncan's upscale clients, shoulder to shoulder with his friends from Alcoholics Anonymous. The gay community, male and female, was well represented and a few couples were there with babies in tow.

The curtains opened to reveal Arisika spotlighted on an unlit stage, her dark-skinned arms and shoulders bare above a long, white sarong. In the background Duncan hummed "Sometimes I Feel Like a Motherless Child," and Arisika lifted her arms and began to sway. Her own mother had recently died tragically, and she danced the anguish, sparing us and herself nothing.

...*Sometimes I feel...like I'm almost gone...*Duncan sobbed out the words, his voice and her movements in perfect synch. She turned and lifted, drooped and fell.

...*A long...way...from ho-me....A long...way...from...home.*

Slowly, she left the stage to applause that was tentative at first, and then thunderous. Her face was wet with tears as she took her bows, and when Duncan joined her onstage, they held hands hard.

Breaks had been scheduled between each piece because of the raw emotionality of the material—"breathers for the audience," Duncan had called them—and everyone sat, subdued, until the stagelights came up again for the next piece, which was "My Father's Drum."

Dressed in black, Duncan paced the stage as he done in the studio, and pounding his chest with both fists sang his opening quatrain:

My father gave me a broken drum
I tried to dance but my feet would stum-ble
It was his best gift, he too was numb
For years I've been my father's son.

Until he reached the scene of the Prince's madness, the piece unrolled just as it had in the studio, but the plot now continued. This time, the King recognized his son as the mad bard in the marketplace, and knew him as his own.

At this point Duncan shifted into narrative, and speaking frankly as himself, told the story of his pilgrimage back to the family home and his front-porch talk with his father. Lowering himself onto the stage, he enacted the whole conversation first as himself, then as his father.

"Mother is still sleeping, son. Shall we go out onto the front porch where we won't disturb her, and have a talk?" He played each of their awkwardness, surprise, relief; he *was* the father, *was* the son.

In the row ahead of me two men stretched their arms across the backs of the seats, making contact. When they turned to look at each other, I saw glistening eyes.

As father, Duncan told the story of the gay family friend, and as son he asked about the years of deafening silence. He shifted his position from one pillar of the porch to the other, showing us both father and son at the same time, and when they had their embrace he sang,

My father gave me a gift so rare
A gift that very few men would dare
To give their daughters, much less their sons
The gift that mended my broken drum.

He held his wounds out for me to see
There in the dungeon I found the key
He turned the mirror so I could see
My father's father looked back at me!

"You're a wonderful audience!" he exclaimed when the applause died down. Everyone laughed with approval and I felt the cohesion that occurs when a gathering of separate individuals becomes a group. "Oh my, aren't we having fun!" he beamed. Adoring, everyone laughed again. "We'll take a ten-minute intermission, and then be back."

He held his pose for just a moment and then with perfect timing turned and was gone, leaving us wanting more.

"I'll be providing some comic relief," Duncan had warned us mysteriously backstage just before the performance, refusing to divulge his secret to anybody but Alex, whose lips were sealed. When the curtain went up after the intermission I wondered if this would be it, but in the dim light a single, dark figure sat hunched on a low stool. Behind her, Arisika hovered like a moth.

Gloria, an actress friend of Arisika's, was portraying Crack Annie, an addict who offered her only daughter to the local pimp in exchange for drugs. I was astonished by her transformation; this minister's daughter, by the magic of theater and great talent, was a street person, broken and helpless in addiction. Ntozake Shange's monologue came through as real, her dilemma worse than horrifying. I could feel the audience freeze. Even though I had seen this piece in rehearsal, I gripped the arms of my seat and held my breath. The daughter's agony of betrayal during the assault came piercingly from her lips, and then from the same lips, the mother's hoarse contrition, and all the while Arisika swayed in the background, her face soft, her body moving gently.

At the end of the monologue the silence in the hall was like an indrawn breath until, from backstage as from far off came Duncan's voice singing "Amazing Grace."

...I once was lost, but now am found
Was blind, but now I see.

And with Gloria hunched over in a position of existential despair, Arisika moved to stage front and danced.

Her burnished skin gleamed like ebony against the white of her sarong and every motion of her trunk and arms and face expressed compassion, forgiveness, identification. We all sighed as she extended her body to cover Gloria's shame and self-hate, her arms offering comfort and haven. She exposed her legs, her thighs, her back, unwinding the white cloths. She wrapped them and herself around Gloria, embracing without blame. She showed us herself unmasked and unashamed as Duncan all but whispered the final lines of the song:

...I once was lost, but now am found. Was blind, but now I see.

There was an uneasy quiet before the applause came, but then it came in a roar. People were crying and when Gloria came out, still in character, the audience applauded wildly. Then she pulled off her wool cap, shook out her halo of hair and smiled broadly, herself again. My own sense of relief surprised me and I rose to my feet, cheering with the others. She gestured for Arisika, who joined her on stage and together they took their bows. They gestured for Duncan who joined them but stepped to the side, leaving the accolades for them. When the curtains closed, we all needed a break.

In the studio over the years, we had tackled the inevitable gender issues which, amongst other things, evolved into a duet for Arisika and Duncan. They struggled long and hard over how to portray themselves, since theirs was not a stereotypical male-female duality, and they eventually created a piece that dealt with the opposite gender as power-figure. It was a work about anger, about victimization and reconciliation.

Now, the lights went down and they appeared in robes from opposite wings of the stage, each carrying an archetypal mask. Side by side they came toward us, placing their masks at an altar in center stage. Arisika began with an incantation:

...A foe with sandals entered my court
He put his hands upon me
With fear he oppressed me
In my halls he terrified me....
O, Queen of the dark chamber
The Lord of my lands caused this shame!...

Bending over, she covered her face with her mask, transforming herself from helpless victim to sharp-toothed defender. His eyes upon her, Duncan began quietly:

...She was always hungry
She was like a caged panther
She wanted Flesh!
She was eating me alive, sucking my warmth,
draining my power
Devouring
I stumbled out
In shame...

He bent for his mask—a great, horned thing—and raised it to his face, removing his burgundy robe to reveal a body naked except for a loincloth. Arisika let her robe drop to the floor also, and putting clawed gloves over her fingers, they squared off.

Their fight was extraordinary! Snarling and screeching, they tore at each other. Stalking and springing, they kicked and they growled. He roared mightily and she let loose, a woman in fury. In rehearsal they had marked out their moves, but with the witness of an audience they let the passion fly! I worried that one of them might get hurt in the melee, but they pulled it off marvelously and gradually let it simmer down with great skill. Turning their backs to us they removed their masks, slipped back into their robes and met at the back of the stage to come toward us again, calmly and slowly. Holding their robes like grain baskets, they sowed imaginary seed.

Two old people work side by side
She moves and he kneels
He digs and she nods
While he speaks to the seed
She ardently covers row by row
Sunflowers will bloom toward late summer.

They had done it! The evening was spectacular and they took their well-earned bows to cheers and whistles. It was a love fest, and the audience stamped for more, not letting them leave the stage. Finally, the lights went down again and everyone grew quiet, settling in for we-knew-not-what. I glanced back at Alex, but he was bent over the sound system, ready to go.

The stage was dark when the curtains opened and then the spotlight found Duncan prancing about in a bright yellow jumpsuit with a long, orange boa trailing over his arms. He held it to him like a mink wrap. The audience began to laugh even before the song began. The pianist played the jaunty melody of the opening bars, and, flinging the boa out with sultry abandon, Duncan sang:

I am the Golden Gate
I hold my head up high
And watch as all your fascinating lives rush by
I'd like to fly away the way the sea gulls do
But I guess I'm too important to!

He was in full form, impersonating a bridge—in drag, for God's sake! We roared with laughter. He was all over the stage and hamming it up like mad, feeding off the delight on the other side of the footlights. We lapped it up, giggling in all the right places, adoring this wild guy pretending to be the Golden Gate Bridge, of all things!

I've got to hold up my end of the world
I am just a working girl with a full-time job
I've got responsibilities...
I know you need me
What other girl could fill these shoes?
But don't you see e-ven celebrities can get the blues?

How he managed to stay in character without giving in to irresistible laughter, I don't know. He was hilarious as he worked the audience like a stripper, slowing down seductively into the next section:

I've half a mind to slide these cables down
And slip into a tasteful, strapless gown

And go to town to see what I've been missing...

In the audience the women squealed and some of the men sank a little lower in their seats. He knew his effect and played it up outrageously, flinging the boa, tilting his chin, thrusting his hips. By the time he sang the final verses, we were his. He two-stepped toward us, arms outstretched and opening up his voice he gave us everything he had:

I know you need me
But I need time to be myself
And I'm a whole lot more
than just a glorified asphalt-ed shelf
There comes a time in every life
When one must break away
I've got to dance my own dance and my own song.
I AM THE GOLDEN GATE!

He had every last one of us in the palm of his hand, in love with him and in love with each other. We had all, in the space of a single evening, been turned into lovers. Applauding wildly with everyone else, I understood that his real genius was to teach the rest of us how to love, by getting us to fall in love with him!

For most of the next year Duncan and Alex were a commuter couple, living and working in their own cities during the week and spending every weekend together—mostly at Alex's in Petaluma. Just after Valentine's Day they decided it was time to take the plunge and set up house together, which meant that Duncan would leave the area and move north. It was not an easy decision for him to make since he would be leaving most of his friends and clients behind, but after much deliberation he made it. He had, during the year, started to make professional contacts and find his place in Alex's community, including forming a trio that sang AIDS benefit concerts. So he pulled up his roots, made his farewells and left us.

It was hard saying good-bye to him, knowing that as he began a new life with Alex our intimate contact would inevitably be broken, but it was time for him to move on, and I had to let him go. It even crossed my mind that this might be a blessing in disguise for me, as it would make it easier for me to let go later on, but I never admitted that to anyone. We kept in touch by phone from time to time, and when, about a year later, the two of them pooled their savings and bought a house together—Laughing Crow Bungalow, they called it—I made the trip to Petaluma for their housewarming.

What they announced as a *housewarming* turned out also to be their *wedding;* a commitment ceremony in the garden surrounded by close friends and colleagues. Alex greeted me, glowing, at the door, a broad grin filling his whole face and his hank of blond hair cascading down his back in a luxurious pony tail. He was solid and strong and when I hugged him he smelled of the clean outdoors.

"You look terrific!" I exclaimed, holding him at arms' length to take in his snazzy white outfit. He laughed and commented,

"You should see my boyfriend!" Right behind him Duncan showed off an embroidered vest over his crisp, white shirt, and then grabbed me up in a warm hug until the next guests came up the front walk.

It was a grand mid-summer party, the back garden in brilliant bloom, the hosts euphoric, the guests in great spirits and the food delicious. Marigolds and zinnias and cosmos and sunflowers grew in colorful profusion, the sunflowers, like tall elders of the gathering, at their peak of perfection.

"We didn't plant a thing this year," Alex and Duncan kept saying to anyone who commented on the beauty of the garden. "We just hauled the soil over from the old house and dumped it here. Everything volunteered itself to us as gifts!" A cottonwood was dense with leaves and the fig tree was just putting out its fruit. Feverfew and borage and tomatoes and artichokes—yellow and purple and red and green—were in full flower and bushed out from everywhere, fertile and abundant.

In the middle of the afternoon, after everyone had eaten and visited and renewed old ties, we stood in an informal circle around the two men and witnessed them pledging their troth. Face to face, they grasped wrists and gazed for a long time into each others' eyes. Clearing his throat, Alex spoke of their connection, of the gift that Duncan was in his life after the devastating death of his longtime partner, Steven, and of his deep and committed love for Duncan.

We were all in tears by the time he finished, and looked to Duncan for his response. For quite a while he kept a steady gaze on Alex, an enigmatic smile on his lips, and then he began softly to sing—apparently taking Alex by surprise.

I'll be loving you—always
With a love that's true—always
When the things you've planned
Need a helping hand
I will understand
Always, always....

Alex broke right down and sobbed in Duncan's arms, choking on the word "always" and breaking down again. They clung to each other and swayed back and forth, finally cracking up with laughter as they told each other secret jokes not for our ears. Then they stood apart again and Duncan, in a quavering voice, spoke directly to Alex.

"I want you to know that I welcome Steven into our household as part of our family." Alex nodded tearfully, wiping his eyes with the back of his hand. Even with the gaiety of the occasion, AIDS was with us in the circle, holding hands with us, making garlands with the flowers and eating at our table.

"Thank you," he responded quietly. Then they again looked long and intently at each other and after taking a deep, determined breath they broke into broad smiles as Alex turned around to us in the circle and cried, "Let's party!"

For the rest of the day we celebrated them with skits and jokes and songs and gifts. We blessed their new house with wands of sage and rosemary, smudging the kitchen and the bedroom and the living-room piano and the garden. And at the end of the day we said our good-byes and went away, leaving them to their life together.

Early the following spring Duncan called to let me know that he had AIDS.

"PCP," he said, slightly out of breath. I recognized the sound of pneumocystis immediately. Too soon! We had all hoped for at least another five years of good health for him. Had the move been too much? Would his T-cell count have remained stable if he and I had not stopped our work together? Tens of questions that I couldn't ask rushed into my mind. "It's under control with drugs right now," he continued, "and the doctor says he expects me to recover from it completely, but it may take awhile." I heard the familiar wheeze, the struggle to get enough air. My heart broke, especially for Alex.

"Duncan..." was all I could murmur.

"Could I ask you this favor—that you let Arisika and Jessica know? I don't think I can handle calling them right now."

"Of course," I breathed, my heart sinking. My senses seemed to shut down like an overheated motor, and for a few moments my mind was a desert of featureless sand. "Are you still working?" I asked limply.

"Modified—for the time being," he responded shortly, with a small dry cough. "I'd love to see you," he said.

"I'll come," was my reply, not yet knowing that within the hour Jessica would call asking me to tell Duncan of her diagnosis of breast cancer.

He was craggier and a shade more pale than he had been a few months earlier, but otherwise he was still very much himself. Our greeting was joyous, and with the afternoon ahead of us we went for one of our favorite "spring crawls" from the old days, meandering in and out of neighborhoods looking at people's gardens. He was one of the few people I knew who enjoyed this simple pleasure as much as I did. Setting out in the direction of the river, our plan was to wander about until we ended up at a little outdoor café that overlooked the water and had, of all things, a train track running through it.

"If our timing is good," he told me, "we'll have the three-o'clock freight to accompany our lunch."

The first garden on our walk showered us with plum blossoms fading from their first bloom, and masses of fragrant daffodils. We knelt in the soggy grass and sniffed their new, high-spring yellow. A few houses down had lilacs in blossom and we ran to breathe in the purple sweetness, along with the memory of every spring we had ever known in our lives. After the lilacs, we continued down the street and around the corner to where we found a border of freesias—pink, white, yellow. Duncan sat down on the sidewalk to meet them at their level, sniffing, and then got up to follow me to some jonquils and early irises.

Like this we made a tour of his neighborhood, appreciating all the flowers and catching up with each others' news. We acted as if nothing was wrong. I heard about the successes of the trio, and the small difficulties of being with a partner after so many years of living alone. He told me about his work, which was more successful here than he had anticipated, and I told him about my husband and what the children were up to, and who was now working with me in the studio. We gossiped about mutual friends and we laughed a lot, glad to be together again.

We were nearing an empty lot by the railroad tracks—a field brilliant with tender new grasses and the million vivid yellow blossoms of wild mustard—when a young man approached on the street. I barely noticed him, absorbed as I was in the greens and yellows of the field, until Duncan placed himself in his path—just enough to greet, but not so far as to frighten. Only then did I realize that the man had Downs syndrome.

"Hi there," Duncan greeted him gently. The fellow looked up tentatively, flushed and then shyly lowered his head. But he gave a hint of an answering smile before continuing on his way. "Have a good day," Duncan called after him softly, making it sound like a prayer. I stopped and regarded him thoughtfully. He walked a ways before realizing I was no longer by his side, and came back to join me.

"I love you," I told him simply.

"I love you, too," he returned, taking my hand gently in both of his.

We sat for hours over our salads and *caffe lattes* in the outdoor café, feeding the pecking birds with our crumbs, talking about marriage—ours and other people's—and commenting on the other patrons' conversations, inventing the stories of their lives. And when the rumbling freight train rolled right through the middle of the café at exactly three o'clock, we loudly cheered it on.

As the sun began to lower over the water we paid our check, complimented the young waitress and wandered slowly back toward the house, taking the long way home by the river via a pathway that had been inundated with floodwaters just a few weeks earlier. I tucked my hand in his arm and he held it there, warm. There was little more we could catch up on that had not already been said, and the future was a subject that had still not been broached.

Just before climbing the steps that would lead us away from the river and back onto the paved streets of Petaluma, we stopped to watch the sunset spreading a blaze of orange across the peaceful flow of the river. Two mallards rose dripping from the water, flew several yards upstream, and splashed down again to land amongst the reeds.

Egrets nest while mallards muse amongst the reeds, Duncan sang in a low voice, singing the phrase from a song he had composed years earlier. Recalling it, I continued the verse:

Timmy and I, as small as tiny squash seeds
float slowly on our tiny leaf-boats toward a rumored sea.
Dreaming of destinations we've never been before,
Zanzibar, Atlantis, the Moon.

"You remember it," he observed wonderingly. I nodded and reached for the refrain, which we sang together:

And the water, the water will lead us.
And the water, the water receives us.
Be a boat, be a light boat on the river.
Be the light, be the laughter in the water.

For a moment we just regarded each other, our lips curved in the smallest of smiles, and then we hugged. He held me very tight and I felt breathless, partly because of the perfection of the moment and partly because I sensed panic in his embrace. When he released me his face had crumpled, and he stamped his foot against the ground.

"You're so beautiful!" he breathed, shaking his head from side to side with a kind of desperate passion. "The sun behind you makes you shine like Mary!" I reached out to touch his cheek and he grasped my hand, pressing it hard against his lips. His whole body was shaking, and for a moment I worried he might be having a fit. The healer in me became very still, listening, but then he relaxed, his face flooded only with love.

"You're the best friend I've ever had!" he exclaimed with heat, making me realize that it was equally true for me. I hadn't ever known anybody, male or female, as intimately as I knew him, and I told him so with a kind of wonder.

"God, I love you," he sighed. We grasped hands and shook them back and forth, giggling. Then, in a steady voice, I said,

"Duncan?"

"Yes."

"I want to let you know something."

"Sure."

I hesitated, not knowing how to say it. "It's just that…I want you to know that…you can count on me…through everything."

Slowly he raised his hands and placed them on my shoulders, holding us at arm's length in the lowering light. His face was mournful, dubious.

"No," he said, shaking his head. It knocked the breath out of me, and I stepped back from him. Rejected. Seeing my dismay, he went on, "I feel too protective toward you. You've been through so much already…and mine…will hurt you…too much." Then he broke down crying into his hands and I leaned against him, handing over my wad of tissues.

"Listen," I told him shakily, "the alternative of not being with you is worse. I can't even contemplate it. Do you understand?" My heart, like an egg about to be pierced by an emerging chick, cracked open and I felt myself spread into love, not only for him but for the entire, gorgeous and tragic rag-bag of the world that he, at that moment, was in the center of. He lifted his eyes and regarded me with a tear-stained face, the space between us filled with love.

There. The subject was out. We were squared off, right in the middle of the universe, facing each other raw in the growing dark by the river. The mallards were shadowy dots amongst the reeds, and the sun left a smear of red at the horizon.

There was nothing more that needed to be said.

During the next several months he had long periods of feeling fit, and was able to carry on a fairly normal routine, albeit with daily naps and early bedtimes. Then there were periods when he seemed to fall apart. Several times I panicked, thinking he might be close to the end.

"AIDS is like that," Alex, who knew too well, cautioned me. "He's nowhere near. Don't worry." I wondered to what extent this was wishful thinking, but Duncan invariably sprang back to normal from these episodes, so I learned to trust Alex's judgment.

Duncan developed a hacking cough during the wet season, which happened to be the earliest and wettest on record in decades, and anything over a whisper produced spasms of choked barking. Every phone conversation became an ordeal for both of us and I begged him to save his voice.

"For what?" he asked morosely, breaking into a fresh bout of coughing.

To escape the rainy weather, he signed up for a two-week meditation retreat in the desert, but after only a week of quiet sitting and slow walking his temperature spiked alarmingly and he was rushed to the nearest hospital, which was several hours away. From there he was sent by ambulance to a large city hospital in Los Angeles where, as an unknown patient with AIDS, he was quarantined and left more or less alone.

When Alex received the news he drove the six-hour trip without stopping, filled a number of prescriptions as soon as he arrived—which controlled the cough and brought the temperature down—and got Duncan out of there.

"I feel great," a clear-voiced Duncan reported to me on the phone several days later. "I even drove halfway home myself. Listen, Alex is bringing me up to the Bay Area tomorrow to see this healer I was telling you about. Would you be willing to pick me up there and bring me home again? That way we can have a visit."

I agreed to his plan because I wanted to see him and was willing to do anything he asked of me, but this new healer-friend of his was someone I did not trust for a minute. She used a pendulum for diagnosis and had informed him, on his first visit, that he did not have to die of AIDS if he didn't want to. It threw him into a tizzy. She told him it was his choice; if he wished to die, he would, but if he chose not to, he didn't have to. This led to some of the most excruciating discussions between us that I have ever held with anybody.

"Should I be preparing for death, or fighting it?" he would ask me in anguish. "I mean, if there's a chance I don't have to die, shouldn't I do anything I can do?"

Her treatments ran the gamut of drinking his own urine in the morning to refusing contact with anyone who might have what she called "negative energy." This group was extensive and included the most loyal of his friends, not to mention myself.

I gathered that she was probably a lonely woman who was captivated by him, and wanted him to herself while he was still viable, and that he was reassured by his continuing power to charm. The poignancy of the whole situation made me sad and angry—and helpless to do anything about it—because Duncan grasped the bit of hope she offered like a lifeline. Alex, when asked about the wisdom of placing mirrors against the windows to ward off the neighbors' bad energy, simply shrugged and replied,

"I don't like it, but it's his decision. I will not make his choices for him."

So I agreed to pick him up at her place, hoping to avoid an encounter with her, but when I arrived he was putting on his shoes and there she stood, pendulum in hand, waiting to speak with me alone. In the privacy of her office she asked her pendulum if I was toxic to his second chakra and it apparently indicated that I was.

"Toxic to your second chakra!" I exploded in the car going back to Petaluma. "What in the world is that supposed to mean?" He winced at my fury.

"She thinks that maybe you're...sexually interested in me. And that you shouldn't be my healer." Inadvertently, my foot pressed the accelerator pedal and we whooshed up to seventy-five miles an hour.

"Duncan, my friend," I said between clenched teeth, "have you ever heard of projections?" He looked sheepish. "Listen," I added, getting my anger barely under control, "just to make the record clear, I adore you and think you're one of the most attractive and charming men I've ever met in my life, but the truth is it has never once occurred to me to be sexually interested in you."

"Never?" he teased with a bit of his old irony back.

"No," I retorted candidly, "not ever. I'm married and you're gay, and that's that. But I think she may have a point about making clear whether my relationship with you is as a healer or a friend. I shouldn't be both. Which would you prefer?"

"Which do you want to be?" Weariness had crept into his voice and I felt him deflating next to me. I had to get him home right away.

"Friend," I answered without hesitation.

"Then let's be friends," he mumbled, already half asleep.

He slept all the way back to Petaluma, and when I pulled into his driveway he awoke and searched his pockets for the house key, realizing he had forgotten to bring it. The only way in was through an unlocked bedroom window, and since he was in no condition to climb into a window, the task fell to me. The window was high off the ground, and by the time I had found enough boxes to stack under it, my shoes were caked with mud. So I made a mess of myself as well as of the house climbing in.

Throughout the whole operation, which took at least twenty sweaty minutes, he stayed in the car, asleep. When I finally emerged triumphant through the front door I tried to laugh about it with him, describing how I had gone in head first and landed in the rocking chair, but he was barely listening.

"Did you close the window?" he mumbled.

"Uh...no," I replied.

"Do it," he said expressionlessly, "and if you got dirt on anything, clean it up so Alex won't have to."

"Say please!" I demanded as I would with one of my children, caught between wanting to sob in frustration and brain him.

"Please," he mumbled, exhausted.

The cough seemed to dry up and disappear with the ending of the rainy season, and although his weight dropped another ten pounds, it stabilized there for the time being. With the help of drugs and a judicious lifestyle—he was now on full disability—he felt reasonably well and was able to function at a decent level of activity. Most of the time.

I would arrive to find him napping on the daybed in his study, the cat, Buddha, curled up on his chest; or meditating in the garden beneath the cottonwood tree. I would tiptoe out until he awoke. Then we'd get ready for a slow walk in the nearby hills or for lunch under the fig tree, and we'd talk.

In the garden one afternoon he read to me from his journal, a rambling chronicle of memories and insights as he came to terms with life as he faced death, and he asked if I thought it were publishable.

"Not as it stands," I told him candidly. "I don't think you've quite found your individual style yet. I'd suggest you write your personal story in more metaphorical terms, so the universal is implicit in your experience. You know, like our old talk-story work."

"Show me," he demanded, bending over his journal to search for an example of how it might be done.

As summer wore on, the sunflowers grew tall and ripened, and the tawny hills of home, dry as tinder, went up in a conflagration that killed twenty-five people and destroyed hundreds of homes, including some of Duncan's finest gardens. Then his father died and shortly after, in a single week, three other good friends. Gloria was ill, too, with liver cancer, and despite the pressure of friends and family, she refused chemotherapy. At about the same time, Jessica's cancer spread into her lymph system and she went home to her family in Santa Fe to die in their care.

It was a horrible time. Both of us were sunk in despair. My social life these days was spent either at bedsides or memorials, and for Duncan singing meant either an AIDS benefit or a funeral. Each new piece of bad news sent me to the beach, for long solo walks along the cliffs, or to the sewing machine where I stitched one brightly colored quilt after another. After Jessica's death her friends scheduled a memorial for her, but I kept the news from Duncan to spare myself the double weight of grieving her death with him by my side—even though I knew that when he found out, he would feel betrayed, which he did.

For me, it was the lesser of two evils.

"I hate this!" he roared one day as we sat eating figs and late melon out in the garden. The melon, a local variety, was so sweet its juice burned the back of my throat and I had a fit of coughing. Absentmindedly, he patted my back until I stopped. "I'm just wasting my time being depressed, I'm not doing anybody any good, so what's the point of sticking around?" He banged his fist on the picnic table, making the melon slices jump, and growled with despair.

"Why don't you write about what you're feeling?" I asked quietly, recalling when this same thing had happened with Jim.

"Write about what—depression?" he spit back.

"Why not? Everyone gets depressed, and it could be helpful to read about how someone else handled it."

"Ha! You think I'm handling it well?" he challenged me.

"You might, by writing about it," I retorted.

Before that week was out he handed me two pieces. The one about depression wasn't too bad, but it was the piece he called *Collapsing Sunflowers* that convinced me that he might have a publishable book in him, which could also be a focal point for our discussions of the hard, real stuff as he prepared himself for the end. It would be a way of summing up the best of himself and using this time well. A last testament.

We were sprawled on the daybed together as I read his pages and when I finished the sunflower piece, I lay my head on his shoulder and wept with the beauty of his writing.

The sunflowers are collapsing under the weight of their own seed. Their tattered leaves hang withered, brittle brown rags that rattle in the least bit of wind. For weeks they have been leaning out further and further at ever more rakish angles toward the front of the border, away from the encroaching shade of the trees, seeking the sun. Only thirteen are still left standing and of these nearly half are bowed almost completely to the ground. The gardener in me wanted to stake them up to prevent their early demise, but I resisted the urge to interfere. The writer in me had made a commitment to observation without intervention.

But it proved too painful to let them lie broken and ruined after their fall. Of the original thirty-four, two thirds have crashed to the ground with broken stems. I have cut the stems back close to the ground, made a collection along the side of the garage of the seed-swollen heads, and returned the leaves and stalks to the earth by way of the compost pile. It has been a season of sadness watching them come down.

The last of the sunflowers stand like ancient crones and withered old men, silently witnessing the decline of their friends. Who would now believe that so recently they vibrated with the raw energy and green stuff of summer, outstretched and alive, embracing the earth, the sky, the sun? They have lived well, fulfilled their destiny. They have completed what they came here to do.

My old friend, the strongest and tallest of the sunflowers, is still hanging on, bent over like a quiet old man, his head heavy with seed as though weighed down with too many memories. His last task in life is nearly complete, to bring the seed safely back down to earth.

A season of sadness watching them come down: Dewey Stewart; Michael del Villar; Martha Imberg; Bill Alvis; Doug DeBeni; Jessica Allen. They have already fallen. Others are bent over nearly to the ground, energy gradually ebbing away. Tom Mapp; George Kronenberger, Julio Suarez, Michael Tarpinian; Liz Cunningham; Don Struthers. Some may recover. Some no longer have the strength to bounce back. Their summer is spent. Illness is claiming so many gentle souls. Who will be next? Who will be left?

Will the strongest and tallest last the season or crash down with the Fall? Who will still be here when the long Winter is over?

Alex complained, a few weeks later, that Duncan had become obsessed with writing.

"Whenever I come home I find him still at his desk, having forgotten to eat and burning with fever because he didn't take his meds!" He threw his hands up in exasperation. Alex, having burned himself out as Steven's primary caregiver for three years, was pacing himself this time. He maintained a full-time work schedule and took time just for himself, with Duncan's blessing.

"I can't use myself up as I did last time," he confided to me. "It wasn't healthy for me, or for Steven, and then after he died I was a wreck."

"Jesus," I commiserated, "you're incredibly courageous to be taking this on again." His lips tightened and he gave a deep sigh.

"I thought we'd have at least five years," he admitted. I put my arms around his broad shoulders and patted his back comfortingly. "This isn't what I had in mind at all!"

"I'll bet it isn't," I acknowledged sadly, "It's no fair." Alex shook his head resignedly and gave an ironic shrug.

"Nothing about this epidemic is fair," he declared, "but life goes on, so I'm gonna make pumpkin jam!" Stepping outside, he brought in the jack o'lanterns from the porch and while we talked and Duncan slept in the next room, he placed them on the counter, grimaced back at their big-toothed faces and then took the carving knife to them. Chopping the bright orange flesh into big chunks, he plopped them into a stainless steel stewpot, and added raisins and apricots and lemons from the garden. The whole kitchen smelled of fall.

Three days later Duncan handed me his next piece "for the book." *Pumpkin Jam*, he called it.

Last night Alex cut up the Jack-O-Lanterns and cooked up the pulp in a big stainless-steel pot on the stove. This morning he combined the pumpkin with raisins and apricots and lemons in a big, orange cast-iron pot and left it simmering in the oven to cook down into jam.

"Could you stir it about every half hour and then turn the oven off in a couple of hours?" He set the timer for me so that I'd remember, kissed me good-bye and headed out to work.

So every half hour when the buzzer goes off, I leave what I am writing here at the computer, enter the fragrant aura of the kitchen, open the oven and remove the heavy lid to stir the ingredients in the big orange pot. A warm, fragrant cloud embraces me as the lid comes off. I am struck by the beauty contained in the pot. It is so pretty, this autumnal stew, so full of fall color, rich orange all dotted with dark raisins and bright yellow gradually cooking down into a lush, bubbling brown. Already in the pantry are the canned pears and figs of late summer. Soon they will be joined by smaller jars of pumpkin jam.

I reset the timer and return to our sunlit study, throwing another log into the crackling flames in the wood-burning stove. The handle makes its predictable screech as I open and close the square black door. The cat is curled up in her usual spot on the side table in the sitting area near the warmth of the stove. I realize suddenly that I am happy.

As I settle back into my wicker chair in front of the screen, I find myself musing about pumpkin jam. There is something about the combination of energies in that kitchen that pleases me greatly. The beauty, the aroma, the warmth on a cold day, the promise of comfort and good times in winter, even the periodic interruption of the timer, a clear voice of order in the midst of rambling thoughts.

Then there is the mystery of the cooking process itself, rich alchemy of change, the letting go of one form, merging into another. And in the center of it all is Alex's love adding the intangible ingredient that makes it all come alive. Peeling the pumpkins, stirring in lemons and raisins and apricots, turning on the heat and then entrusting me with the delicious task of checking up on it from time to time.

The ingredients are simple: little more than pumpkins bubbling in a pot. It's love that makes it something splendid. Your love helps free me to see the beauty, to feel the warmth, to bask in the aroma, to respond to your invitation to pause in my search for meaning to help stir the pot.

Provisions for winter. A warm place to call "home." Someone to love. Someone who loves me.

Simple pleasures. Profound gifts.

Jack-O-Lanterns transformed into jam.

The next six months were the most intense writing times on the book. Often there were weeks when he turned out two or three pieces, each one a gem. Between Alex and me, we managed to convince him that balance was essential: that he had to notice when he felt weak or hungry, and to eat; that when he was tired, he had to take a nap. His immediate response was to write *The Man Who Burned Up While Surrounded by Blue*, the story of an artist dying of AIDS who spent his last forty-eight hours sleeplessly producing his finest work.

"It's a fine piece, but you're not dying tomorrow," I said dryly after I had read it. "Eat lunch."

His writing was close to the heart, down to earth and pure poetry. He wrote about Alex hanging out the wash; about an appointment with the acupuncturist; about the death of an old lover. His facility with metaphor was remarkable, and being the musician he was his ear was flawless. He was discovering the extent of his gifts at this, the eleventh hour, and more than once he told me wistfully that if by some miracle he survived, he would become a healer using music and writing as his vehicle.

"Like you," he said thoughtfully. "We'd work together and do the most fabulous things. But it's too late."

"Never too late," I retorted too sharply, painfully aware of my own loss and how much I would give for another twenty years of working with him—but all I said was, "Every second that you do this well, you're showing the rest of us what it means to be fully alive."

"Do you suppose," he began, his eyes twinkling with the old mischief, "that I came in this time in order to die like a pro?"

"I suspect it has more to do with *living* like a pro," I offered. "I think the trick is to learn how to *live* 'til we die." His eyes got a faraway look and he began scribbling furiously on the yellow lined pad he kept by his side. I took my cue and left the room, and by the time I went home later that afternoon, he was well into a new piece called *Live 'Til You Die*.

When, one day a few weeks later he lost his footing in the kitchen while making himself a sandwich for lunch, it became clear that he could no longer be left alone when Alex was away at work.

"Suddenly, it was as if my knees were water," he told me on the phone. "I tried to carry my weight with my arms on the kitchen counter, but they're not so strong anymore." There was a catch in his voice.

"Did you get badly bruised?" I asked.

"Not too bad. But I just had to lay there until I had the strength to crawl back to the bedroom and hoist myself into bed." My brain flashed an image of the fallen giant redwood where, lifetimes ago it seemed, we had sung our hearts out in the woods. "I'm OK," he assured me almost cheerfully. "Buddha came and sat on my hipbone while I was on the floor. She seemed delighted to have such an unexpected treat in the middle of the day!" We laughed.

"Where are you now?"

"In bed. I'm writing up a list of potential caregivers. Alex says it's time. Can I count you in?"

"Of course. You sound positively cheerful, m'dear," I observed.

"I don't feel bad, actually," he admitted. "It's sort of like being on the river, you know? I've been coasting for awhile now and it's been great, but we've always known there were rapids up ahead. So it's getting kind of exciting to come in closer and closer to the whitewater. Alex thinks I'm out of my mind."

"You might look at it from his point of view," I suggested.

"I know." His voice suddenly turned sober, pleading. "Please be there for him, no matter what happens. People have been coming into the house as if they were only coming to see me."

"You're the star—again," I noted. "Be careful of that."

"You think I'm doing it?" he asked incredulously.

"Not specifically, no," I replied, "but more sensitivity to him on your part will probably heighten everyone else's sensitivity as well." He took this in quietly and for awhile neither of us spoke. Finally, without responding specifically to what I had said, he asked if he could read me a new piece over the phone.

"It's sort of long," he told me. "Are you sitting down?" I stretched out the extension cord, and lay down on the living room carpet to hear his new piece. He called it *Fear of Winter.*

The brilliant leaves of the season are everywhere in evidence. Fiery liquidambers and Chinese pistachios are like bonfires blazing in the landscape. I love the yellow exclamation points of roadside poplars against the darker greens of redwoods and oaks. The way they break through the horizon of the earth to embrace the sky inspires me back into life, back from the edge of despair where I have recently stumbled so precariously.

Oh, there is still fear as the shadows lengthen. An ancient fear whispers in my blood as frost creeps out across the land. It is the fear of being caught out in the cold without protection, vulnerable to attacks by hungry wild things that rove the land in their various guises, stalking their prey singly or in desperate packs. It is the fear of being neither smart enough nor strong enough to stave off physical or spiritual assault by the forces of destruction. I fear being out of control. Being a victim. Being helpless. I fear being caught out too far from home.

"It is only fear," I remind myself. More often now I remember to breathe

when the fear assails me. "It is only an old, historic fear. You don't have to give in to it."

But the despair that could yet claim me comes from an overwhelming season of sadness. A season of loss and grief. My sadness bears witness to much more than my own vulnerability, my illness, my dialogue with Death. What a precarious thing is life! My mind turns to the plight of those who have no home, those who are hungry. The challenge of their lives intensifies as the days and nights grow colder and darker. The recent national and regional elections do not bode well for those in need. It seems we are entering yet darker times.

"Am I doing enough?" again I wonder. "Is it fair for me to experience happiness and contentment as long as there are endangered species, including my own, in our world, in my neighborhood?"

War, disease, loneliness, poverty. They sit huddled against my front door.

One of them has gotten in. He eats at our table and sleeps in our bed. His hollow eyes stare back at me in every room of the house. When I move, he moves. He probes the dark corridors and halls of my body. He is not content to be confined in one cramped cell. He ranges freely here and there. He knocks at locked doors inside my mind and gently but firmly demands entry. Like the snowy egret at the side of the road, he watches me dispassionately, observing my movements, body, mind and soul.

He poses a question. A hard question about life and connection. "What are you doing with this precious time?" "Are you loving well?" "Are you living fully?" "Will you be ready when it's time to let go?" It is the same question in different forms.

It is the question the seasons ask us again and again, making us aware of our deep-seated fears as the cold of winter creeps in toward the hearth. Then at the very darkest hour, the seasons turn, awakening once more our hope, our faith, renewing once more our sense of openness and wonder as spring slowly, inexorably renews the land. We try to protect ourselves from the changes by locking ourselves inside our houses and cars. We light up our supermarkets and offices so brightly, no shadow can lurk in an unexpected corner. Yet all the while Death is watching, courting our attention in a hundred different ways.

"Wake up!" Death whispers, as the leaves slide down, brushing against me, falling among the fading zinnias and carpeting the grass. "Wake up!"

He whispers as I walk along the river and encounter the abandoned litter of the homeless, old mattresses and blankets, shopping carts, cardboard boxes and crates, here a doll, there a tiny shoe. Where have they gone, the men and women who assembled these living rooms under the broad trees of summer that now stand leafless in vacant lots, their tortured forms offering no protection against rain and raging winds?

My mind races back to the house. Have we done enough to prepare for winter? I think of the woodpile neatly stacked within easy reach of the back door and the walnuts drying in the sun. I think of the well-built walls and insulated roof. I think of Alex and our love for each other. I think of mornings with hot biscuits steaming from the oven and perhaps a friend or two stopping by to share them with us. I am reassured. We will last another winter. But what about the others?

Life and Death are holding hands. They work long hours together, offering their lessons, posing their questions in a myriad of forms. Light and shadow in ever-shifting patterns play across the changing face of the land, trying to catch our attention, urging us to slow down and consider. "What are you doing with this precious time? Are you loving well? Are you living fully? Will you be ready when it's time to let go?"

The yellow poplars stand like prophets and evangelists in the landscape. "Prepare!" they warn. "Prepare!"

The first caregivers meeting was called for the following Sunday, and Duncan and Alex's whole community, it seemed, was there. The house was packed with people and Duncan held court on the sofa, greeting each arrival warmly, his face gaunt but translucent and his eyes like beacons lighting everything in their path. When we settled down to the business at hand, he introduced us to his hospice nurse, a soft-spoken, slender woman by his side. Then we all had to say our names. Alex slanted me a look and we shared a secret smile. Duncan was in his element.

"I'm Johnna," she said, looking around the room. "Duncan and Alex certainly have a lot of friends! That's good, because you'll all be needed to help." She told us what to expect from hospice and what precautions we should take for our own safety. She reassured us that we should not hesitate to call for one of their volunteers any time we felt unsafe or overwhelmed. "Don't try and lift him yourself if he falls," she warned. "Call us. We can be here in less than five minutes."

She and Alex organized a telephone tree and a schedule of shifts, and Daniel volunteered to coordinate the weekly schedules. Michelle offered to bring dinner every Tuesday. Housecleaning and cooking chores, laundry, help in the garden, massages for whoever needed them—all these were addressed and set up.

"I want to make it as easy as possible for Alex," Duncan explained, acknowledging especially the friends who had been there for Alex when Steven was dying.

"Daniel and I will set up a notebook with a copy of the calendar in it, and it'll have information about drugs and food intake and Duncan's general state—all that kind of stuff," explained Alex. "It will be on the kitchen table and you can look in it and jot down your own observations when you come for your shift." Then he grinned. "Feel free to leave notes for each other, too."

"Love notes!" Duncan chimed in. Everyone laughed.

The gathering had a party-like atmosphere, and after the business meeting was over Duncan organized everyone into round singing. "This is much too heavy," he complained. "People have to have a way of expressing their feelings!"

Alex got up suddenly and slipped out of the room. I followed him into the kitchen and we worked silently together slicing carrots and celery, unwrapping cheese and putting mixed nuts into bowls. His whole attention was fixed on the task at hand, like a meditation to keep himself calm.

"It's hard," I remarked, stirring sour cream and yogurt into a bowl for a dip. Alex's exhalation was more like a snort. From the other room came Duncan's rich baritone leading everyone in *"Dona Nobis Pacem"* while Alex, releasing tension, sliced fiercely at the bread and stuffed the slices into a bread basket. Then he whammed the cheese onto the cheeseboard and slammed the cheeseboard onto a serving tray, and whisking it up with a single motion, strode toward the living-room door, tossing over his shoulder a pistol-like, "Yup."

Later that week, during the first of my regular shifts at the house, Alex had returned home for lunch and was eating it on the back porch while I hung the laundry on the line. Duncan lay in the bedroom taking his mid-day nap. I hung up several pairs of large-size blue jeans, large T-shirts, large socks. Boy wash. Alex munched on his sandwich and organized the red binder on his lap into categories: the weekly schedule of caregivers projected three months in advance; daily medications; informal comments on mood swings and food intake; emergency phone numbers for hospice, the doctor, the police.

"Alex," I remarked, taking two clothespins out of my mouth and stuffing them into my pants pocket, "I hope that when your time comes, you will get taken care of as well as you are taking care of Duncan."

"Won't happen, I expect," he replied matter-of-factly, not missing a beat. I spun my head around to look at him but his expression was not bitter, just frank. "When I took care of Steven," he went on, "I realized that I'm just that kind of person. I'm capable and reliable, that's all. I may not be an artist like Duncan, or Steven for that matter, but I'm totally dependable. And I'm well aware that there aren't too many people like that."

"You're probably right," I agreed, "but I still hope someone will be there for you, as you are for him." I shook out a pair of stiff-wet jeans and pinned them to the clothesline first one leg, then the other.

"I don't think anyone is going to be left to do it, to tell you the truth," he declared. "I don't understand why I got off being HIV negative, and I'm not really sure I'm glad about it."

"Alex!" I felt I'd been punched in the stomach, but before I could respond we heard a clunk and shuffle in the kitchen as Duncan approached slowly with his walker.

"What're you guys talking about?" he asked reasonably.

"What do you think?" Alex muttered darkly.

"I was just telling Alex that I hoped when his turn came, he had someone like himself to help him out," I responded, planting a kiss on Duncan's graying beard before pinning a towel to the clothesline.

"I'll second that, honey," Duncan said, in a voice he might have used to make reservations at a Chinese restaurant. He plunked his walker onto the top porch step, and with concentration made his unstable way down to the garden. My instinct was to reach out and help him down, but Alex's quick glance told me to let him do it himself. Duncan pulled over a garden chair and landed heavily into it, catching his breath before making eye contact with Alex. Then he said feelingly, "I'm sorry this is so hard on you." For a few moments they gazed steadily at each other and I draped a sheet over the line, keeping my hands and eyes busy with the sheet. This moment was theirs, not mine. "If there were any way of changing things...."

"Well, there isn't," Alex declared, swallowing hard. "I hate it—at the very least, I want more time with you!"

"I do, too," Duncan said sadly, "but I must let you know that I'll be ready to go fairly soon, and it would be easier for me if you accepted that." A pair of socks hung limp in my hands as I froze. "I want to finish the book, and design that front garden I promised you, and do a few more concerts with the trio..." Alex and I both released our tension with a peal of relieved laughter and in unison shouted,

"A few more concerts?"

"Why, yes," he replied with aplomb. "The trio has two more house concerts scheduled, and one at Santa Sabina next October." I started uncontrollably laughing, spilling the bag of clothespins all over the porch, and Alex just stared down at the man he had wedded, his eyes full of wonder.

Alex badly needed more time off than he was getting, and he asked if I would spend a night there after my regular shift so he could get away for awhile. I agreed to do it. When I arrived that day, Helen was just leaving and she let me know what Duncan had eaten that morning, what his energy was like and when he had last slept. She had prepared lunch for us, and said she'd call me at home when we would have a little more time to talk. New friends, through Duncan, we chatted quietly in the kitchen before she left.

He was at the computer in the study, working on a piece about a day spent at the beach where Alex had spread Steven's ashes. He was trying to get the sense of waves washing in and mingling, replacing each other continually while being part of the same sea. I looked over his shoulder, nuzzling him "hello" and read:

We continue until it is time to change. Change direction. Change our names. Behind us, the sound of thunder is growing dim. Waves crashing in.

Waves flooding out. Waves intermingling, overlapping, merging. Waves embracing and letting go. Waves dissolving and melting again and again back into source, back into one.

"What do you think?" he murmured.

"I think you're a miracle." I wiped the tears from my eyes. "Capitalize *source?*" I suggested. He considered it thoughtfully, trying it both ways.

"Yeh," he finally agreed. "Made you cry again, huh?" he teased, reaching out a finger to poke me in the ribs. I spurted away from him in mock horror and went to the kitchen to put away the groceries. Glancing through the information binder I caught up on the caregivers' network remarks for the week, and checked his med tray. Then I filled the big pot with water and put it up to boil for his sterilized water, checked the hamper for dirty laundry, read Johnna's most recent hospice report, and trussed the chicken I had brought for roasting.

Early spring flowers—lilacs and freesias and daffodils and delphiniums graced every surface in the house, masking the antiseptic smell with freshness. Neighbors came to the door with little bouquets from their gardens, peering in behind me for a glimpse of Duncan, who had asked not to be interrupted while he worked. In less than two years, these two gay men had won the hearts of the people in this Italian working-class neighborhood—people who probably had not knowingly interacted closely with gay men or women before.

"How did you do that?" I asked the two of them one day when they were telling me about the family across the street. "Aren't homosexuals anathema to good practicing Catholics?"

"It's easy," responded Alex, who himself had grown up in the Church, waving his hand toward the front window. "We just keep up our front yard," he said.

"I need a break before lunch," Duncan announced, getting up unsteadily from the computer and stretching out his back before reaching for the walker.

"It's beautiful out," I declared, strolling into the study from the kitchen. "And weeds are growing like mad in the garden. You up for a little weeding?"

"A little...," he replied cautiously, clunking and shuffling slowly toward the back door with his walker. The earth was moist and fragrant, the tender sprouts so green they broke your heart. In the garden beds everything was coming up at once—cosmos and marigolds and zinnias, borage and feverfew and delphiniums and a thousand baby mustard plants.

"The mustard must go," he said, lowering himself to the ground and plucking with delicate fingers at the small prickly leaves.

"Let's eat them for lunch," I suggested, starting a little pile of green between us.

"I never would have thought of that," he observed. "You always come up with good ideas."

"You do, too," I countered, "we're very alike that way. It's just that right now you're a bit preoccupied with other things." He responded, and soon we were engaged in an engrossing discussion about attention and creativity and the uses of unexpected opportunities. It was like old times, both of us full of ideas and feeding off one another's imaginations. Oh, how I would miss this man!

He sat back, rubbing his bony knees. "I'm going to miss you so much," he mused, echoing my thoughts. Call and response, like in the old days. "Such a simple thing—weeding a garden with a friend—but with you it becomes an epiphany!"

"It's not me, Duncan," I said pensively, "it's *us*. Believe me, I can't make this kind of magic without you." Thinking, "though I wish to God I could." He regarded me for awhile, munching on a handful of baby mustard sprouts and then he began to hum very softly in his throat. I looked up startled, for it had been at least a year since we had sung an improvisation together. In a quiet voice I joined him, humming the third above his note and then sliding up to the sixth. We held it until breath ran out, and he sang a simple melody of three tones, first slow, then fast. Then backward, then inside out. I followed him and then jumped ahead, off the beat. We were a bit rusty at first but we picked up speed and spirit and were soon in full play, racing all over the scale and teasing new sounds out of the air. He slapped his skinny thigh rhythmically, a huge grin on his upturned face, and for the next quarter hour, sitting in the wet grass beneath a springtime sun, we sang our song.

While he napped I put the chicken in to roast and boiled up new potatoes and the deep red beets he loved. Above the sideboard Alex's old family clock ticked away as the kitchen grew steamy and fragrant, and I tidied up, washing the dishes left in the sink and wiping off all the tiled counters. Then I curled up in the study to edit a difficult piece called *To See the Wild Geese Fly.*

When Duncan awoke about two hours later, signaling me with a "ding" on his handbell, the garden was in shade and the air had grown chill. Groggily, he struggled to pull himself to a sit and, after using the portable urinal he handed it to me for emptying.

"Don't forget to put on rubber gloves," he reminded me, handing over a fresh pair from the box in his night table. "Have a good afternoon?" he yawned, painstakingly smoothing out the layers of rubber sheeting and towels beneath him.

"Peaceful," I replied. "I've made some progress on *Wild Geese.* Ready for supper?"

"Hungry as a bear," he grinned, sniffing the air. "Smells fabulous." When I brought dinner in he examined his plate eagerly, like a kid, and I placed it carefully on his lap. Retrieving my own plate from the kitchen, I sat in the armchair by his side and crossed my legs under me. It was very cozy, just the two of us in the dusk eating a quiet dinner together. He lit the candle on the night stand, the candle that most likely had been their lovemaking candle, and as the twilight deepened we saw each other silhouetted through the flickering glow of candlelight. My chest ached for what once had been, and I brought myself sharply back to the present.

"Mm-m. This is delicious!" he declared, smacking his lips on the first bite of chicken. "What did you put in it?"

"Lemon mostly, and garlic—some rosemary."

"From the garden?"

I nodded. "Like the beets?" He sucked a small beet into his mouth and chewed enthusiastically, his lips showing red in the corners.

"You jazzed them up with something...?"

"Guess," I said provocatively, grinning as he tasted another one with concentration.

"Balsamic wine vinegar? And mustard—is that what I'm tasting?"

"Bingo."

Like that, in the quiet intimacy of a meal together we spent a peaceful hour, and had settled in to do some editing together on *Wild Geese*. We each had a working copy of the manuscript on our laps, and after so many years of collaboration, we knew how to use this fulcrum of shared work to turn over and over the deepest issue of our lives: How can we live well while we are alive, and die well when it is our time to die?

During this period I observed him come more and more into the truth of his situation, courageously and with humor, as if in the course of each week he matured the equivalent of a year. We were leading each other into new territory and following each other into new territory; it was another improvised duet like the ones we had been singing all those years except that this time the song was of life and death itself. And we were learning to balance on the knifelike edge between them in a dance of growing grace.

"OK," I said, "this sentence on page three, second paragraph that begins: ...*Our only option is to move forward, continue on into unknown territory, accepting the adventure on its own terms, complete with surprises and unforeseen detours.*

"Mm," he murmured, peering down at the page through his bifocals and finding the place.

"I would end the sentence there so that you don't overstate the metaphor. The more subtle you keep it, the better." He read the sentence to himself first one way, then the other, his pencil stuck between his teeth, considering. Suddenly his bowels erupted, fortunately onto the rubberized pad that was kept under him for just such emergencies. My first reaction was to jump up and grab the phone to call hospice. I was already in the doorway when I realized he was gazing calmly in my direction, a look of patient resignation on his face.

"Let's just leave it for the time being," he said quietly, "and finish this section." He motioned me back to the bedside and continued reading from *Wild Geese*.

As we make our approach, the fruit starts to sing, exuberant and shrill. We pull up across the road from the huge, mottled trunk and its overarching branches and shut off the engine.

"I'm thinking we should cut all the way to the line that begins:

Through the open window spills the sound of a multitude of black-birds..."He looked up at me for my opinion.

"Why?" I asked. In fact, I agreed with him but wanted to know his reasons for making the change, as if I were teaching him the craft of writing for his future use.

"Because it's another case of overstatement, I think. What I want is for you to hear the blackbirds singing, not hear my voice telling you about them." He looked up at me for approval, blithely ignoring the fact that he was lying in his own shit.

"I agree," I declared simply. "You are such a quick study! You know, you've become a real, honest-to-God writer in just a couple of months!"

He placed both palms together at his forehead and bowed. Then he breathed in a huge sigh, carefully removed his glasses, handed me his copy of the manuscript and hauling himself up onto his elbow, dramatically announced,

"The time has come."

"What do we do?" I asked frankly, placing the manuscript pages on the chest at the foot of the bed.

"First," he remarked impishly, blowing out the candle, "we get some more light in here so I can see the extent of the damage." I turned on the overhead light and blinked in the glare as he lifted his coverings gingerly and peered inside. "It's contained, thanks be for small mercies," he declared, taking his time to consider a course of action. I looked for, but did not see any hint of self-consciousness or shame. "If you'll position the walker right here against the bed, I'll try and lift myself up from the mess without spreading it. This is a two-person job."

In my heart I sainted Alex right there and then. Duncan flashed me a quick grin as he hoisted his bulk up and heaved out of bed, placing all of his weight on his arms and hands grasping the walker. My job was to follow alongside as he shuffled the dozen steps down the hall to the bathroom, holding his towel like an unpinned diaper fore and aft to prevent dripping.

"Gloves," he cautioned me again, pointing to the box in the night-stand. "So far...so good," he grunted as the two of us made our un-steady way toward the bathroom, negotiating the turn through the door like trapeze artists exchanging places on a tiny, high platform. I wanted to titter, as if I were watching this absurd scene in a French farce rather than playing in it myself. At the tub, we had the next hurdle to face. I turned on the water, finding the right temperature and observed,

"Duncan, if you sit in the bathtub I'll never be able to get you up again."

"Good point," he allowed, biting on his bottom lip as he steadied himself on my shoulder and awkwardly lifted one leg up and over the side. "So...I'll stand," he panted, one leg in and one leg out of the tub. How were we going to get his other leg in without me getting in with him?

"Shouldn't we call hospice?" I asked in a small voice. I think I had begun to pray.

"We can handle this," he gasped, adamant, hanging onto the tiled wall and heaving his other leg in, tottering alarmingly to regain his balance. Bending for the soap he began to scrub while I sluiced him with the shower-hose. He soaped and I rinsed what, only a year ago, had been the firm, Adonis-like body of a young man and was now mostly loose skin over a large volume of big bones. He was totally concentrated on standing, his knees occasionally buckling out from under him. Supporting him by leaning my weight into him, I realized that neither of us felt mortified by my witnessing this most intimate of indignities.

"Trust, huh?" he remarked, reading my thoughts. "We're pretty impressive, don't you think?" He grunted as he tried to shift his weight to gain a better foothold.

"I'll say," I agreed, aiming one last sluice of water to his crotch before preparing for the next stage of the operation.

Getting him out was another proposition altogether. His knees were really starting to give way, everything was slippery with soap and the way out was somehow a much further distance to negotiate than the way in.

I tried grasping him around the waist, but couldn't find the right hold. I tried bracing myself against the sink and extending my arms, but they wouldn't quite reach. His legs were trembling. We both started to laugh at the same moment, as everything slipped and jerked between us. I was certain he would fall and I would go down with him. Even down to skin and bones, Duncan carried a lot more weight than I did.

"Whoops!"

"Steady. Steady. I think I've got you."

"Wrong foot—damn! Snag the walker!"

"It's right here!"

"Put it into the tub!"

"How?"

"I'm going down...."

He almost did fall, but more from laughing too hard than because of actual weakness. By the time we made our shaky way toward the bedroom we were convulsed, already telling the tale to each other between hoots of riotous laughter.

"And then he says—'put the walker in the tub!'"

"And she screams *'How?'* even before the words are out of my mouth!"

I was soaked to the skin, my hair loose and stringy when we got him safely back, squeaky clean and stark naked, into the bedroom. I lobbed a fresh T-shirt into his lap after settling him in the armchair, and cleaned up the mess on the bed, laying down fresh pads and towels and rubberized sheeting. Then I tossed all the soiled linen onto the wet bathroom floor and discarded my rubber gloves, helping him back into bed and sinking into the armchair myself. I was all tuckered out and breathing heavily, as if I had just run a marathon. He turned on the bedside lamp and in its warm glow we gazed at each other in perfect admiration. Tenderly, he reached out his arm and smoothed down my disheveled hair.

"Thanks, honey," he whispered.

"Any time," I responded lightly. We shared a smile.

"Want to finish *Wild Geese?*" he asked, as if we had just taken a short break for a stretch and a cup of tea. I picked up the pile of papers and handed him his copy of the manuscript. Finding our place, we went on:

In thin white lines against the stormy dark sky the snow geese are flying directly through the beautiful arc of color upon color, the ancient symbol of promise and hope, modern symbol of diversity and community.

"You don't think those last two phrases about symbols isn't overdoing it?" I asked.

"Why?"

"Oh, I don't know—it brings the emotional impact of the image back into a conceptual framework, and I'm not sure you need it." He regarded the lines for several minutes and then said,

"No. I like them there. I want to underline the point."

"OK."

I can almost feel the rush of wind from all those strong, magnificent wings and I long to be with them. My spirit flies up and joyfully I join them, honking and flapping my great white wings as I find my place in their formation and, merging into air, we head toward home.

He read his own words with a kind of awe.

"I think I'd either use the word 'strong' to describe the wings, or 'magnificent', but not both," I suggested.

"I want both," he insisted without hesitation.

"OK, but maybe we should check and make sure you haven't used the word 'magnificent' before in the piece. It's one of those words that loses power if it comes too often."

"I'm sure I want both words here, even if I have to take it out somewhere else," he said, definite. I read the paragraph over again to myself, still not sure he was right when, from beneath the sheets came a sound not unlike the honking of a goose as another bout of diarrhea came gushing through. We just looked at each other, expressionless. My heart sank way into my shoes and in a little voice I asked,

"Hospice?"

"I'll do it myself if you'd rather not." He looked disgusted this time, not with me but with his body. Well, if his body was going to betray him, I certainly wouldn't!

"Of course I'll do it," I stated firmly, slipping on a fresh pair of rubber gloves.

"Let's just do it here," he sighed, wearily lifting first one thigh and then the other as I mopped at his buttocks, holding his scrotum first to one side and then to the other so I could reach into his creases. Meanwhile, we told each other little private jokes and commented wittily on the varieties of human experience in the world. He suggested a duet and began a drunken humming, which set us into another bout of hilarity. With ease and élan I wiped the shit off his butt; with dignity and grace he allowed me to do it.

Between us, strangely enough, was the rare gift of unsullied peace, a once-in-a-lifetime experience of perfection. Between us at that moment was the love that passeth all understanding, made flesh.

It wasn't more than two weeks later that he got dressed in his best dark pants and black turtleneck sweater, switched from the walker to an elaborately carved cane, and appeared in a local Talent/No Talent show. When he first proposed it I went running to Alex, alarmed.

"If Duncan makes up his mind to do something, you know he's going to make it happen," Alex shrugged resignedly. We were whispering heatedly in the kitchen while Duncan napped in the bedroom next door.

"He can hardly walk!" I insisted.

"Don't look at me!" protested Alex, throwing up his arms in exasperation. "You know what he's planning, don't you?"

"No. He wouldn't tell me."

"Ready for this? A Cole Porter torch song—plus an impersonation of Marlene Deitrich."

"Oh my God!"

"*Plus*, he's going to tap dance!"

I just gaped at him incredulously, but in fact when the day came Duncan stood tall and radiant on the stage, poured out "Falling in Love Again" in his most throaty, seductive voice and managed a wobbly little soft-shoe, hanging onto the microphone the whole time. Coming closer to the audience, he changed the words to "Falling off-stage again," cried "Whoops!" and lurched over the lip of the stage in a planned, well-executed fall. We all gasped until he came up grinning, and took his bows. The crowd gave him a standing ovation.

"Can't just lie around in bed all the time," he quipped to his adoring fans surrounding him at the end of the show, altogether done in by that time and ready to collapse into Alex's care.

By the end of summer—considerably longer than either the doctor or Johnna from hospice had expected him to live—Duncan was maintaining a fairly steady course with the help of a barrage of drugs. The rest of us, however, were totally burned out. I dragged myself there each week, trying hard not to resent him for hanging on, and wondered how Alex could bear the strain. "Compassion fatigue," someone called it.

In June, Duncan performed what we all expected would be his last concert with the trio, none of us guessing that there would still be two more to come, and between August and early October he completed the design of the dry-watercourse front garden and several new pieces for the book.

Mostly now he lay in bed calmly, apparently enjoying being waited on. I found myself impatient with him and tried to mask it. He knew me too well not to pick it up right away, so when he smiled his knowing, wise-man smile I let the irritation show.

"We still need an introduction for the book," I declared crankily. Still, what I *really* meant was, *"I* need your written acknowledgment in the book of my part in all of this!" It was an awful moment and I detested myself for the need to be recognized, but his attitude of the detached prince was driving me crazy. He nodded calmly but said nothing.

During this period, Alex sliced through a tendon in his hand at work and was in a cast for six weeks, becoming another patient in the house. The accident forced him into passivity, and being an energetic man with few physical outlets now for his energy, he had bouts of depression and once or twice slammed cans of cat food against the kitchen walls.

Daniel, who had been something of a ministering angel throughout, still maintained the regular flow of caregivers through the house, but was overwhelmed by the summer comings and goings of us all. He looked exhausted and seemed to have reached the end of his emotional tether altogether. So when one day I arrived having misunderstood when I was expected to show up, the whole thing exploded into smithereens.

"Daniel wants to speak to you," Duncan announced solemnly as I walked into the bedroom after depositing groceries on the kitchen counter and glancing at the folder to make sure he had taken his morning pills. He had the phone loosely dangling from his hand and reached it over to me with a grimace of apology on his face. I took the phone.

Before even saying hello I was assaulted with a barrage of outrage and was accused of exclusivity and selfishness and every kind of shallowness of character imaginable. Trembling with shock, I held Daniel's angry invectives away from my ear and stared wide-eyed at Duncan, who turned his face away.

"Daniel!" I tried to out-shout him, "what are you talking about?"

"You were supposed to come yesterday and because you stood us up everyone else had to…and Alex couldn't leave the house…and I won't do this anymore if people can't keep their commitments and…." The invectives went on and on and I simply placed the receiver against my hip and let him holler into my flesh.

"Shut up and listen!" I finally yelled when he had come to the end of his venting. "There was a misunderstanding, that's all. I'm sorry if it caused trouble, but for God's sake, you could have let me know at the time!" We went back and forth for awhile and then, still angry and unresolved, both hung up with a bang. Duncan lay there, helpless.

"You OK?" he asked softly.

"Noo-o," I sobbed, breaking down and falling to my knees where I could bury my face in his bony chest. He wrapped his arms warm around me and held me while I cried with great, racking gulps. Alex came in and sat on the floor, his good arm on my back. Surrounded by their two big, warm bodies I let loose the months of tension and grief that had held me suspended between living my own life and living Duncan's dying, and wept my heart out.

When at last I was able to come up for air, I began to explain to Alex that I had thought that today was when I had agreed to come, and he shook his head and said No, it was yesterday, and then I said…and then he said…

"Could you do this in another room?" begged Duncan in a pained whisper. We left the bedroom still arguing, both hurting down to the bones. After awhile, with a lot more talk in the kitchen and the expression of mutual regrets and apologies, we admitted that while we were overwrought and angry it was not really at each other, but at something else entirely.

Once again two weeks later, I reminded Duncan that the book still needed an introduction. This time I was not choked up because after much negotiation with myself I had let go of my need for recognition, either from him or from the public. With relief, I had come to accept that the experience of doing together what we had done was sufficient reward for me. He picked up his binder, his nostrils flaring slightly with amusement, and removed a small sheaf of papers entitled, *Introduction*. I just stood there, the papers rustling in my trembling hand, trying not to cry. He chuckled, kissed the back of my hand and said,

"Sit down and I'll read it to you."

I have been HIV+ for over ten years now. Since January 1994, I have been diagnosed with AIDS. Spiritually, it has been a turn of events that has intrigued me considerably. Initially I was terrified by the spectre of death I was facing. But through it all, I have welcomed the virus and the pilgrimage I knew it would take me on.

The place where life and death intersect has always fascinated me. Perhaps it's because I'm a Scorpio, sign of death and transformation. Fall and Spring are my favorite seasons when the potent mix of death and life is so rich, and the days are alive with energy and portent. The air is unusually sweet and musty, and the evening light is nothing short of mystical. I tingle with anticipation as each new day unfolds. I practically live outside.

I grew up in Oregon, where the land was verdant with trees and flowers. Even as a child I found beauty in brown shriveled bracken as well as in lush green. Nature was abundant with astonishing treasures. To hold a cat's skull was to hold a prize at once awesome and sacred. It contained a mystery I somehow understood and was strongly drawn into, but could never have articulated. This is still pretty much true.

I entered upon the writing of this book with the naive perspective that life and death are separate entities. When you are alive, you live. When you die, you're dead. Simple. Neat. Through the process of paying closer attention to what is really going on, in talking with others, in uncovering some of my own motivations and aversions, I have come to see that life and death dance together constantly, the one lending meaning and context to the other. There is always the new and the falling away, always the rich composting and renewal. Always the intertwining of one with the other.

There are no points of arrival, only the process of transformation. The falling leaves and declined growth of summer represent a kind of death, a

passing away. But in the truest sense, there is no death, no loss of energy. Only transmutation to new forms. The fallen leaves, twigs and branches make a thick mulch of dark humus that by Spring is alive with worms and their castings, a fertile layer of new soil. There is an awesome preparation of each season by the one that precedes it. Summer's lush growth collapses into Fall, providing the ingredients for the rich and secret alchemy of Winter. By Spring, the alchemist has provided the dark, living medium out of which new green explodes. It is a perfect run around a timeless track. Each season passes the baton to the next, and then drops back.

Here, a loose sob inadvertently escaped my lips, and I buried my face on his bent leg. He lay a gentle hand on my shaking shoulders. "Go on," I said finally, mopping at the tears with the back of my hand. I sat on the bed close to him and lay my head on his shoulder. We readjusted the pillows behind us, and he continued reading.

The major cycles of the heart often parallel the cycles of the year. As I learn to listen to the messages constantly offered by my body and my psyche, I come into closer alignment with the greater cycles of which we are all a part. The more time I spend in nature, the deeper and sweeter my connection to the seasons, both inner and outer.

I have written this book for you and also for myself. It is ultimately a personal journal in which I can trace my own process and discover my own path as it unfolds before me. It is a personal journal meant to be shared.

I have wanted to share my experiences of living with AIDS, and to chronicle the shifts and evolution of my physical, emotional and spiritual states through the four seasons of the first year of disability. I wanted to leave something tangible behind that family and friends could hold after I am gone. I wrote this book so that I would be remembered, at least for a time.

It is a huge and awesome adventure, this moving slowly, inexorably into the final and full embrace of death. It is an adventure that excites me deeply, deserves my attention, is something, I think, worth communicating. It is a journey we must all engage in sooner or later. If what I have written helps another human being struggling with illness, or with the ambivalence of living on in such a difficult age to have courage and a clearer perspective, to hear their own voice in mine, I will be thrilled to have made a positive dif-

ference in the world, to have strengthened the web.

Thank you for picking up this book. May its contents bless you.

I had all but held my breath through his reading, and now I laughed and cried at the same time.

"God damn!" I exclaimed in a voice muffled by the pillows, "you did it!" I stood up and stomped around the room. "You did it! You *did* it!"

"So you like it," he said mildly, still scrutinizing the manuscript and making small corrections. "You don't think it's too straightforward—I mean, it's the first thing in the book." Tearfully, I shook my head and reached for a tissue to blow my nose.

"It's perfect," I insisted. "It totally knocks my socks off. Don't change a comma."

"You approve, I gather?" he teased, catching my eye with his blue-green ones, now so deep in their sockets. They had an otherworldly glow. "Well, thank you," he said with a lilt, placing the pages with meticulous care back into his binder. He lay his head back on the pillow and just concentrated on breathing. I lowered myself into the armchair and, resting my hands in my lap, sat quietly with him while the clock in the kitchen tick-tocked and all the neighborhood sounds of lawnmowers and laughter and the occasional bark of a dog provided a background wash of simple life music. He slipped into a calm sleep and after awhile I stood up, kissed his brow, and tiptoed out of the room.

As the days progressed I felt a subtle, but persistent uneasiness as he drew himself more and more inward, choosing solitude rather than interaction, focusing on death rather than life. Now that I needed a best friend more than ever, my best friend had found a more interesting friend than me—Death.

What about *me?* I wanted to yell at him. You're not the only one going through this, mister!

Like a woman scorned, I was consumed with jealousy for the one who had usurped my place in his affections. To my great dismay, I was jealous of Death!

For perhaps the first time since we had met those many years ago, I was of no importance to him. As I watched the mosquitoes of my mind buzz fitfully around this new disturbing insight, I worried that some-how I had let myself be used. Here I was on a beautiful afternoon, sit-ting indoors in a darkened room at a sickbed, instead of being out there playing in the sun, getting on with my own life. It had been forever, it seemed, that a dying man had claimed the best of my attention. He had been my first priority for so long I had even shortchanged visits to my own children! His whisper cut through the cloud of my whirling thoughts.

"One more thing." On his face was a smile of such sweetness and poignancy that I melted, mentally telling my family that he would not be with us much longer. Reaching for his binder, he pulled out a sheet of paper and handed it over to me. *Acknowledgments,* it read. I scanned the page without registering a single word and placed it face down on my lap. His eyes, deep in their sockets, seemed to swim.

"Read it later," he said. "It goes before the *Introduction.*" Everything was moving in slow motion, like a dream. I nodded and just sat there. "The doctor is seeing the first signs of dementia." He announced it sim-ply, without affect. I had nothing to say. "I'd like you to take some notes for me, please?"

I picked up the pad and a pen and waited.

"I'd like to be right here for three days, if possible. If not possible, then at least for a full twenty-four hours." I wrote it down and looked back up, taking the dictation as if I were writing his instructions on how to plant a rosebush. "Please light candles—as many candles as possible. I'd like to be surrounded by flickering light when I go." I wrote it down.

"No body bag, please. I'd prefer being brought to the crematorium by friends, if any of you are willing, without any professionals involved." I wrote down his words exactly.

"Keep the memorial time down to an hour and a half, and don't let too many people speak, so it doesn't drag on. I'd like one reading from the book, and me singing "Danny Boy" on the tape you'll find in my study." I wrote it down assiduously. He rubbed his fingertips gently to-gether. "And help Alex…," he ended in a whisper, his face at last crum-pling into grief.

After a few chest-racking sobs, his face came back to stillness and he looked luminous, burning from within, at complete peace with all things. It was done. I had no choice but to follow his lead, and then he weakly lifted the arm closest to me, opened for me to enter, and warmly took me in. We cried together, a deep satisfying cry. Then he handed me *I Am Worn Down,* and asked me to read it only after I got home.

Later that night I lit two tapers, placed them on the mantelpiece and curled up on the sofa wrapped in my orange and purple nine-patch quilt, one of the first I had made. Taking *I Am Worn Down* ceremonially out of its folder, I settled down to read:

I am worn down. A smooth stone in a stream bed. Sun dappled, wet and tumbled, one among many. I had thought to be the mountain, majestic, viewed from miles around, a place for pilgrimages and the dispensing of wisdom.

My wisdom is in resting here and feeling the water about my bones.

I did not go peacefully down the mountain. I did not approve. I did not agree. I did not understand how I was being shaped. Overwhelmed by blinding torrents, I crashed down gullies, lodged in crannies against twisted roots, tried to dig in, tried to hide. I tumbled brutally against other stones. We believed in the myth that we were contenders. We jockeyed for place, desperately competing to hold our grip on the mountain.

Sometimes I'd come to rest for awhile. The current would toss me off to the side. I'd look around to get my bearings, catch my breath and start to adjust. Sometimes I even got comfortable, totally forgot my dream of the mountain. I'd start to settle, find my place, accept my fate, turn away from the mountain altogether. Or so I thought.

The mountain is a dream that won't go away. Even in my deepest sleep the dream festered and grew, ready to erupt again into painful, compelling consciousness.

I thought to settle, to be done with the mountain, to establish my sanctity on some little slope. But the mountain always shook me loose. A crack would open. A storm would come. Wrenched back to the current, pounded incessantly by water, by stones, I was forced to lose my latest grip, to slip ever lower down the side of the mountain. I was thrown against others' raw, rough edges. Resisting loudly, we clattered and cried. I seldom trusted or understood the work of the mountain, the painful plunges over jagged ledges down into boiling pools. Torn further and further from the glory at the summit, I despaired of the dream, being forced to let go.

Yet the mountain has never let go of me. I carry it with me. I am born of the mountain. I have been on the mountain the entire time. The mountain has never abandoned me. The mountain is in me, over me, around me. There is more to a mountain than its highest peak. We are all the mountain. I grasp the mountain and the mountain shakes me loose. I let go of the mountain and the mountain carries me. It molds me and shapes me and delivers me smooth at the end of the journey.

I am worn down. Here at the foot of the mountain I rest. A child may pick me up in wonder, feel the mystery in her palm, press me smooth against her cheek, taste the mountain in me full against her lips; then toss me back, captivated by another stone or a frog or flower, dragonfly or fern.

Dappled sun, singing water, other stones touching me, other stones holding me, resting here together, supporting one another. The touch of fallen leaves floating by, the flick of minnows, the slime of snails, rotten roots we have clung to, they all pass by. The memory of a child's cheek, hand, kiss, release.

Kiss. Release.

I had thought to be the mountain. I tumbled down here. It is enough. Oh, it is more than enough.

A week later it was clear that the doctor's diagnosis was premature because Duncan had an unanticipated surge of energy which, after a few days of alertness, good appetite and interest in what was going on, we realized was not just a fluke.

"That's AIDS," Alex claimed at the monthly caregivers' meeting. Duncan was present in the room with us, fully dressed and chomping on celery sticks. Even the hospice workers were surprised by his comeback, and then even more astounded when, a few days later, he decided to exercise his legs and try to walk again.

"Let me push against your hands," he panted, pulling his knees up toward his chest and then flexing down against my palms. In fact, even though his muscles had gone to flab, there was still a remarkable amount of strength behind that push. Within a few days he had pulled himself up to standing with the walker and a day later made it alone to the bathroom, then to the kitchen, then into his study.

"I walked the length of the driveway today!" he announced proudly to me on the phone. "To the sidewalk and back." To be honest, I assumed he was elaborating on the truth but when I came that week, we walked slowly all the way up the street together, greeting neighbors as we went, and then turned around and made it all the way back home again.

Even unflappable Alex, who had learned not to be surprised by anything Duncan did, was astonished. And then when the trio began rehearsing at the house for the October concert at Santa Sabina, Alex and I had hysterics over the kitchen sink, speculating on whether Duncan's next scheme would involve a deep-sea diving expedition to the Bahamas, or climbing the Eiffel Tower.

"Or a trip to Hawaii, maybe," said Alex wistfully.

The convent of Santa Sabina includes a cloister and an intimate lady chapel, and is available to the public for retreats. Harriet and Susanna, who run the retreat and concert program, had heard the trio perform an AIDS benefit concert many months earlier and had invited them to sing in the concert series the following October.

Out of deference to Duncan the date was kept, although everyone understood that there was little chance he would still be alive on that date—much less be in a condition to perform a concert! But despite all our expectations, rehearsals were scheduled, Duncan's voice and stamina held up, and when the concert day dawned cool and clear he put on his bright yellow corduroy shirt and Alex carted him and his wheelchair, pee-bottle, special water and medications to the convent, I brought a big bouquet of sunflowers for the altar, and the three men performed their last concert together.

Everyone was there. The chapel was crowded with friends and family and curious strangers who knew of Duncan as a living legend and wanted to experience this fellow before he died. I sat way in the back. When the procession of the three of them came down the center aisle with Duncan proud and upright in his wheelchair and the opening song filling the chapel with great lust and vigor, I sat there stunned and teary along with everyone else.

It was a tour de force from beginning to end. Duncan was, remarkably, in full voice throughout the program, encores and all. There wasn't a dry eye in the house and they received a standing ovation that wouldn't stop. Finally, Duncan held up a hand requesting silence and as the crowd quieted down the three of them simply placed their hands over their hearts and bowed.

"This," he began quietly, speaking into the microphone, "is what AIDS looks like." The other two, each of whose lives had been deeply touched by the epidemic, told their stories and then Duncan spoke about his current medical status and how much time it was expected he had left. He spoke eloquently of how it felt to be him right now, of what he now understood about acceptance, of how much he had learned about love. He thanked Alex, turning to him in the audience, and wept without covering his face.

"You are a brave man, my love," he said. "Thank you from the bottom of my heart." We all held our collective breath as they gazed for a long moment at each other.

Then he spoke about the book—"our book," he called it—and he asked me to stand.

"We've done this together," he explained, "and the process has been a gift to me at every stage." I blew him a kiss from the back of the chapel. Then he winked in my direction and told the audience, as if in confidence, "We're best friends." Everyone laughed.

The next day, after sleeping until some hour of the afternoon, he called to compare notes with me about their triumph.

"It was a foretaste of Heaven," he exclaimed wonderingly. "Sitting up there with all that love pouring out to me from every direction I realized that if I love life so much, I am bound to love death as well."

And I, still on the sidelines of *his* experience, thought to myself with a certain degree of bitterness, am going to lose the very friend who is able to speak those words to me.

"Did you think I was dying?" he asked me candidly the following week.

"Yes," I replied directly.

"That's what the doctor said, too," he commented. "Well, I didn't."

"Then what were you doing?" I asked pointedly.

"Thinking about things," he replied. "And one of the things I was thinking about was that I wanted to do two more concerts—one with the trio, which we already did, and the other one a solo concert around the book." I was indexing the manuscript in preparation for layout, and did not dare look up. "I've called Santa Sabina and they have offered the chapel for the Sunday right before Christmas."

If he had planned his announcement for maximum shock value, it worked. Alex, stirring a pot in the kitchen gave a strangled yelp, and I simply stopped breathing.

"You've done what?" shouted Alex.

"Can't just sit around," mumbled Duncan, sorting the pages of each section into stacks for numbering.

A publisher in New York had expressed interest in the book and held the manuscript for four weeks, finally sending it back with regrets, saying it was "too mushy." Hoping that Duncan might have a bound book in hand while he still could enjoy it, I suggested we publish it ourselves and have the pleasure of designing the cover and seeing the whole process through from beginning to end. So, working with various gifted friends, we selected typeface and book size, made layout decisions, produced line drawings and created an elegant cover of a sunflower rising in an evening sky. In a few short weeks, with Duncan maintaining a good level of energy throughout the whole process, we were just about ready to send all our material to the printer.

"Did we decide to put a blank page between each section?" he asked one day, shuffling through manuscript pages before handing them over for the last time.

"Only when the last page of text ends up on the right-hand side," I answered.

"Oh. That's why there isn't one here…," he murmured distractedly. Alex was looking over his shoulder, massaging his back and carefully placing manuscript pages on the bed in the order he received them.

"Here's my idea for the concert," Duncan declared as soon as the last page was laid down with the others. It was as if he were checking off the remaining tasks of his life from a list in his head, shifting from one to the next without any transition. "I want to read six selections from the book and alternate each piece with a song. David has agreed to be my pianist." He lifted his hand to meet Alex's face and gently fingered his beard. "I'm going to keep to songs that everybody knows—'Tis a Gift to Be Simple,' 'Danny Boy'—songs like that."

I began humming one of my favorites, a simple melody that began with the words, "How could anyone ever tell you, you are anything less than beautiful...," and which always made me cry. "Will you do that one?"

"Harriet and Susanna won't let me *not* do it," he laughed.

"Would you like Alex and me to do some of the readings?" I asked, carefully sliding the bulky manuscript into a large manila envelope which Alex held open for me. Hefting its solid weight, I hugged the bundle to my chest.

"No!" he answered, adamant. "I want to do the whole thing myself."

"If you think you can," I shrugged, with a skeptical glance at Alex, who shrugged back. On the morning of the concert, however, he realized his mistake and called contritely to ask if it wasn't too late to change his mind.

"I wanted the day to be completely my own," he panted over the phone, "but that was pretty selfish of me. I'd really rather we did it together, so does your offer still stand?"

Again, the chapel was packed with family and friends, this time including people who had come from out of town for the event. The day was overcast and very cold, although in the stone chapel the press of people raised a great heat. Harriet and Susanna had placed boxes of Kleenex at the ends of every pew where the community had been gathering since three o'clock, and were showing latecomers to the last available seats. It had the air of a memorial service, except the deceased was expected to attend.

The atmosphere was hushed and holy, and people were already crying when Alex, David and I wheeled Duncan out onto the altar. The four of us, without having planned it, had dressed in purple, Duncan the most resplendent of all in a bright magenta shirt. We left him in the center of the altar after setting the brake on his wheelchair, and Alex and I took our places at the microphone to his right while David sat down at the piano on his left.

We had forgotten to prepare a cup of his special water, so I reached for the bottle I had left beneath a small table by his side, poured out a cupful and began to place it on the table's lace covering, but he reached round and took the cup from my hand, smiling into my eyes.

"Thank you," he whispered, holding my gaze for one intimate second. It was just a simple, ordinary gesture, but it had the effect of melting all my boundaries and gentling me into a state of pure love. What passed between us in that moment was the essence of our whole friendship—intimacy and mutual struggle, pain and laughter, giving and taking. And it set the tone for the whole concert.

What I remember of that day was grace: an uncontainable, joyous expansion that lifted me above the mundane and caused me to be an altered instrument for the words of his writings. I was transformed into a me that was more than myself, a me who had merged with him, with the others in the room, with the universe.

His voice, for the first two songs, was wispy but then he seemed to receive an infusion from somewhere, and it opened up and poured out like vibrant honey, ecstatic. Everything in the world was contained in those sounds coming through his used-up body, and we all heard it and felt it as a miracle. In the chapel, the people sobbed and clasped each other tight.

Alex had just finished reading *I Am Worn Down* when the skies opened and pelted the chapel roof with rain. At first the sounds were unidentifiable; then they grew into a hard, arrhythmic pounding of the elements which became the music itself.

"Let's just listen," Duncan suggested, closing his eyes and letting his hands rest gently in his lap. For a long while we sat in the darkened chapel in communal silence listening as the rains beat hard against our walls, bursting into stronger and wilder gusts before finally letting up into a gradually diminishing patter. When nothing was left but a drip-dripping from the eaves, Duncan opened his eyes, smiled up at the vaulted ceiling and bringing his palms together at chest level sang,

Tis a gift to be simple,
tis a gift to be free,
tis a gift to come home where we ought to be...

We sang along with him, arms around each other and swaying as Susanna and Harriet emerged from the vestry to pass out trays of votive candles until every face, glistening with flowing tears, was illumined by a tiny flickering light.

"Silent Night, Holy Night," sang Susanna in a gentle, high soprano as she came toward the altar, toward Duncan, with her candle. She leaned over him, whispered something in his ear at which they both laughed, and hugged him before placing her candle on the altar, bowing and returning to the congregation with her hands folded at her chest.

One by one we all followed her, singing the ancient Christmas carol over and over, each of us bringing our light up to Duncan with our love and our farewells, our shared memories and tears. After a final embrace, we added our candle to the others flickering on the altar and moved on, making way for the next person, and the next.

It was true communion. People embraced who had never met before, weeping together for their fallen, but risen, friend. The mass of lights burned on the altar like the fire from which the phoenix arises, giving warmth and promise and hope. And when the last person had come forward and gone, and the candles were gutted and only Harriet, Susanna, Alex and I were left in the chapel, Duncan slumped in his wheelchair breathing shallowly, and fell hard asleep.

I half expected he would make his exit that night while in such a state of grace, but there he was on the phone first thing the next morning.

"We are splendid!" he cried, euphoric. "You brilliant, gifted, magnificent woman! You read like an angel! Did you hear what happened after the second song when my voice came back? Was that a miracle, or what?"

"Unbelievable!" I agreed. "The whole day was a miracle and you, dear love, were in a state of grace. I am in awe! I'm still in an altered state—how in the world do you do it?"

"With a little help from my friends," he laughed, feigning modesty.

It could not last, of course. His flame had burned brightly and was almost out. He was ready to leave, and had stoked the fire to give himself the necessary push for take-off. A week later, Christmas, he was ready to go, except that everyone had left town for the holidays.

"Don't you think it's strange," he mused, "that all my friends should be gone just at this moment?"

"Oh, Duncan," I joked, "you know you always like to create as much drama as possible!" He lifted one eyebrow, flared his nostrils and retorted,

"Timing, my dear, is everything."

Just after the New Year, once his friends had returned, in fact, in the middle of the night with Alex fast asleep beside him and the cat curled on his chest, he slipped away with none of us to witness his leaving. That evening I had been reluctant to go home, sensing I would never see him again but Alex insisted, finally pushing me out the door after nine. All day I had watched from the doorway his semi-comatose state. He would smile and wave his arms and hum unrecognizable songs to people I could not see. Before leaving I kissed his brow, encouraging him on his journey, and he gave me a lovely crooked grin as a farewell.

When I arrived the next morning he lay unbreathing in their bed, slightly shrunken but beautiful, dressed in his favorite shirt and lying beneath his favorite quilt, surrounded by candlelight. With the cat purring on his chest, staking her claim for the last time, he lay peacefully amongst his friends who came and went, just as he had wished, with the sounds of laughter and weeping and quiet talk all around him. For twenty-four hours—not the three days he had originally requested—he remained among us. And then in the dark of the moon, after all the guests had left the house and the candles went out one by one, he was lifted from the bed they had shared and carried through the dark garden, past the fallen sunflower stalks and brittle winter weeds, across the new, dry watercourse and out into the waiting night.

Dappled sun, singing water, other stones touching me, other stones holding me, resting here together, supporting one another. The touch of fallen leaves floating by, the flick of minnows, the slime of snails, rotten roots we have clung to, they all pass by. The memory of a child's cheek, hand, kiss, release.

Please light a candle for me when I go. For me, for my spirit, and for your own. In my own way, when I reach the other side, in whatever form it takes, I too will be lighting a candle for you. May its light join with the other lights that guide you. May the love we continue to share help sustain you. May you always remember how precious you are. Never underestimate the power of a single candle. Thank you for helping to light my way home. Kiss release.

Kiss, release.

Kiss, release.

Kiss

release.

Epilogue

ON THE DAY WHEN DEATH
WILL KNOCK AT YOUR DOOR,
WHAT WILL YOU OFFER TO HIM?
OH, I WILL SET BEFORE MY GUEST
THE FULL VESSEL OF MY LIFE.
I WILL NEVER LET HIM GO
WITH EMPTY HANDS.

RABINDRANATH TAGORE

his is an agony for me to write, and I'm not certain I can do it. I've considered sending the rest of the manuscript off to the publisher without this Epilogue, but the timing of events seems to mandate that I tell this story, even though my wounds are fresh, raw and painful.

While I was still grieving Duncan, and gradually putting my life back together again by writing these stories, my younger sister Leslie was diagnosed with terminal cancer of the pancreas, and told she had only a few more months to live.

"You know," she observed to me philosophically on our way out of the examining room in the hospital, "I'm not altogether surprised by the diagnosis. I had a feeling something was about to change radically and, while it's not that I particularly want to die, somehow, I think it's my time."

The news had just been quite unceremoniously delivered by a poker-faced doctor who breezed in holding the CAT-scan films to tell us that she had a "garden variety tumor" and would die of it very soon. I gaped, and came close to attacking him with my fists, but Leslie took the news calmly, later claiming to appreciate the lack of wimpiness in his approach.

"Don't like dewy eyes," she declared, lighting up a cigarette as soon as we had cleared the hospital doors. "Anyhow," she announced with one of her characteristic, provocative grins, "I know just what I want you to do with my ashes."

I kept my face as straight as I could, my heart thumping painfully in my throat. A mill of people on their way to their appointments—some hobbling on crutches, mothers with crying babies, medics with stethoscopes slung over one shoulder—vied for space on the sidewalk. I wondered how many of *them* had just received death sentences.

"What?" I finally managed to get out.

"You know that high mesa in New Mexico I've told you about—the one I've always been too chicken to climb up myself but have always been dying to get to?" She chuckled while I inwardly gasped at her choice of words, no doubt deliberate. She always got great satisfaction out of shocking her older sister. "There's where I want to be, and you guys'll get to take me!" Her eyes gleamed with devilment as she continued. "It's this vertical ladder, and if you look down you get totally dizzy and..." She only stopped her monologue when we got to my car, and then she said,

"Hamburger! I'm starving." Which, with cancer of the pancreas, she literally was and would continue to be, until it killed her.

Leslie, who was always as smart, feisty, and witty as she was beautiful, was a born iconoclast who came of age during the sixties and used it intensely, living the passionate hippie life up and down the coast of Northern California. She had a penchant for unusual men and perilous lifestyles, and for years rocketed between her far-out adventures and the safe-house of my stable little family in Berkeley. After a particularly disastrous affair or mishap, she would stay close to us to regroup, lie low and hang out with the children until she got her wanderlust back, (or her older sister's worry would get on her nerves,) and off she would go again to her next wild adventure.

Indeed, I worried about her all the time, afraid that this time she *would* fall off the cliff, or trust the wrong person, or smoke too much dope. But she kept us all laughing with her stories and one-liners about the characters she was meeting, and the kids adored her to bits no matter what she was up to, which was almost always completely original.

Her creations over the years were always unique. An unschooled artist—she had never been able to stay in school long enough to be trained in anything—she made room-sized macramés, tapestries painted on canvas, jewelry made from ancient amber beads. She turned an interest in photography into an archaeological search for unknown Anasazi ruins in the Southwest, and a love for animals into a career of running the hottest veterinary clinic in town. As one of their clients said at her memorial,

"The place has lost its soul." And as an old boyfriend described her, "I have never been so in love with anyone else in my life—and nobody else has ever pissed me off as much as she did!"

Eventually, she settled down with a succession of dogs and cats, rather than men, for company—("Men make fairly good pet substitutes.")— and with her very successful work at the veterinary clinic. While my children were growing up, we spent a good deal of time together as a family, but I still felt I played the reluctant role of older-sister/bailer-outer, rather than friend. She talked to me when she was troubled, but when things were going well she kept her life a secret; and when it came to sharing with her my ongoing work and passions, she showed no interest. So that once the children had grown and scattered in separate directions, our paths tended to diverge and we talked to each other only when we had to.

Which meant that we talked about mother.

For as long as I can remember, my mother and sister were locked in a battle of wills, which, even when Leslie was a small child, were ferocious. Willful, clever and mischievous, Leslie would, by age three, provoke havoc by pouring water out of a second-story window onto the landlord's head; paint the radiators with the hateful cod liver oil; lock herself in the bathroom and smear herself with shaving cream. My mother, grieving the recent death of her beloved brother in World War II, could not handle such a live wire and, and in a stunning, many-layered betrayal that she repeats to this day, declared,

"Leslie is so bright and appealing, and you so dull and unattractive that I have to break her spirit so you won't feel bad."

The consequence was mayhem on a daily basis, and the resultant depression for me. Leslie, with every fiber of her being, protested her treatment and raised a racket. Witnessing their screaming fights from the time I was a babe myself, I tried to stop them, to get between them, to protect my baby sister. As we grew older, I felt that my presence would at least keep my sister from getting killed, but it was clear that I could not do much more than that. All I succeeded in doing, when we were younger, was to create a minor buffer between them, like the umpire in the boxing ring, and take onto myself the reflected blows from both sides. As we got older, I was so used to my place in the middle, that it didn't occur to me for years that I could take myself out.

The day after her diagnosis, Leslie began to get her worldly affairs in order. She tore up old lists of to-do's—("Oh good, I don't have to take that Stop Smoking class now!" Slash)—and she organized her will. She asked a close friend and neighbor to be the executor of her will, and announced to her staff at the veterinary clinic that she had just enough time to train a new person to do her job. She arranged for the sale of her house, and made provisions for the care of her dogs. Her valuable collection of Southwest artifacts she contracted with a dealer to sell, and all her original artwork was earmarked for me to distribute throughout the family. Hospice was called and a first visit scheduled, and her two closest friends, as well as my daughter Rebecca, pledged to see her through to the end. As each task was completed, she checked it off her list and began giving household items away, encouraging every visitor to walk away with something.

Otherworldly affairs, however, she didn't want to talk about. I was clearly left out of her calculations, and she pointedly ignored what I had to offer. She had never wanted to know about my work, nor my experiences helping others prepare for death, and she had no interest to find out about it now. The fact that I had just completed a book on the subject was irrelevant to her, and when she was doubled over in pain and the morphine pump had broken down, I was not welcome to offer my expertise with non-drug related pain relief.

Nobody was allowed to cry in her presence—("You're going to have to bring your own Kleenex if you do that!")—and at the hospice nurse's offer to discuss the deeper aspects of what was happening to her, she warned,

"Don't get all whispery on me. I don't want any of this enlightenment stuff—I'm going to do things *my* way this time."

During that first week after the diagnosis, when she needed help getting to and from the hospital, we spent a lot of time together and it was a bit like the old days. We reminisced about the past, inevitably talking about our parents and the childhood strife we had experienced in that household. We noted the irony of the fact that she would be dying at about the same age as our father had, and she spoke warmly of her love for my three children, Michael, Rebecca and Ethan, adding that my husband had always been a good friend to her.

"I wonder what my life would have been like if mother had loved me," she mused sadly one day.

"I've wondered that a million times," I confessed, "but she was so troubled she couldn't really love any of us. You got the most frontal attack, but it wasn't just you." She ignored the challenge, not for the first time, never having been able to acknowledge that my brother and I were equally victims of our dysfunctional family. She lit a cigarette and walked into the next room, her habitual mode of avoidance, but I followed her and persisted.

"I've got some pictures of the two of us when we were very small, shall I bring them?"

"Sure," she shrugged, so the next day I brought an album of photos from our childhood which showed two little girls, she giggly and naughty, and me repressed and unkempt, looking like a child refugee from a war-torn country. Clearly, neither of the sisters was in very good shape. I hoped we might talk about our *collective* past, but after a cursory glance at the photos, she closed the album without comment, lit up a cigarette and changed the subject. I sighed with disappointment as she went back to her own personal regrets and unfulfilled hopes.

"You know," she said, "I never wanted children because I was afraid I'd be the same kind of mother I had."

"That's sad," I allowed, "but you've been a wonderful aunt to my kids, and I don't think I've ever told you how much I appreciated that." Her eyes misted over.

"I think I could finally have children now," she remarked poignantly. For a moment we gazed at each other warmly, two women with a common understanding. This was not something we did often.

"I wish we could have gotten to know each other without mother around," I told her sadly. "I was looking forward to it for after she died."

"Too late for that—too late for a lot of things," she chirped, picking up the tempo with her quick-tongued style before anything got too sentimental. "Anyhow, the last challenge in my life," she declared, rubbing her hands together like a chef ready to make the first, juicy slice into a roast pig, "is to get *you* away from mother!" Before I had a chance to register my shock, she was chattering away on another subject and stubbing out her cigarette. I waited for her to take a breath.

"Hold on," I interrupted, my heart sinking with what I had to say, and the response I guessed it would receive. "I'm my own person, and I decide how I run my relationships. Nobody *gets me away* from anybody else."

For years I'd been trying to impress upon her that taking sides in the battle between her and mother would be lethal to me, because *neither* of them really gave a damn about my welfare, and that either I stuck with both of them, or I ditched both of them. And that I found their continuous bickering sickening, embarrassing and outrageous. But she had never been willing to talk about it, and wasn't now. In a gesture of dismissal, she flung herself from the bed, lit up another cigarette and went into the next room to pack her sweaters into boxes.

After that, we never spoke to each other in confidence again.

Never having felt safe in the presence of mother, Leslie passionately defended her right to not allow mother near her now. I could not blame her now, nor had I several years earlier when Leslie stopped coming to family gatherings, refusing to be under the same roof with mother unless it was absolutely necessary. My sister had no intention of changing their status just when she was so vulnerable, and mother, understandably, became hysterical. Leslie insisted it wasn't her problem and looked sorrowful when she said it, but she was not about to relent.

For me and the rest of our family, this situation caused anguish. Not only did we have to run interference between the two of them, but it made it impossible for all of us to grieve together. My brother Leon tried to force a reconciliation between them, but Leslie was adamant, and stubbornly resisted.

"I think it might do both of you some good," I offered mildly one day, remembering the turn-around in Alice's family just at the end. Even Duncan had been able to approach his father, in a situation at least as delicate as this one. Why couldn't mother and Leslie let down and do it, too, "showing each other their wounds to see," as Duncan had put it. Leslie gazed past me to the dogs, then the TV, and then the kitchen. Then she sighed unhappily, admitting in resignation,

"It'd do everyone some good." She stubbed out her cigarette angrily. "OK. I'll give it a try."

I was proud of my brother for insisting, and proud of her for agreeing to it. For me, though, the agonizing question was: To be there, or not to be there? All my attempts to break our triangle over the years had ended in failure—each time, a new crisis would be precipitated, and I would get dragged back in. Inevitably, I would try to interpret them to each other yet one more time, insisting to each one that the other was human with weaknesses rather than the incarnation of all that was evil. Each time, I hoped that this might finally be the treaty to end all treaties. It never was.

Now was my last chance to make a statement, to myself at least, that their conflict was their own, and not my responsibility. On the evening before the fated day, I sat on my sister's bed while she quipped one-liners about the next day's visit, wondering how to let her know I wouldn't be there. My chance came when she said,

"When you get here tomorrow, I want you to…"

"I'm not coming." I spoke quietly, adding, "This is between the two of you." Her sudden expression of pure, abject despair will be etched in my memory forever. Holding my breath, I also held my ground. She looked down at her spidery hands, and for a long while said nothing.

"Do what you have to," she choked out finally, not looking up.

"Can you understand why I can't be there?" I begged. In a dispirited voice laden with disgust, she repeated,

"Do what you have to." Not since she was a small child had I seen the extent of her terror, nor felt such a desperate surge of protectiveness toward her. I worried I might not be making the right choice, but it was too late to turn back, and I suspect, had I done so, I would have regretted it for the rest of my life.

But my sister had learned early not to be passive to the challenges her life brought her. By the next day she had arranged, without our knowledge, to have all her neighbors, plus children and dogs, present in her living room when mother arrived. And the half-hour visit—a tea-party bedlam of people (and pets) who were strangers to my mother—passed without a single significant word spoken between bereaved mother and dying daughter.

I was out of my water, not for the first time in my life. These two people, for whom I had been the third angle in their triangle, the middle horse in their troika, the grounding voice in their trio, were much too foxy for me to outmaneuver. I always landed flat on my nose, not knowing how I got there. This time, when my mother called wailing about the humiliation she had received at Leslie's hands, insisting that I intercede for her, I said shortly,

"No." My fantasies of forgiveness and last-minute reconciliations, it seemed, were not to be. During wakeful, agonized nights I told myself to let go, to drop expectations, to let them do it their way. If only I could talk to Duncan or Alice about it....

My mother, however, hadn't been around for eighty-two years for nothing. This was a woman who had survived a Depression childhood caring for her crippled mother; the untimely death of her beloved brother in the war, and the loss of her husband while still in her forties. Her life had been riddled with disappointments, none of which had broken her yet. It would hardly have been like her to take the current crisis sitting down, so two days later she arrived at Leslie's house and stood in the street, staring at the windows until someone noticed her. My daughter Rebecca, who was staying with her aunt, came out, listened to her grandmother and then took her by the elbow, steered her into a car, and drove her home. For the rest of the afternoon, Rebecca told me later, she tried to explain to her why Leslie chose not to see her. She told of past indignities and abuse; she reminded her of the kind of scenes she had been witnessing since a child. She told her gently, but she told her firmly, repeating her stories until she was sure she had been heard. And then she left to return to my sister.

That night an unexplained fire broke out in the downstairs bathroom of Leslie's house, flames shooting out the windows. Firetrucks, with sirens blaring, sped to the scene; the house had to be evacuated, the dogs rounded up and neighbors reassured. My sister, by that time fairly close to her final coma, insisted upon taking the stairs under her own steam and, once in the nighttime street, Rebecca told me the next day, revived enough to rise to the challenge of the moment. In a raspy voice she got cars moved, dogs put behind doors, and firemen charging through the right door to put out the fire.

Also that night, unknown to any of us for two days, my mother became deathly ill with explosive diarrhea, dehydrating herself until she was half unconscious, and knocking her phone off the hook in one of her forays to the toilet. It was that continuous busy signal that got us over there when the fire crisis was finally resolved.

To me it was if, after fifty years of walking down the same street from the bus stop, I realized I was actually treading a quicksand path by an alligator-infested swamp. I knew it had not been much fun being in the same family with the two of them, and that their continuous dramas were a drain on my energy, but never had I guessed at the extent of the danger, and their power!

My sister's deterioration happened quickly. Within a few weeks her weight had gone down to eighty-five pounds. A morphine pump, which she named *Fred* after her tumor, also called *Fred,* was attached to her side, feeding her at ten-minute intervals. She went from looking sweet and delicate, to frail, to cadaverous. She would show us her skinny thighs, skin draped like cloth where once firm flesh had been.

She spoke to me once about taking her own life when the time came, and I did not protest. She claimed that hospice would help. I thought not, but we didn't discuss it further, and when I questioned the nurse, she shook her head. I wondered if Leslie were hoarding drugs, but I never asked.

My brother wanted to try one more reconciliation with mother, before Leslie's appearance became too shockingly emaciated, and this time Leslie agreed weakly, promising not to call in the neighbors. Again, I chose to stay away. It was just as well, because they managed to mutually provoke another sad and ridiculous fight, and the meeting ended with the usual stalemate, except that this time it was for keeps.

Shortly thereafter, Leslie's caregivers asked visitors to stay no longer than ten minutes at a time, and to my dismay, I was included in the rule.

I wanted to insist upon special privileges as her sister, but recalled that just two years earlier I had guarded Alice's door in a similar way. Now my heart went out to Christa and Greg, knowing what it felt like to be branded an interloper by the guardians of your own flesh and blood.

Although I kept hoping for some final acknowledgment of our sisterhood: a royal wave (my sister did a perfect mime of the queen of England); a smile of resolution or mutual regret; an eleventh-hour recognition of the life we shared, I got none of these. Only once, earlier in the illness, did she recount to me a dream she had, in which she came to a grand, old house by an endless, bright lake. She knocked on the door, and it was answered by people she loved on sight, who she really would have liked to live with.

"And the windows," she said, "everything was windows, and they shone with a light I can't even begin to describe."

"Really," I murmured non-committally.

"I really liked that dream," she'd admitted.

"Sounds pretty classic," I commented. I wanted to tell her about dreams of light before death, and that she had probably experienced something real, and that I hoped she was comforted by the precognition. But I simply nodded, holding down my enthusiasm for fear that she would reject both the dream and me together.

She died in her sleep late on the night of the May new moon with Rebecca at her side, after several days of ragged, labored breathing. She was, by then, a tiny, waxen woman of skin and bones.

I hardly recognized her.

After the deaths of Lynn, Jim, Alice and Duncan, although I ached with grief and loss, I found myself in a heightened state for weeks. I saw the world newly through a vivid lens: colors were more intense, time felt incredibly precious and life itself was a gift to be savored. I missed them terribly. The presence they had been in my life was now an empty space, a kind of black hole, but my heart had been jerked open by each of them, and for the time being, even through the depths of my grief, it remained full.

My sister's death, however, has left me bereft. It is three months now since she died, and I am still knocked off balance, like a child whose see-saw partner has slid off her side without warning, leaving me to plummet to the ground with a painful crash.

We had not finished being sisters, Leslie and I. Too much was still unresolved, too much life unshared. Our friendship, so contaminated by mother's venom, had never found a way to ground on its own footing, with ourselves in the center. Our lives had gone in different directions and we hardly knew each other! The ultimate intimacy I had shared with my friends as they lay dying was, with my sister, more like an ultimate vote of no confidence.

I am crushed by this loss, haunted by the specter of the relationship we never had. During sleepless nights, I write long letters to her in a thick notebook I bought for the purpose, telling her things I could never say to her in life. I rage in fury at our whole family system, and I try and describe to her what it has felt like to bear witness to such abuse. I use words like *torture*, and *nightmare* and *despair*, and I remind her that jailers use similar tactics to break down their prisoners, and that I didn't break! I beg her for respect and I tell her of years of loving her helplessly. And on some days, I just let loose and give her Hell!

I am drained and dizzy and agitated by this loss, unable to concentrate on anything or anyone else. I seem incapable of sleep, although I am exhausted; unable to recover my energy or interest in my own work and life. My mother's needs loom constantly, and her anger and confusion are now focused upon me. All I can do is duck, dreading that the demands of ordinary life may require more attention and strength than I have to give.

Six months ago, when we sat in the examining room peering at the CAT-scans which showed her enlarged pancreas, the doctor claimed that a tumor of such a size had to be growing there for at least two years. My heart gave a lurch as I recalled an incident that had occurred two years earlier, and I wondered with horror if it had any relation to the inception of Leslie's cancer.

My oldest son Michael, who lived on the other side of the country, was visiting for a weekend and wanted to see both his aunt and his grandmother, so I took a chance and invited them both for dinner together. They rarely saw each other at the time, but as Michael was beloved to them and would be the center of everyone's attention anyhow, I presumed they would behave for the duration of a family meal. But I was wrong. Within an hour, mother and daughter were at each others' throats, hurling insults across the table without a tick of care for the rest of us in the room. I observed a much too familiar wince of pain cross Michael's face, and like a tiger protecting her cub, I sprang. For the first time in half a century of putting up with their self-absorbed bickering, I kicked them both out of my house.

After Michael left, I sat down and wrote them each a letter, swearing that unless they got some counseling for their problem, I would have nothing more to do with either of them. I suggested mediation, therapy, a lawyer—whatever it took. I agreed to go into counseling with them, if they thought that might help. I told them that their battles had compromised me all my life, and that I felt contaminated by them. I protested their total lack of consideration for me and everyone else around, and I declared that never again would one of their fights ever happen in my home!

Then I waited. No response. After a week, I learned that mother had shown the letter to my brother and asked if he thought I had gone crazy. When he claimed to agree with my perspective, she decided he had gone crazy too. Much later there came a curt postcard from my sister, calling me self-righteous.

So, for the next two years I kept my distance from them, waiting for some break in the stalemate. The passage of time took some of the edge off, and gradually they each meandered their way back into contact, but with Leslie I still had hopes of a change, and so I emotionally held out, waiting for some acknowledgment of the mutuality of our lifelong problem. If Alice and her family could make peace when she was almost dead, I figured we could pull it off while we were still in our primes.

But Leslie began complaining of pain, fatigue and weight loss. The doctors didn't take it very seriously and prescribed painkillers, calling it stress. I figured I knew what the stress was about, and hoped it might lead eventually to our reconciliation.

For about a year, that was the story. Leslie didn't go to the doctor again, no doubt not wanting to know more, and I kept waiting for the great *denouement,* uneasy, but unwilling to either entertain other possibilities or go back to my pattern of being the older sister-caregiver. Then her pain got worse, and worse. So when one day she called in desperate pain, this time I phoned everyone I knew at the hospital and got her an immediate appointment for the CAT scan that, within days, found the large tumor in her pancreas.

After Leslie died, I began searching through boxes of family photographs for every picture of her I could find. There she was as a baby; there a dimpled little kid already a Shirley-Temple beauty at three; in grammar school, already looking miserable; there the summer camp renegade, followed by graduation pictures taken by boyfriends—all the way up to the person lying in bed, wan and shrinking, with *Fred.*

For her memorial, I created a collage of her life on a large tackboard, recalling with each photograph what had been happening when it had been taken—where we lived, who else was around, what was happening in my own life at the time. I wanted to understand who she was without me, why we had failed as sisters, how *I* might have been different without her.

After the memorial, I kept the collage in the dining room for two months, passing by it several times a day to stop and muse. There she was, about four years old on Santa Claus' lap, her face filled with a child's longing and hope.

"I had to break her spirit so you wouldn't feel bad." I am haunted, haunted by these words. When mother repeated them to me just a few months ago, I tried to point out to her how insulting they were, not only to me and Leslie, but to herself as well. "I don't care," she spit back.

I swallow down the tears and stare at Leslie, age sixteen, with the family dog, her long hair pulled back from her face. Already, her high beauty and sharp tongue were getting her into trouble with other girls. There she is at her wedding—a marriage that would last less than a year—in her white gown. I had taken her aside after witnessing an awful argument over which shirt the groom should wear, and asked if she really wanted to go through with this.

"Eh!" she shrugged her shoulders with rakish abandon, giving a wicked giggle as she swept down the stairs for the start of the ceremony.

Another day I pause by the photo of her hugging my small children. Those were the good days. She took over for me when I gave birth to my third child, up to her elbows not only in my oldest two babies and their diapers, but in the quarts of rose-petal jam I had been cooking on the stove when labor started.

"OK, I've added another pound of sugar, and it still won't thicken," she sang out, phoning me at the hospital. "What do I do now?"

Years later, there she is, laughing with her colleagues at the clinic where, they tell me, she kept everyone, clients and staff alike, on their toes and in stitches most of the time.

Like that, I kept her with me for eight weeks, perhaps more intimate than we had ever been in life. And I wrote to her every day in my notebook, arguing, questioning, reminiscing, and still I don't know what really went on in that mind and heart of hers.

I did this until the exercise began to irritate me, and then it was time to put her away. Ritually, with candles lit and curtains drawn, I unpinned the photos one by one, remembering and crying, grieving the past and preparing to move on.

It may well have been her time to go, as she said, and perhaps it was also my time to have her go. Reassessing my own life through her death, I am clearing a lot of old skeletons out of their cobwebby closets and steadying myself in the center of my own life, apart from the triangle. The triad is dissolved; the third player is no longer here and the first, a sad, unfulfilled woman, is already deflating.

I am the one who is left and the world, to me, is a wonder.

I'm not nearly finished grieving, and have no idea how long it will take. I must come to terms, not only with my sister's absence, but with what feels like my failure to have come to resolution with her. We were not able to do, it seems to me, what we came here to do, which makes me disappointed and angry—with myself, as well as with her.

I await my own feelings of forgiveness, toward Leslie, toward mother and toward myself, wishing it were possible to try this sisterhood again from the beginning, with the knowledge I have now. In reality, though, I was not the one to determine Leslie's life nor my mother's, and cannot expect great changes at the last minute from mother, but must simply carry on. My own life is the only one I can master.

So—once the sadness of years has faded and the well, which is now so depleted, has filled again, I will take a deep breath, have a good look around and take the next intriguing step in my dance.

For further reading, here is a selection of some of my favorite books:

BACKGROUND MATERIAL

Stanislaw and Christina Grof, *Beyond Death: States of Consciousness.* Thames & Hudson, 1980

David Meltzer, Editor, *Death: An Anthology of Ancient Texts.* North Point Press, 1984

Eknath Eashwaran, *Katha Upanishad.*

Alice Bailey, *Death: The Great Adventure,* Lucis Press, 1985

Lyall Watson, *The Romeo Error: A Meditation on Life and Death,* Dell Publishing, 1974

Sherwin B. Nuland, *How We Die: Reflections on Life's Final Chapter,* Vintage Books, 1993

THE NEAR-DEATH EXPERIENCE

P.M.H. Atwater, *Coming Back to Life: The After-Effects of the Near-Death Experience,* Ballantine Books, 1988

—*Beyond the Light: What Isn't Being Said About the Near-Death Experience,* Birch Lane Press, 1994

—*Future Memory,* Birch Lane Press, 1996

REINCARNATION

Joseph Head & S.L. Cranston, *Reincarnation: The Phoenix Fire Mystery,* Warner Books, 1977

Jenny Cockell, *Across Time and Death: A Mother's Search for her Past Life Children,* Simon & Schuster, 1993

Dolores Cannon, *A Soul Remembers Hiroshima,* Ozark Mountain Publishers, 1993

AFTER-DEATH

Michael Newton, *Journey of Souls: Case Studies of Life Between Lives,* Llewellyn Publications, 1994

Sukie Miller, *After Death: Mapping the Journey,* Simon & Schuster, 1997

CHANNELED BOOKS ON AFTER DEATH

Geraldine Cummins, *The Road to Immortality,* Psychic Press, 1932

Cynthia Sandys & Rosamond Lehmann, *The Awakening Letters: Varieties of Spiritual Experiences in the Life After Death,* Neville Spearman, 1978

Jasper Swain, *From My World to Yours: A Young Man's Account of the Afterlife,* Walker & Co., 1977

Ivan Cooke, *The Return of Arthur Conan Doyle,* White Eagle Trust, 1963

Jane Sherwood, *Post-Mortem Journal: Communications from T.E. Lawrence,* Neville Spearman, 1964

Helen Greaves, *Testimony of Light,* Neville Spearman, 1969

CAREGIVING

Anya Foos-Graber, *Deathing: An Intelligent Alternative for the Final Moments of Life,* Nicolas-Hays, 1989

Sheila Cassidy, *Sharing the Darkness: The Spirituality of Caring,* Orbis Books, 1994

Charles Garfield, *Sometimes My Heart Goes Numb: Love and Caregiving in a Time of AIDS,* Jossey-Bass, 1995

Rebecca Brown, *The Gifts of the Body,* HarperCollins, 1994

Mark Doty, *Heaven's Coast: A Memoir,* HarperCollins, 1996

Duncan Campbell, *Candle In the Night: Four Seasons in the Life of a Man with AIDS,* North Star, 1996

For information regarding the author's work
with movement and sound, please write:

Carolyn North
c/o Amber Lotus
P.O. Box 31538
San Francisco, CA 94131

The author with Duncan Campbell after
his final concert at Santa Sabina.

Carolyn North teaches sound and move-ment for healing, and has been helping people prepare for death for the last five years. She is the founder of the Daily Bread Project, a hunger organization in Berkeley, California, and was responsible for building the world's first load-bearing, rice-strawbale house. She has three grown children and lives in Berkeley with her husband, Herb.

Birth is not a beginning,
death is not an end.
There is existence without
limit. There is continuity
without starting point.

CHUANG TZU